*Praise for*

# This Is US

The *New* All-American
Family

"In the interest of full disclosure, I s~~____~~ve
with David Marin, the human being~~____~~.
A single guy adopting three little N~~____~~[
started reading *This Is US* and I fel~~____~~e
writer. This guy can make the crazine~~____~~n
turn a trip to McDonald's into an absorbing read; and mostly he can
stir your heart by describing the life of his new All-American family
in a way that makes you wish he'd "adoct" you as a well. The love is
palpable; the prose throbs with life; the insights sparkle. I gave it to
my husband to read, even though he doesn't 'normally read this kind
of book,' and he laughed, read ahead of me, kept quoting passages out
loud, and even offered to write this blurb for me. It's deeply gratifying
when a good human being turns out to be a good writer and storyteller.
Another reason to read this lovely book."

—**Julia Alvarez**, author of *How the García Girls Lost Their Accents*,
*In the Time of the Butterflies*, *Return to Sender*, and
*Once Upon a Quinceañera: Coming of Age in the USA*

AN INDIE NEXT LIST SELECTION:
*Great Reads from Booksellers You Trust*

"David Marin has written an important and moving book. He poignantly describes the soaring exhilaration and quiet satisfaction of becoming an adoptive father. He also captures the maddening frustrations of dealing with the child welfare bureaucracy. This book should be required reading for all adoption social workers and all prospective adoptive parents."

—**Jeff Katz**, founder, Listening to Parents

"In telling the story of how he adopted three young, bicultural children, David Marin is wise, warm, funny, insightful, passionate, persistent, and occasionally (and justifiably) outraged. As a single, middle-aged, affluent man who wanted more than anything to create a family, it should have been simple for him to provide a home for this trust-hungry trio. It was anything but. In *This Is US*, Marin recounts with unsparing honesty and wry humor the formidable challenges he surmounted: a crazy-making bureaucracy, a mean-spirited boss, a suspicious and prejudiced society, and his considerable naïveté as a first-time parent. Yet he also shares the joys and victories with which he was richly rewarded, not the least of which is the unconditional love of two boys and a girl whose lives—once constrained by fear, abuse, and neglect—now overflow with happy and intriguing possibilities. This remarkable book should be required reading for anyone who wants to adopt, had been adopted, or works in the adoption field. For the rest of us, it is an eloquent reminder of the primal power of kinship."

—**Richard Mahler**, co-author of *Secrets of Becoming a Late Bloomer* and "Southwest Storylines" columnist at *Desert Exposure*

"David Marin opens our eyes to the profound significance men make in the lives of children. If every man could understand the heart-warming and life-changing truths David so personally reveals in *This Is US*, America would be a stronger country."

—**Meg Meeker, M.D.**, author of *Strong Fathers, Strong Daughters: Ten Secrets Every Father Should Know*

"Inspiration is a word used too freely and too frequently. Yet, David Marin's honesty and humanity in telling the story of how he became a father against the odds is just that, an inspiration in the truest sense. *This Is US* fills the world with the breath of hope."

—**Jacquelyn Mitchard**, author of *The Deep End of the Ocean* and *Second Nature: A Love Story*

"Single dad David Marin's quest to adopt two boys and a girl from the California foster care system brings new meaning to the phrase 'against all odds.' As he and and his beautiful children—and their happy and healthy lives—demonstrate, there are many ways to create a family. The essential ingredient is love."

—**Jessica O'Dwyer**, author of *Mamalita: An Adoption Memoir*

At EXTERMINATING ANGEL PRESS, we're taking a new approach to our world. A new way of looking at things. New stories, new ways to live our lives. We're dreaming how we want our lives and our world to be...

*Also from*
EXTERMINATING ANGEL PRESS

The Supergirls: *Fashion, Feminism, Fantasy,*
*and the History of Comic Book Heroines*
by Mike Madrid

Jam Today: *A Diary of Cooking*
*With What You've Got*
by Tod Davies

Correcting Jesus: *2000 Years of*
*Changing the Story*
by Brian Griffith

3 Dead Princes: *An Anarchist Fairy Tale*
by Danbert Nobacon
with illustrations by Alex Cox

Dirk Quigby's Guide to the Afterlife
by E. E. King

Snotty Saves The Day
by Tod Davies

# This is US

## The *New* All-American Family

## DAVID MARIN

Portions of this book first appeared, some in different form, on the
Exterminating Angel Press online magazine at
**www.exterminatingangel.com**

EXTERMINATING ANGEL PRESS
*"Creative Solutions for Practical Idealists"*
Visit **www.exterminatingangel.com** to join the conversation
**info@exterminatingangel.com**

Cover photo by Sarah Marin-Gutierrez

Interior photo by Esther Bubley, Library of Congress,
Prints & Photographs Division, FSA/OWI Collection
[LC-USW3- 037939-E]

Book design by Mike Madrid

ISBN: 978-1-935259-34-3
Library of Congress Control Number: 2011931918

Printed in The United States of America

# Contents

*For my three shooting stars.*
*I made a wish when I saw you.*


*For my mother and sisters. You were right.*
*I didn't know what I was doing.*

## Notes

All names are changed except for mine, our pets, and nationally known characters. Conversations are based on extensive notes and my best recollection.

*This Is US* has graphic descriptions of my children's lives before they entered my home. Life is cruel to the offspring of felony, and many suffer more than they, but for them, my heroes and my life, their escape from calamity to bursting with joy makes them, like yellow wildflowers blooming in the ash and aftermath of a Santa Barbara fire, even more amazing and beautiful.

## *Prologue:* The Robbers

My ornery side drove us to Pappy's, a Highway 101 truck-stop-diner popular with meth-toothed rednecks with eyes like burn holes. The last time we visited they stared at us until I stared at them. I parked near the sign with busted lights and misspelled slide-in words: STEAKS, MILKSAKES, AND OTHER SPECAILS. After lunch we'd visit the La Purisima Mission outside Lompoc, 27 miles south of Santa Maria. But first I had three little bellies to fill.

We walked through the front vestibule into the dining area, a mix of tables and booths. The hostess took us to the back. Craig, my four year old, climbed into the booth and I slid next to him, draping my arm across the back. Adriana, my six year old, and Javier, who'd turn nine in a few days, sat opposite us in straight-back chairs. All 40 people in the restaurant knew we'd arrived.

When I was exiled to Santa Maria (forced out of a job by a superior who disapproved of my adopting as a single parent), I heard Santa Maria had a problem with "all the Mexicans." An employee at Pulitzer Newspapers in Santa Maria, where I became vice-president of advertising, told me his neighborhood was great until "the Mexicans" came. A business owner, not knowing that I was adopting three chocolate children, told me he didn't do business with "the Mexicans." After my newspaper published a story about a young fieldworker arrested for burying her stillborn baby in her backyard, it published a letter-to-the-editor from a woman imploring fellow citizens to get rid of "these animals." The woman evidently preferred burning the baby into a sippy cup of ash ($1,000) or burial in a field of strangers ($5,000).

The mother was released after authorities confirmed the baby was stillborn.

i

A few months earlier, millions marched against immigration "reforms" that singed the word 'criminal' onto the foreheads of people like my children. Politicians like former House Speaker Newt Gingrich suggested we bus to Mexico three million adult illegals (1% of the U.S. population), but not their four million American born citizen children.[1] At 50 people per 50 foot bus and the space in between, the 1,136 mile long caravan would stretch from Arizona to Seattle, visible from space.

It was nasty out there and getting worse.

Adriana picked up the children's menu and said, "Listen up, everybody," a phrase I used. She read aloud. Dressed in her favorite pink jacket, she wore the earrings I got her for Christmas. Every time I put them in I winced.

Listening to Adriana, Javier pushed up the sleeves of his dinosaur print shirt to reveal two watches, a digital watch and the new secret agent watch my sister, his Aunt Diana, gave him. The scrawniest child, he savored the thought of each menu item. To Javier, food was sacred. When I first met the kids, in a rare mention of his "real" house, he said, "When I was little, I sneaked into the rabbit cage, got the carrots, washed them and ate them."

Craig wore a blue Winnie the Pooh shirt and Buzz Lightyear tennis shoes. One heel had a flashing red light I covered at night so it wouldn't scare him. At 24 pounds, he was like a baby, but bigger.

After my children moved into my home, he and Adriana had nightmares about "the robbers." I was often awakened by Craig's little knuckles rapping on my bedroom door. I knew it was him and I knew why he was there. His hair wet with sweat, he'd scream as I took him back to his crib. I'd sit on the floor for 30 minutes at 2 a.m. with my

---

1    Pew Research 2009 Portrait of 11.9 million unauthorized immigrants. 59% are from Mexico, a fairly constant number over the past 30 years. 33% are from Asia, Central or South America, the Caribbean, or the Middle East.

forearm touching him so he'd know I wasn't leaving. I whispered, "No more robbers," like a lullaby until he fell asleep. Then I tiptoed away.

Adriana didn't sleep without a ray of light. A noise outside? The robbers. A light on when we got home? The robbers. On the way to school I told them the robbers will never come into our house and if they do, Bam! I'd slug 'em. We made it a game and we played it often.

"Daddy, after you slug them, then what?" said Craig.

"I'll kick them in the stomach."

Javier, from the back seat with caution, "Then what?"

"I'll rip off their arms!"

"And throw them in the river!" Craig added.

"That's right."

"Daddy," Adriana said, "If you throw them in the river will the crocodiles get them?"

"Oh, yeah," like a world famous expert.

"Yeah!" with glee.

After a year squishing robbers, knowing their old family had nothing worth robbing but guns or drugs, I asked Adriana what the robbers took. What was the loot? What scared and scarred for so long?

"What did the robbers take?"

"They take us, us kids."

That's not good.

"Who are they?"

"The social people. And the police."

Imagine. Night, sirens, black boots and guns, screaming, strange guys hiding in the closet or jumping out the back window. And then, the robbery, children in pajamas in separate police cars, peeled apart, placed in foster homes and then worse, returned to the place they were rescued from.

And, um, imagine: Me tearing the arms off the police and throwing them into the river...

Without care that her baby teeth were gone, Adriana ordered a hamburger. Javier picked grilled cheese. Craig wanted the usual— macaroni and cheese. Each child ordered with a smile and a "please." We practiced manners at home.

I ordered meatloaf and extra napkins. I'd already used one to dispose of the sand in one of Craig's shoes after he'd dumped the contents of the other onto our seat.

We got the usual stares, from truck drivers, tattooed girlfriends, and a lady around fifty years old who looked like she dried her hair at an automatic carwash. She ate lunch with her potbellied husband. His white t-shirt was clean and tucked into his jeans. I didn't know what they were thinking, but we had their attention.

A Hispanic woman using her cell phone at a table fifteen feet away turned and watched me and Craig play rub-the-face, his favorite game. I opened my hand wide, stretched my thumb and index finger apart, placed them on his temples, and then slowly dragged my hand down his face. She smiled.

Craig climbed onto my lap and gave me a blue crayon to color the reindeer on his placemat. Adriana finished the find-the-word game without help, she announced. Then she and Javier leaned toward one another and colored in tandem. Each watched the other carefully. Like synchronized swimmers, they colored their own placemats but worked on the same objects using the same colors. This huddling behavior was odd; usually, they were eagerly independent. Maybe they felt people watching.

I sensed trouble, too. Several times, my right eye saw something outside the window, but when I turned I saw nothing but gray sky. I accepted that people were curious about us and I happily shared our story, but today we got one smiler and rude stares. I didn't stare back today, but instead focused on the three angels who had my heart.

While eating, we discussed our last visit to La Purisima Mission, established in 1787. We ate fresh corn tortillas made by ladies dressed to period, and fed pieces to cooped chickens when the ladies weren't looking. As our plates emptied the napkin pile grew. The children were full and happy.

It was time to rock and roll. Or, not.

As we left Pappy's through the same door we entered, a California Highway Patrol officer in mirrored sunglasses and hat came through the door on the opposite site of the vestibule—the side with the window. Instead of turning left into the restaurant he walked through the vestibule—toward us. Seeing him, Javier waited and politely held the door open for him, just like we practiced.

I expected the officer to keep going, but he stopped. He wanted to talk. Why?

"You may have been a witness to something. I just want to know if you saw anything. Why don't you ask the kids to wait inside?"

"Okay," I answered evenly, not wanting to alarm my children. They were watching, so they understood when I shooed them back into the vestibule and told them to wait. None of my children liked the police, Adriana especially. A few weeks after we met, a police car stopped next to us at a red light. I watched Adriana in the rearview mirror.

"Javier, look, it's the police. It's okay. We have a car. We can get away."

I stood face-to-face with the officer. We were twenty feet from the vestibule. Did Craig expect me to throw him in the river? Maybe something happened at the gas station we stopped at before lunch. At the highway exit red light, a Highway Patrol officer ahead of us stared through his side view mirror. My eyes watched his. Was it him? The shades matched. He was young, a few inches shorter than me, with red blond hair. He could have been my little brother.

"We got a call from someone who thinks there might be something inappropriate going on here."

"Is that right? Like what?"

"Well, are those your kids?" He kept his sunglasses on. I did, too. It was a Ray-Ban vs. Vuarnet showdown.

"Yes, they're my kids. They're adopted, obviously. They grew up here. I adopted them through Santa Barbara County."

The adoption process included vetting by two counties and fingerprinting three times. My path to fatherhood was so long I could have a trail named after me. I didn't explain that to him. Part of the system, he knew how it worked. I wanted our chat to end. The best thing about police contact was the getting away.

He wanted proof. I remembered asking Scott, the social worker who helped me adopt my children, what would happen if I traveled out of state, say to Utah. Was there a piece of paper, something, to prove that Javier, Adriana, and Craig were mine? Scott slid three forms across the table.

"This is what you're looking for, these are the Utah Papers." At the final adoption hearing the judge signed them. I put them in a box.

"I really apologize for this," the officer said. "I'm just doing my job. Someone called, and we have to check it out."

"I understand." But I didn't. Did someone in the restaurant really call to report a triple felony? And what were they doing now, eating dessert? Or, had the officer been following us for miles, wondering why three Mexican children were in a car with a white male in his forties? Was he a weekend Minutemen Project[2] devotee, using Kmart night-vision goggles to spot aliens in the San Diego brush?

"Is there any way you can prove they're your kids?"

If I had the Utah Papers with me, we could finish and go. But I

---

2   Founded in 2004, Minutemen patrol the U.S./Mexican border and report sightings. Among their stated goals: the elimination of car pool lanes, a reduction in the risk of terrorist attacks on schools and temples, less leprosy, and lower utility bills. Gilchrist, 2008.

wanted us to be a normal family.

"Regular parents don't carry papers around. I don't either."

He was perplexed: Too much brown and too few adults. I was unmarried. Would he bother me if I had a wife? Were there more of him out there, unable to contemplate single male parents? Men can love, be patient, supportive and multi-task. Men play catch or fly kites with their children because it's fun. The instinct to parent is gender-neutral. And men have biological clocks. I worried throughout my thirties about becoming too old to have fun with children. Men yearn the same as women. And if they are self aware they know they have to give what they want or it's not fair.

He wondered. "Again, Sir, I'm just doing my job. You never know, we have to check these things out. It is unusual, if you think about it—you and these kids."

He must have turned right when he emerged from his cocoon.

"Has anyone actually alleged anything? Was someone offended that my son was sitting on my lap? We were coloring. Is there something wrong with that?"

Maybe I should've stopped letting Craig sit on my lap in restaurants. But he was just a little guy, still learning to hug—he got up close, looked into my eyes for two or three seconds, and then lunged at me. It's good no one saw me brush Adriana's hair. Outsiders didn't get that I was all these children had—the mom and the dad, as Adriana put it. She and Javier made Mother's Day cards for me at school.

"No, no," the officer said. "No one has alleged anything. Can I see some identification?"

"I know you guys have a job to do." I gave him my driver's license, forgetting that it had my old address.

"So, you live in Oakland?"

Oops. I offered up a little brown card with my new address. A woman at the DMV gave me the card when I moved to Santa Maria; she told me to keep it with my license.

"No. We live here. It's on this card."

He read the card, but did nothing. He didn't call in. I thought he'd let us go.

"So, uh... there's nothing inappropriate going on."

Was he making a statement or asking a question?

"What are you talking about?" Frustrated, I again asked, "Does someone have a problem with me?" What did the caller care about? If he/she/it was worried about the children's well being, I wonder if he/she/it called the police after seeing a 10 year old working in the strawberry fields. That was illegal, until they were 12.

"No. I was...um.... The caller must have been wondering...." His voice faded.

"You must be joking." My ears were warm. In my youth, when I didn't have three trusting souls looking at me through the glass door, I would have told him to fuck off and left, daring him to come after me. Being a father changed me, made me less impulsive, less prone to anger.

"Right. Well, okay...." He turned to go. "Like I said, I'm just doing my job."

"Have a nice day," I said to his back.

I got the children and, as always, we held hands across the parking lot. We were four feet wide and one foot deep. I helped Craig into his car seat while Javier and Adriana buckled themselves into the jump seats in the back of our Land Rover. I pretended nothing happened.

"Daddy, what happened?" Adriana asked.

I hesitated. "It was nothing. Someone lost a dog and the policeman wanted to know if I'd seen it anywhere."

I silently abandoned our Mission plans. I didn't want more trouble. So we went to the park near home. As the children played I watched through the trees to see if the curious cop/robber just happened to be driving by…

I felt bad about lying to Adriana. Should I have explained that some people didn't think we were a real family or worse, didn't want us to be a family? Did I warn her that although this won't happen often, it would happen again? Would it be helpful if I went to the police station with my children, found the Chief and said, "This is us; we're going to be around."

There must be a better way.

# 1. Angels in the Yard

The old brown man labored on the pedals. His tricycle carried a wood box filled with fresh tamales and long, ribbed churros rolled in cinnamon and sugar. His thumb, a crooked stump like those he pulled from August strawberry fields when he was taller, now rang a child's bicycle bell. I parked in the street and stood. I hoped to see children playing—maybe I'd see mine—but it was quiet. The 1950's single-story foster home had green trim. The dead grass yard had one small tree with bare winter branches. When I turned to scan the neighborhood, the young men watching backed into the shadows. Each house had a used car lot in the driveway and angels in the yard.

I smelled good dirt in the fields 90 feet behind the house and across the road. During the windy season, early January through late December, crops and chemicals gave a distinct odor to Santa Maria, a Santa Barbara County slab of dirt clawed by stooped and hooded fieldworkers. They came the year Napoleon was born, 1769, lashed to the lowest post, drawn to California to work at the missions and fields or, if work was short, gathered and auctioned like livestock.

Faces wrapped in bandanas, they worked more than 700,000 harvested acres of vegetables and field crops worth hundreds of millions. Top crops included strawberries, broccoli, cauliflower, and lettuce, so delicate every head was touched by human hands. I never figured out if the bandanas were to keep chemicals and dirt from their mouths and lungs, or to hide their faces from neighbors, teachers, or federal agents.

I took a deep breath and waited for Willie, a Santa Barbara County social worker I met a few months earlier during the foster care licensing process. He'd act as translator. Waiting for a man I'd met once to introduce me to three strangers I'd love and raise was not the typical path

1

to fatherhood. But it was mine. I'd never been a father—there were small mammals with more parenting experience than me—but I had what I needed: a license from the county, a desire to experience unconditional love, a reckless curiosity about the unknown, and no fears, except of dying alone.

It wasn't supposed to be this way. After getting my license, I was supposed to sit with a social worker, review pictures and biographies, and look for a good match. We'd chat over a cup of county coffee and I'd rank my selections, check references, and then meet him or her—like hiring a gardener. Instead, a phone call:

"David Marin."

"Hi, David. My name is Scott. I'm with Santa Barbara County Social Services. I have five little Hispanic kids, ages two, four, six, eight and ten. Can I bring them over?"

"Huh?"

"They need a place to stay right now."

I don't think so...! "I'm single. I'm at work." I ended the conversation. What the hell was that about? I called Social Services and complained, telling them not to call me with five kids.


But I needed some. That week, I watched co-workers leave work early because it was the first day of school. When would that matter to me? I wanted it to. But, five? Right now? Taking five was nutty. On the other hand, my mother raised five alone after my father died young. I'd need a bigger house. And a van and bunk beds. And a bigger dining room table, two sets of walkie-talkies, and a good therapist. A good-looking therapist would be even better.

A week later Scott called.

"I'll place the older two girls with their fathers if I can find them. If

2

I do that, are you open to meeting the youngest three?"

"Are they available for adoption or are you just looking for a place to put them?"

"Well, both, kind of. They aren't legally available for adoption yet, but they will be. We need a place for them to stay. Right now they're in three different foster homes."

"Three seems like a lot. I'll think about it."

"Do you know how this works?"

"Not really. I attended adoption classes to get my license, but the classes dealt with how kids get into foster care, not out."

"We are required by law to work with the parents. If we want to stop working with the mother, like in this case, we have to get court permission. It's called withdrawal of services." I'd heard about that in the licensing classes I took. Withdrawal of services was a precursor to termination of parental rights. After termination, the only way to get your kids back was to steal them.

"There's a hearing on October 8. I'll call you."

Who would take three kids at once? How would I raise three from a standing start? On the other hand, stuck in Santa Maria, a sleeping pill between San Luis Obispo and Santa Barbara, I had plenty of free time.

Scott called a week later. "I've placed the older girls with their fathers. The little three are left."

"Neither father wanted to take them?"

"There was no chance. Would you like to meet them?"

I'd led an interesting life, traveled to 11 countries, jumped out of airplanes, graduated from law school, and I had three holes-in-one. But at night I imagined the worst: sitting alone and retired on a Carmel Valley porch, watching families drive by to barbeques, nodding my way. My original plan: wife, children, four bedrooms, a wrought-iron fence, and a pony in the back near the shed with the ocean canoe, had eluded me. It was time. I was ready.

"I'd like to meet them."

"I haven't met them," Scott said, "but I understand they're good kids. The withdrawal of services hearing is around the first of November."

"I thought the hearing was in October?"

"It was postponed. I'll call you."

I waited for Scott to call. I wanted to meet the kids. They were around town somewhere. I wondered if Scott would let me drive by, look at them, or check their water meter. I imagined what they would be like. Most fieldworkers were small. What would they think about me? What would I feed them? How would I feel? Did they like spaghetti? If there was a little girl, when did I get her ears pierced? After two weeks of waiting, I called Scott.

"When can I meet the kids?"

"The hearing got postponed until late November. You can't meet them until the hearing takes place. It doesn't make sense for us to introduce you to the kids, or them to you, if the court does not let us withdraw services."

"Can you tell me their names? How old are they?"

"Let's see. I haven't met them…" I heard shuffling papers. He hadn't met me either. What he was thinking?

"There is a boy, two, his name is Chris, or Craig.

"There's a girl, four, her name is Adriana. And a boy, Javier. I think he's six."

I made notes on my office To Do sheet.

"The little one. Is he Chris, or Craig?"

"We're not sure."

"What's their story?"

"They've been in the system their whole lives. The mother is in jail. There is a 50/50 chance she'll stay there."

"What if she gets out?"

"She'll be deported."

"Where's the father?"

"Well, that's the thing. It's possible the five children have five different fathers. It's hard to find them because we don't know their names. The kids are American citizens. They were born here in Santa Maria, or Santa Barbara. I'll call you."

In early December, Scott called. I'd waited almost two months.

"The hearing is on December 16. I want you to go ahead and meet the kids."

I'd have children by Christmas! Even if they weren't mine, I was sure Scott would let them come over. Where else would they go? I'd need them on Christmas Eve, too. My family always opened one gift on Christmas Eve.

"Do they speak English?"

"I don't know. Do you speak Spanish?"

"Not really." My father was Puerto Rican and three of my four siblings spoke Spanish, but I wasn't a language person.

"Does the foster mother speak English?"

"No. I can have a translator meet you at the house. Better yet, call Willie, he speaks Spanish. Ask him to help. Are you sure you want to do this?"

"I am."

"If you're not sure, you have to tell me."

"I'm sure."

"They've had a tough life."

"That's okay."

After work I resisted driving by the foster home to steal a look because I worried Social Services might spot me stalking them. That ight, I called my sisters and mother and they offered to come to Santa Maria to help if the kids moved in. They knew I'd waited a long time.

I awoke Thursday with a cold and a day of appointments. I canceled everything except seeing the children. As the meeting approached, my anxiety rose. I'd learned in my licensing classes that adoptive parents were seen as saviors, at first. Then, memories of the harm children were rescued from faded and they began to look back. They wondered why it was, exactly, they were removed from their home. Mothers were forgiven, the social worker told us. Fathers, known or not, were forgiven too. Then the enemy became the system, a villain that trapped them in the deadest part of the world, where they hid in the dark, seething at their perceived mistreatment.

It got worse. Within four years of exiting foster care at age 18, 25% of foster children were homeless, 40% on public assistance, and 20% in jail. Only 2.7% would make it through college (one tenth the rate of other kids)[3]. 25.2% had Post Traumatic Stress Disorder, two times more than the rate experienced by war veterans[4]. All facts aside, I wanted to help my children see through the darkness, past their past. I'd give them a chance to rebound, like me. After all, it's never too late to have a happy childhood.

I waited outside the foster home for Willie. He was a big man with a bad knee. He took a box of eleven donuts out of the white county car. We shook hands.

"Thanks for coming," I said.

"It's my pleasure. Are you ready?"

"I'm ready."

"Donut?"

"No, thank you."

3    CA Foster Children and Education Report, 2008.
4    Northwest Foster Care Alumni Study, 2005.

We walked to the front door. It opened like a fairy tale. I saw Adriana first. She was a beautiful four-year-old girl with a long, black ponytail and used clothes. She was sweet and dimpled. Her little brown ears were pierced. Behind her I spotted Craig, or Chris, also in old clothes. His plump cheeks narrowed his eyes, making him look like a chubby Eskimo boy. He was adorable, with deeper dimples than his big sister. His teeth were perfect white, but dull at the tips like he'd been gnawing on bones. He was shy, but sturdy enough. Their older brother, Javier, was at school in first grade.

The foster mother was a Mexican woman about 50. Mimosa. She looked older from the sun in the fields.

Willie introduced us.

"¿Como está, señora?" I said.

"Bien, gracias." Her hair was gray and she wore swap meet clothes. The living room had a couch and a loveseat, both covered in throws and an old television in the corner. The floor was clean and empty. There were no toys and no sounds. Did they really live there? It was like they came in the back door when I came in the front door. The kitchen had a tortilla maker and a wooden dining table surrounded by six matching chairs, each with a torn pad with stuffing falling to the floor.

The children were excited to see donuts and sat at the table. Adriana gave Chris, or Craig, a donut and a napkin. They stared at me and I stared at them. Willie and I sat on the loveseat. Mimosa sat on the couch. I looked at the kids. They continued watching me. I didn't know what to say.

"You can ask her anything you want," Willie said.

"How are the kids?"

He asked. She answered. He translated. "They're good."

"What do they like to eat?"

"Hamburgers," he translated again.

"Do they have any clothes?"

"Nothing," Willie said, without asking Mimosa first. "They had a tough time in their old house. They arrived here with nothing."

"Do they have any toys?"

Again, on his own but in a funeral director tone, Willie took a breath and said, "It wasn't that kind of a home."

*What other kinds of homes were there?*

"How long have they been here?"

"Four months."

"When are their birthdays?"

"Well," Willie answered, without translation, "we don't really know, the mother didn't cooperate with us, she wouldn't share that information. But I think we can get that information."

Mimosa had a question for me. Willie translated. "Where is your wife? She wants to know where your wife is."

"Tell her I don't have a wife."

He told her. She wondered.

Willie didn't know I understood Spanish better than I spoke Spanish. I listened as he spun my being single for Mimosa, telling her I was an attorney and the vice-president of a local company and that I had a Mercedes (pre-Land Rover) and lived in a big house on the other side of town. She nodded.

Mimosa had another question. "She wants to know what you will do with the kids when you are at work."

"Tell her I'll put them in preschool so they can learn new things." Willie told her. She nodded and smiled.

"So, is the little one named Chris, or Craig?" I asked.

On his own, Willie said, "No one knows."

"Can you ask Mimosa what his brother and sister call him?"

"Craig."

That was the name we'd use.

The children finished eating and ran towards us. Craig was a good little runner. He slid to a halt in his worn socks and started dancing. He was a bad little dancer. Adriana came closer. She stared at me and smiled. Delightful.

I was there to ask Mimosa questions about the kids, but what questions? They were just children. I assumed they had their rabies shots and nightmares and that one might wet the bed, but I didn't care. The social worker who taught my classes told me that a lady to whom she gave a two-year-old boy gave him back because he wet the bed. "That lady went to the end of my list," she said.

"Are they nice kids?" I asked.

"She says she wishes they were hers."

She came from Mexico across the river, poor and hungry. She'd been in the States for more than 20 years, she told me later, and could not go back. She didn't say why, but sometimes she stared out the window. She was a good cook and cared for the kids. They trusted her.

She told Willie that Javier did well in school and we all nodded; that was good.

Craig climbed onto Mimosa's lap and pointed to the cheek he wanted kissed first. He didn't speak; he grunted. Was there something wrong with him? He was two years old. When did children start talking?

Adriana climbed onto Mimosa's other leg and said, "¿Estoy bonita?" She was asking Mimosa if she, Adriana, was beautiful. She was. I decided right there to take them. I'd spoil her first. My lap had plenty of room. I wanted them there. I'd give Craig all the kisses he needed. Adriana, too.

On the way home, I called Scott. "Hey. I met them! Finally. They're great kids."

"I'm glad. Are you sure you want to do this?"

"I am. I'm going back tomorrow to see Javier. He was at school. I'm getting a cold and won't last much longer today."

"You have to tell me if something goes wrong, or if you change your mind."

"Don't worry. I have the patience of a slab of granite."

"There are people in Social Services who think I'm making a mistake; they are opposed to this. I'm sticking my neck out for you."

I heard him, but it didn't register. I was thrilled to meet the children. I had a license I earned. I didn't care what people in Social Services thought.

"Everything will be fine," I said.

The next evening I returned to Mimosa's to meet Javier. He walked to me and offered his hand to shake. Craig was behind him and did the same. His hand fit between two fingers and my thumb. Adriana was there, too. She stood by my side and looked at me.

Javier was a little big brother with a delightful smile. He was too small to play football. Maybe thoroughbred racing. I'd stand by the rail and yell at the coach.

"How are you, Javier?"

"Good."

"My name is David."

"I know, my sister told me."

"How was school today?"

"Good."

He didn't look around much. And he was thin.

"You're in first grade, right?"

"Yeah."

"Do you like it?"

"I like math. Math and lunch."

Like his siblings, his teeth were brilliant white and perfectly spaced, like domino dots. His hair was a curly black mop over his ears, months since cut. Saving eight dollars, I imagined.

Their six dirty tennis shoes had six holes. I saw Adriana's toe sticking through an old sock. They were ready to eat dinner—bread with peanut butter and a glass of milk. They stood near me, not knowing what to do, a few watts of feelings, a beginning, a reason to wonder.

As days passed, the mere thought of them added years of depth and maturity to my life. They took me to a new place, awaking feelings I wasn't sure I had: trust, caring, and responsibility for others. It was like they walked in from the fields and gave me a tablet, inscribed with this: If you want love, give love.

If I pulled it off, this would be their last stop in foster care. They would not spend their lives in the dirt picking strawberries until their fingers bled and their backs ached from the stoop. Not that it was dishonorable—all work was honorable—but it was too low, paid less, and you weren't eligible for Social Security because you'd be long dead by 65.[5]

The children were slight, but I wasn't starting a rugby team. After a few weeks of regular meals they'd be like new – at least physically. Filling bellies, however, was easier than tending troubled minds. Why were they in foster care? No one told me. "We have some files," they said. A year and a half later, I'd finally see what happened on their last night with their mother. I realized that the two-month delay before I met them, explained as postponed legalities, was likely a ruse to give time for Adriana's bruises to heal.

Now that I'd met the children and knew a little about them, I wondered about their emotional health. When the light went out at night, did they sleep or see shadows? What did they remember of their mother and their transient lives?

5   Fieldworker life expectancy: 49 years. Antonio Velasco, M.D., Farm Workers in the 1990s. Forty-nine is akin to Somalia (United Nations report) and thirty years less than in the U.S. (CIA World Factbook, 2008). Camels and catfish live longer.

When I was seven, my mother called me and my two brothers and two sisters to sit on her bed. She told us our father would not come home from the hospital, but was instead going to heaven because God needed him there. Melanoma surgeries seemed a cruel way to take him, but if God needed him, an engineer, more than we needed him I imagined God had a big project in mind, like a bridge to heaven. I spent many years looking for that bridge. But I never found it.

To avoid the pain of his young death, I told myself every day don't think about it until you're 18 because it hurts too much right now and when people are 18 they are adults and they can think about anything they want. It was a strategy that helped my bleeding, broken heart, but, alas, by the time I was 18 and ready, having blocked it out for over ten years, there was nothing left to see or feel. I sort through old photographs instead. My childhood ended then. I was thrown out of school 10 times and arrested five times. I led a life that was, like my father's, timed to end at 36 years old. Until I realized I would outlive him—that there was no direct relationship between the father dying and the son—I had no long-term plans. Given my experience, I presumed Javier, Adriana, and Craig were doing what I did, struggling with memories—blocking out their own lives. My memories made me want to hurry. Through understanding and explanation, I wanted to help them before their pain metastasized, like mine, from memory to rebellion, permanently roosted in their psyches like the beaked shadow of dark-winged bird.

It'd be a shame if they turned out like me.

## 2. Train, Train, Go Away

Unlike normal people, I needed a license to become a parent. My saga began 256 miles north of Santa Maria. Before I met Javier, Adriana, and Craig, I lived on the Oakland side of the San Francisco Bay area, a fascinating multi-cultural dysfunction. My favorite day was Sunday when I'd breakfast at Jack London Square and watch giant praying mantis shipping cranes lift port cargo from ship to shore. I loved Oakland's unique people and places. Plus, I didn't get stabbed.

While managing a group of advertising sales people at the Oakland Tribune, a wood chip of a formerly stout newspaper, I watched my supervisor, Martha, complete California's licensing requirements to adopt a child.

Like most states, California did not permit adoptions until the child, or children, lived in the adoptive home for six months. In the meantime, a foster care license was required for placement of children into the home. After six months, the legal process of formalizing the adoption began. That process, I learned later, can take forever.

Martha had a six-figure income and a stay-at-home husband. Her situation was ideal; mine wasn't.

"Can single people adopt?" I asked, not knowing it was permitted for heterosexuals in every state except Nebraska (now allowed).

"Absolutely."

"I've always wanted kids. What do you think?"

"I think you should go for it. It's the greatest thing ever. Here's what you do...."

In July, I attended an evening adoption orientation meeting in a county building on Broadway Street in downtown Oakland. Besides the armed guard ensconced in his 9-11 bulletproof booth, I was the only white male in the building. I wondered why there weren't more males there, and if they'd come if they knew they could. Our culture not only doesn't celebrate males as parents, we're hardly recognized at all. The latest immigration "debate" accuses Mexican mothers of looking for a better place for their children when fathers seek that future as well.

Our biological clock is different than a woman's. Since men can technically produce children in our sixth or seventh decades, our clock instead winds down on our ability to raise children, attend high school graduations ("Who's the guy in the wheel chair?"), spend quality time, and help them grow. Thus, downtown Oakland.

Thirty curious people ate free cookies. One of the speakers was Bev Carter, an Alameda County social worker. She told us that Alameda County had 5,000 children in foster care. California had 98,000. 32% were six or younger. 40% were white, 32% black and 19% Hispanic.

"The licensing process requires 10 weeks of classes," Bev said. "I'll teach the classes. We'll conduct interviews, check references, and perform a background check. You'll need to give us fingerprints, take a physical, and turn in a written biography."

"There are," she added, "more than 500,000 children in foster care in the United States. About a third are available for adoption right now."

*I only needed one—no one would notice.*

"Do we get to choose the kids we want?" a lady asked.

"You do. Part of the application process requires you to review a list of behaviors exhibited by foster children, like fighting, or hoarding food. These children have had a tough life. You do get to pick certain characteristics, like age, gender, and ethnicity. We may not have what you want, and if you want a young Caucasian, you're in the wrong place, but we'll try."

"After that, assuming you're licensed, the social worker assigned to you will write what's called a Home Study. It's an in-depth report evaluating you as a prospective parent, summarizing your qualifications and recommending you for a license. Once that's finished, you'll sit with your social worker and review files, look at pictures, and read about the children, looking for a good match. You get to decide."

"How much does it pay?" a lady asked.

"Well, people taking foster children do get paid. You'll find out how much after you've taken the ten-week course."

*Clever.*

"What if we don't like the kids we get?" another lady asked.

*My competition was shrinking.*

"We try to match you with children you'll like. Here's how it works from here. Unless you contact us to decline, you will be in the October classes. We have your name and address from when you called about orientation. We'll mail you the specifics about where the class is, and the days and hours. If you don't get anything in the mail by August 15, call Social Services."

I called on August 16.

"You're not on the list. You'll have to wait and take the classes next year."

"I don't want to wait until next year."

"Too bad."

I found the director and left a thoughtful voicemail. In October, I drove five miles south on Highway 580 and parked next to an ugly brown government building near the Oakland Coliseum. My parenting experience would begin in the shadows of the city.

I had 12 classmates: three married couples, an unmarried couple because it was illegal for gays to marry, and four singles. Three of the singles were female. I thought I might connect with one of the women there, but what a debacle to date someone in an adoption class, have it fall apart and then limp to the finish line. No Distractions. The other male had a foster child at home already, but needed to renew his license. Altogether, we were nine households. Three wanted to be foster parents, six wanted to adopt. With 5,000 waiting to be adopted, each of us would need to take 833 children. I'd need a bigger place.

The training regimen selected by Alameda County was Model Approach to Partnerships in Parenting, or MAPP. Our first class was a hand shaking, "Pleased to meet you," session. Each student got a three-ring binder and a set of forms called a Profile. The Profile would be about me. It was the foundation of the Home Study, prepared by Bev to recommend me as a foster parent, or not.

We met from 6:30 pm to 9:30 pm every Tuesday night. We explored issues faced by foster children: rejection, fear of abandonment, violence, abuse, blood, drugs—it was touching. Bev, a petite, book smart and charming woman in her late 40's, was a gracious and forthright advocate for Alameda County children. She was soft-spoken, but tough. On occasion she preached about how we should raise our children. A classmate objected to Bev telling us spanking was not allowed. He eloquently made his case, but she said, "No. No hitting and no humiliating." Those were her main rules. "They've been hit enough. We're not going there anymore." She did not negotiate.

Bev explained how children get into foster care: "95% are there because of their parents' problems with drugs or alcohol."

I wondered if there were sweet children out there who needed a place to live because their parents died in a car crash, but no. This was not a Superman movie with junior popping out of a capsule in a barley field. Alameda County kids arrived bleeding and in a bad mood.

"Our children have had a hard life. And they react to that in a variety of ways, including fighting, skipping school, lying, stealing, wetting the bed, hurting animals, or lighting fires."

*Hmmm, except for hurting animals, I did everything on her list....*

We learned about separation anxiety—children being taken from parents, siblings, relatives and friends—and how this feels to them (bad). I'd been there with a father taken from me.

"Many children have parents in jail, if they're still alive. These children do not have good role models."

I knew from psychology textbooks that some experts thought personalities were formed and fixed early in life, before eight years old. I thought if I got young children I'd have time to heal them before they did anything bad.

Bev taught us how people attach to each other and how hard it is for children to attach to adoptive parents, especially if they've been pin-balled from one foster home to another. When to trust? And we learned the importance of maintaining "old-world connections," as Bev called it, a lifeline to their cultural past.

Finally, we discussed how our lives would change. It was important, she said, for us to ask for help, something I never did. Second, we'd need to tap into our network of family and friends for support and babysitting. I had no family within 800 miles and socialized with a grand total of zero couples with children.

Bev was not shy about telling it like it was—the beatings, fear, anxiety and distrust. Like an anatomy professor, she was curious to see if we'd run from the bleeding. All 13 stayed. Of the six households wanting to adopt, Bev told me years later, four did so.

I went online to find children to adopt. Many states posted photos and biographies. Some children were already broken. Others were sweet. All had a "Why me?" look. The reading depressed me and made me angry at the parents. Why did they leave their children? Why did they beat them? On one site I saw a family of five abandoned children, all with the same disease, all projected to die within five years. The reading took away your religion.

17

Then I found www.nwae.com, a consortium of four Northwestern states, and there they were, Eduardo and Rosario, cute little Hispanic children in foster care in Washington. She had a bad eye. He liked trucks. I decided I wanted them. That weekend I went to Michael's Arts & Crafts and bought Rosario a wicker basket and two ceramic bunnies.

Our last training class was a graduation party with cookies and cakes. I got a certificate with my name on it and two MAPP coffee cups. I told Bev about Eduardo and Rosario, and she agreed to rush my application. We made an appointment for her to interview me in my home—The Essex condominiums in downtown Oakland.

I arranged the visit for an evening following the housecleaner so everything was shiny. I put Piedmont Grocery fresh-cut flowers in my vase so Bev wouldn't think I was too busy for the little things. We sat next to my sixth floor window overlooking Lake Merritt. We saw joggers circling the lake and geese chasing cats. It was December 9, 2002.

"I've read your application and everything looks good."

"Did you get the fingerprint results back yet?" I wondered if the background check uncovered three arrests before I was 14 years old and two after that.

"Yes, everything is fine."

Bev had a pile of files and she took notes. After our meeting she would prepare my Home Study. She confirmed my age and income (I was promoted to director over five newspapers and made $7,500 per month).

First, we discussed my home. Bev described it in her Home Study report as "spacious and light-filled," "very neat," and "furnished in an appealing manner." No mention of the flowers.

"Tell me about your desire to adopt. Why do you want children at this stage in your life?"

"Well. I've always wanted children and I've simply grown tired of waiting. I don't want to be like those women I read about in Newsweek years ago who put career before family and looked back, at age 40, wondering why and too late and what happened. I enjoy children, watching them learn, and teaching them."

"You have some nice things here. Those three-foot-tall glass vases, they might get broken."

"They can break whatever they want."

"How come you never remarried?"

"After my divorce I took a year off from dating to figure out how I got myself into a bad marriage. I settled on the speed of it—we decided to get married 90 days after we met."

I skipped this part: I've dated a lawyer, belly dancer, marathon runner, massage therapist, artist, secretary, administrator, reporter, restaurant manager and a psychology student. And, um, blonde, brunette, black hair, and twisted, short, long, straight and curly. And, um, Spanish, Asian, Black, Danish, German and French. I asked out a woman I saw on the back cover of a marine biology book she wrote, another I saw profiled in the newspaper, and a third I admired as she delivered the TV evening news. I dated one woman who laughed at the wrong time at the movies and another with a pink living room: furniture, rugs, even the lamps. I felt like I was getting x-rayed in there. One woman dumped me via e-mail. Another I'm going to let go if she returns my phone calls. Several made me listen to Aaron Neville sing Yellow Moon. The best were the smartest. The worst spent money I sent to buy food for her kids on small D breast implants, saving "more than $200," she said. I've done it all. I've dated everyone but a nurse and a Canadian. There was no one left for me but Maureen Dowd.

"I'm not sure why I'm still single. I worry I might like being single. My career moved me around. I was terrified of having children and getting divorced again, and I have a built-in dilemma—I'm attracted to smart, accomplished women, but they're more inclined to pursue a career than embrace motherhood. And, thinking I would die young like my father, I did not want my wife to go through what my mother went through."

"You haven't died young."

"No, and that miscalculation went further than marriage. I never had long-term plans, never saved for retirement, never took my college education seriously, and never expected to live past 40."

"Why do you think you'll be good at this?"

"I relate well to kids. I lost my father when I was young, so I know what it's like to miss a parent. To wonder."

"That will help a lot. What kind of kids do you want?"

"As we discussed, I have two Hispanics in mind."

Half of my family was Puerto Rican. I traveled there many times in my youth to visit three sets of aunts and uncles and a dozen cousins. My ex-wife was Costa Rican. I had Hispanic blood and an Hispanic attitude. Plus, I liked enchiladas. I didn't want to get into a best home contest with cheerful couples wanting white children.

"Are you interested in African-American children? We have a lot."

"I'm open to anything, but I am half Hispanic, so that's my first choice."

"What about children who have been exposed to drugs prenatally, or children whose parents have a history of mental illness?"

"That's okay, I guess." I knew from class that nearly all foster children were exposed to drugs or alcohol and that saying no might end my candidacy. Plus, I didn't care. I knew children from spacious households with dedicated parents who ended up in a bad way and I knew children raised in despair who took flight.

"What about children with severe disabilities?"

She checked the "No" box as I nodded in agreement. A single guy with no family around…not going to happen.

"Tell me about your parenting experience."

*This won't take long.*

"Well, I've babysat," *for about 20 hours...*

"Are you open to allowing contact between your children and their natural family?"

"Oh, sure." I'd change my mind later.

"How do you want your children to turn out?"

"I'd like them to be good people and to feel like they can do whatever they want in the world. I'd love for them to go to college, but if they're healthy and happy I'll take that too."

"That's great. I think you'll be a good father."

*I'm winning!*

"I got your physical back; that's fine. And your fingerprints came back negative from the Department of Justice and the FBI. Your references are confidential, you can't see them, but they all highly recommend you as an adoptive parent. You are described as steady, fair, and a good listener, but headstrong at times."

"It's true."

"After the Home Study, two things need to happen before you're licensed. You need to take a one-hour safety course and someone from Social Services will visit for a safety inspection."

"I'm ready."

The Home Study she wrote said, "David impressed the worker as very much the way his references characterized him. He appears to be a thoughtful, bright, very responsible man with a genuine fondness for children... David has a very "rational" aspect to his personality, and is quite honest and straightforward... David demonstrated a real warmth and desire to create a nurturing, appealing, appropriate home for his children... While he does not have direct parenting experience, he does seem to have a feel for children's needs, and a strong willingness to go out of his way to meet those needs... He does need to create a more solid base of support... and is aware of this need. With that one caveat, the worker very highly recommends him as an adoptive parent. It is recommended that the home of David Marin be approved for the foster-adopt placement of two children, male or female, ages 1-7, race open."

I trusted Bev and appreciated her counsel from day one. The safety course, however, had a snag: the people teaching it didn't want to. It was cancelled in November and then in December. Finally, several of my classmates and I met in a government building near Hayward, down the road from Oakland. I walked to the security counter. A guard stared at a computer screen.

"Hi. Where is the adoption training safety class?"

"It's cancelled."

"Why?"

"We had an anthrax scare. The building was evacuated."

"If the building was evacuated, what the hell are you and I doing standing in it?"

"It was evacuated," he yawned. "Everyone came back but the people teaching the class."

Three months had passed while we waited for the state to hold a goddamn one-hour course. I had two children I wanted. In the parking lot, I called Social Services with my cell phone. I left the director a little voicemail. She called in ten minutes.

"We aren't responsible for teaching the course. We just schedule it."

"What is the new date?"

"I think I can get someone there next week."

"I'll look forward to your call." I wondered if Alameda County's 5,000 children in foster care was partially the fault of...Alameda County.

After I took the safety course I e-mailed Eduardo and Rosario's social worker—the rescuer cometh—but it was too late. After 48 months in foster care, 20 months more than average, they were placed in a home. It hurt. Even though I hadn't met them I told people about them and I wanted them and I had rose strewn plans now broken because Social Services had the kinetic energy of a bag of grapefruit.

I thought about a different approach. My license didn't compel me to adopt through the county. Friends suggested going overseas. People did that for many reasons, mainly to avoid getting a child exposed to drugs or because they wanted a baby that wasn't too dark. But drugs and alcohol were worldwide problems and a Caucasian baby was hard to get in the United States. And expensive. (I e-mailed an agency about a white child I saw online. He cost $24,000 they wrote back, asking nothing about me.) Besides, working full-time, I'd be foolish to try to raise a diapered youngster on my own.

Nevertheless, I made an appointment for a county person to come to my home for the safety inspection. Following the script, I bought a fire extinguisher and a first-aid kit. If all was well, I'd get my license right there. Then I'd call Bev and we'd review files. Soon I'd take a daughter or son to the playground, holding hands across the parking lot.

My new boss, Kevin, the executive vice-president, limped like an old Green Bay Packer linebacker. He fancied himself a Master of the Universe like the author Tom Wolfe described in *Bonfire of the Vanities*, but after I bought a new briefcase he soon had a $300 briefcase and after I hung a $10 Velcro dartboard in my office he soon mounted a $300 electronic board in his. Those were not the actions of a true Master. When he found out I was taking adoption classes, he took me to lunch and told me it was too much and a bad idea. A father, he did not understand someone wanting children. He often cursed and ridiculed women late for meetings because of their "fucking" kids. Since I wasn't looking for family planning advice, I ignored him.

Three days before I'd get my license, my best friend Greg, one of my adoption references, and Martha, my old boss who inspired me to adopt, both told me to reconsider. Both said it was a bad idea. Both said I did not know what was going to happen. I thought they were warning me about the challenges of being a single parent: It's a lot of work, no time to play golf, etc. I was touched they cared.

Twenty-four hours before I'd meet the licensing social worker, Kevin came into my office, put his foot up on a chair, and told me he was stripping me of half of my responsibilities. "Most people at our level," he said, "would resign if this happened to them, which wouldn't bother me a bit."

Later that afternoon, he came back into my office, tossed an e-mail onto my desk from a headhunter looking for a director at a newspaper 256 miles away and said, "This would be a good place for you to raise your family." At a meeting a few days later, he told my colleagues that I had resigned, "To raise a family somewhere else."

I was finished, ousted by a three-ring circus of boss, best friend, and mentor. It was a devastating blow. I canceled the licensing visit because they didn't give children to unemployed people. Worse, since foster care training and licenses were not transferable from one county to another, I'd have to start over. I took the new job in Santa Maria.

When I asked Kevin why he did what he did, he said, "You'll figure it out in ten years."

That weekend, I figured it out in ten hours, I found an attorney, and after moving to Santa Maria, I sued Kevin. Two weeks after the lawsuit was delivered Kevin didn't work at the Tribune anymore. But the company chose to defend him anyway.

We would engage in a two-year battle punctuated by the law firm defending Kevin trying to interfere with me adopting my children.

# 3. Colorado Boulders

Blown to Santa Maria by cannon, I arrived in a bad mood and with one rule: Do Not Tell Anyone You Are Adopting Children Because You Cannot Afford to Lose Another Job.

According to Mapquest, Santa Maria had one main road. Worse, if your town was named after a boat you should see water, but not here. I thought about giving up, but I wanted children and a family. I called a real estate management company and rented their biggest house. I didn't realize I was moving to the white side of town, and I didn't realize the jail I jogged past contained my children's mother.

After months settling and recovering from my wounds, one night I visited the www.nwae.org web site where I found Rosario and Eduardo. You're a fool, I thought: Move. On.

What do you know, their photos were back on line! Perhaps the adoptive parents gave them back. I'd bring them to Santa Maria and....I called Santa Barbara County Social Services and explained my situation and they agreed to license me if I faxed Bev's Home Study and got fingerprinted again and I called my mother and sisters and they were happy and I was happy, but when I called Washington Social Services the woman said someone put their photos up by mistake so I called the county and said there was no hurry anymore.

I thought about quitting, or getting a pet bird. I didn't have to send e-mails to Washington for a bird and no one ever lost a job because they had a canary. I thought about moving to a smaller place, too. What the hell was I doing in such a big house? When people on their evening walks passed my house they looked past me to see who else lived there, but it was just me. If I lived in a studio no one would look past me—that was the rule—people in studios left each other alone.

Then, on October 3, my office phone rang. I'd been on the anthill for six months.

"…my name is Scott. I'm with Santa Barbara County Social Services. I have five little Hispanic kids, ages two, four, six, eight and ten. Can I bring them over?"

Well. I met them and I loved them and now I was days away from having three children. Time to nest! I gathered string and shiny objects and made a bowl of sticks in the crook of a maple tree. I found a red race car bed in my newspaper classifieds. The owner delivered it for an extra $25. He said he and his wife had 33 foster children before taking a break. I wondered if my children had already slept in the race car.

I had an antique walnut bedroom set with two twin beds I bought for Rosario and Eduardo. It was for Adriana now. I bought a thin wood-and-fabric contraption to replace the box-spring; she'd be low and not fall too far if she rolled over the edge. Lowering her bed four inches was the first of many odd actions I took to make sure the children were safe. I was paranoid that if something bad happened Social Services wouldn't let me keep them.

I shopped Walmart for supplies. I had no idea what I was doing, but instead of my ignorance stopping me, I delighted in the challenge, excited and proud. The children were so sweet, helpless really, and brought me such joy. For the first time in my life I had a purpose. I knew I knew nothing and I knew I'd make mistakes, but who cared? We were in Santa Maria. The whole place was off the record.

I bought pink sheets and a quilt for Adriana and a comforter set for Javier. Finding a Hispanic doll, Dora, surprised me, but Santa Maria was 67% Hispanic, more than four times higher than the national rate, so it made demographic sense. Adriana would be thrilled with a doll in mirror image. I put it on her bed to use as a pillow. I bought a big brown stuffed dog and put it on Javier's bed for his pillow. Craig's pillow was a soft stuffed airplane. I saved whatever money pillows cost because I needed three car seats. After thinking that pillows was a weird way to save money I bought three at Kmart. At the grocery store I pretended to shop for me and three children. There were cookies, candies, and ice cream, items I never bought. I reached for frozen French fries and fish sticks, but why now? And, um, how will I go grocery shopping with three little kids? I'd need a store with licensed childcare.

The big day arrived: December 16. As required by law, before severing the rights of parent(s) Social Services had to first win a judge's permission to stop working with the parent(s). It's called withdrawal of services and that's what it is—Social Services withdrawing its services. The hearing would free the children to spend time with me. The notion that I'd have them for Christmas poured joy into me. My mother and sisters would come to Santa Maria after Christmas to help me get settled—a period of time I estimated between three weeks and fifteen years.

In dreams before I slept, I imagined the children and me going to Nipomo, an exit ramp north of Santa Maria. We'd turn right off Highway 101 and right again and hold hands as we walked through Holloway's Christmas Tree Farm. We'd take a saw from the rack, choose a tree, saw on it, and cut it down. We'd drag it out to where the tractor comes to pick us up. We'd ride on the tractor to the booth up front, pay and go home, make hot chocolate and a wood fire and listen to Bob Seger sing "Little Drummer Boy" and John Lennon sing "This is Christmas."

I called Scott for his update. He'd want to speak first. He said nothing. "Do you know what time the hearing is today?" I asked.

"The hearing was yesterday."

I was grateful to Social Services. "What happened?"

"The attorney for the county didn't show up. Nothing happened. You can't see the kids until the hearing takes place. I'm sorry. I know you're disappointed. I think it's re-scheduled for the end of January. About five weeks. I'll look it up and let you know."

"Why didn't the attorney show up?"

"She had a cold."

*What about our Christmas?*

I felt my face turn red getting mad—at myself. Why did I agree to meet the children before the parents' rights were severed or the withdrawal of services occurred? No sensible adoption attorney would advise a couple to do that. Worse, to prevail legally it's helpful to have an adversary. Social Services wasn't even sure of the identity of the fathers of my children. Without knowing the names of the fathers, how would Social Services serve notice of legal proceedings, send a blimp over Mexico?

Bev warned us in training about social workers who tried to place kids before severance of parental rights: "They may use you as a temporary shelter." I blamed myself because I assumed the risk.

For the 44th Christmas in a row, I would not have kids. I called Scott. "Is it okay if I buy the kids Christmas presents?"

"I don't know. I'm not sure."

"They don't have any toys."

"You were not supposed to meet the kids until the severance hearing. The meeting was a mistake."

I made a face.

"All right, but only if you leave them anonymously. You can put them on the porch."

"They don't have a porch."

"I'm worried you'll confuse them."

"I'll leave the presents near the door."

I bought Craig a Winnie the Pooh book. Javier got a fire truck. Searching for Adriana's gift, I noticed that coloring books, watches, toys, whistles, and shirts had the Hispanic girl, Dora "The Explorer" on them. Instead of provincial to Santa Maria, Dora was likely a national phenomenon. Adriana might know her. I would have looked stupid acting like I'd discovered a Hispanic doll. Now, no one will ever know.

Adriana got crayons and a Dora coloring book to match her pillow doll. As I wrapped the presents I decided to not leave them in the dark. Six days before Christmas I called Scott. "I don't want to leave the presents by the door. I want to give them to the kids."

"I'm worried they'll mention the word adoption. No one is supposed to mention that word until we write a communications plan for the kids. We have to write a plan so they know what's happening to them."

"You know the situation better than I do. Will the withdrawal of services hearing go as you plan, or not?"

"I think it will." He paused. "Don't tell anyone I said okay, but go ahead."

I liked Scott, even though I'd never met him, because he didn't mind breaking the rules with me. And according to Willie, he had long hair. He was about improving lives, not capturing the most money. I imagined Scott to be a skilled recycler with thin, friendly children.

After work I drove to Mimosa's house. I stood in the dark in a suit and tie. Guys leaning on their cars watched me holding a bag of toys. Adriana spotted me through the window and jumped from the couch. I loved it. The door opened and she was there. I hugged her and kissed her on the cheek. She gave me a kiss, giggled, and held my hand. Inside, I saw seven kids instead of three. Which ones were mine? I smelled carne asada taco meat and tortillas on the griddle. My mouth watered. I knew Mimosa would invite me to eat and that I'd say no because I always said no. I didn't want her to run out of food.

Craig ran to me and reached up with his brown doll arms, more in question than gesture. I picked him up and kissed his chubby cheek. He hugged me tight. Javier stood by smiling. After putting Craig down, Javier and I shook hands. I rubbed the top of his head. My fingers disappeared in the depths of his hair.

I got my bearings and sat down. Seven children stared at me like meerkats. I handed out three gifts.

"I got a truck," Javier guessed.

"Javier," I said, "who are these two girls?"

"They're Mimosa's daughters."

They looked like grandchildren to me. A sick one clutched a box of tissues. "And who are these two?" I said, gesturing towards a girl and boy.

"She's Flora, and that's her brother, Jeremiah. He's my friend." I guessed that Flora and Jeremiah were also foster kids, meaning that Mimosa had five foster kids and two grand-daughters. That's a lot of tortillas. Jeremiah told me that Mimosa, who didn't drive, was taking the children to Santa Barbara to visit her sister for Christmas. Eight seats on the Greyhound bus; seven if she holds Craig.

Watching my three show their presents to the other four, I realized it was difficult for the ones who got nothing. "Your presents were so big," I white-lied, "I couldn't carry them all. I'll bring the rest tomorrow."

"When?" the sick daughter asked.

"After dark; after work."

"What will I get?"

"It'll be a surprise."

It was time to go. Adriana, who I'd never heard speak English, stopped me with a tug on my pant leg. "Can we open our presents tonight?" she asked. Her eyes were pools of chocolate.

I glanced at Mimosa, but her look said no.

"No, princess. Wait until Christmas; it's only six days away."

"Princess? He called me princess." She twirled, smiled and I loved her. I wanted to give her the biggest hug in the world. Her dimples melted me.

Stopping me at the front door, Javier said, "Do you want me to show you our rooms?"

"Sure. Let's go."

We got Craig and Adriana and walked down the hall. It was the first time the four of us were alone together. I had to watch all three at once. My head went back and forth like a windshield wiper.

"I sleep here," Javier said, pointing to the lower bunk. "Jeremiah sleeps up there."

"Where does Craig sleep?" I asked.

"He sleeps with Mimosa," Adriana answered.

"And where do you sleep, princess? Where is your room?"

"I sleep there," pointing to a bedroom with two mattresses on the floor. All four girls slept there.

Not for long.

As I left we exchanged little hugs and kisses on the cheek. I went to Kmart to shop for the other kids. I got a Cinderella doll, a huggable dog, a jewelry making kit, and a cheap digital watch. The next night, Jeremiah opened the door. The other kids were playing in the back but heard the commotion inside. Craig ran to me and reached, and when I bent down he gave me a kiss. Adriana gave me a kiss. Oh, goodness.

"How are you, sweetie?"

"Good. Did you bring me any toys?"

"No, sweetie. I came to bring toys for the other kids. Do you want to help me?"

"I'm helping!" she announced to the group. Everyone else just get back!

Javier was happy to see me. When I said, "You're a good boy," he swooned like Ray Charles.

Mimosa didn't mind if these kids opened their presents. Maybe she knew they had other presents in Santa Barbara. Six kids climbed on the couch to watch. Adriana gave the dog to the sick daughter. I told her how to hug it before she goes to sleep.

"I know how to do it," she said.

As the kids unwrapped gifts I saw Adriana's Dora book on the floor.

"Adriana, what did you get?" I asked.

"A Dora book and colors."

"Do you know Dora?"

"She's the explorer."

*Alrighty then.*

"Javier, what did you get?"

"A fire truck. Do you want me to show it to you?"

"Sure."

Adriana brought me her coloring book and crayons. The book cover was torn and half the crayons broken. I looked for scissors to help the other daughter free Barbie from her little pink box while I explained to Jeremiah that I'd get him a new present after Christmas because he already had a watch. Javier got the new watch. It fell off his little wrist unless he held up his arm like the Statue of Liberty. I was happy to need a present for Jeremiah because it gave me an excuse to return after Christmas.

Adriana sat on my lap while Javier and Jeremiah tried to set the new watch. Meanwhile, one of the other girls asked me to help get Barbie's maid outfit free of the wrapping while Craig lifted the fire truck onto my legs. I noticed the other girl struggling to open her jewelry making kit and I told her I'd help her, but I didn't because there were too many kids and I was losing track. In a few minutes, her gift finally unwrapped, she came to me.

"Can you help me put this back in the box?"

"Why? Don't you want to play with it?"

"I want to save it for Christmas."

It was time to go. I knew weeks would pass before I saw the children again. I worried what they'd think.

"When will you come back?" Adriana said.

"After Christmas. You're going to Santa Barbara for Christmas. I'll bet you have fun. I'll come and see you after Christmas. In about five weeks." I tried to be positive, but the words tumbled out of my mouth like Colorado boulders. The children didn't understand Social Services miscues. Five weeks were an eternity to them—and what if the hearing didn't happen? Maybe Scott was wrong and the county would lose. Not seeing the children again would be a fiasco, for me and them.

"I'll miss you," Adriana said, sinking my heart. Why is it when your brain registers a sadness you feel it in your chest? It hurt me to think of them wondering, "Will he be back? He appeared from nowhere. Will he disappear the same way?" I worried about them waiting, watching by the window, one by one giving up, walking to the dark two-mattress room, Adriana throwing the stupid Dora coloring book away, hating me for hurting her.

I hugged Javier and kissed his forehead. "I promise I'll be back, but I'm not sure when."

"Okay."

The next day I called Scott. I presumed he was evaluating me. I told him I delivered the presents, as promised, and—what a guy!—added four more today. He was pleased, but puzzled at the number of children in Mimosa's house.

"The kids are great. This is what I've been waiting for. I understand you have your challenges there, but I'd appreciate you and your folks getting on with your business so we can make this happen."

"Okay. I'll move forward, but I have to tell you, there are people in my office who are opposed to this."

"Is that something I need to worry about?"

"No."

He miscalculated.

# 4. Cinderella Story

The delay was excruciating. I wanted golf partners, but it wouldn't last when I had children. Socializing with couples with children was odd. I floated between worlds. Scott said the hearing was January 26. Four months after learning their names I'd see the kids again. I wanted to play with them and I wondered if Javier was still holding up his arm. I called and learned that Scott was gone on vacation. I felt betrayed. I wanted to lay into someone, but if I yelled they might not give me my kids. I asked the woman if she knew about my case and she said no. I asked if the attorney was in court today and she said yes, but she didn't know why.

That night my mother and sisters gasped in disbelief. I complained about the bureaucrats and told them that the social worker placing the kids with me never asked to meet me and didn't know the kids. I went to bed numb, wondering when I'd see the kids, if ever. I felt like I was waiting to see if I was pregnant.

The next morning I called at 9 a.m.; no answer. I called the operator. "The unit is not in."

"What does that mean, the unit is not in?"

"No one knows where they are. The entire department is gone."

Was that legal? I called later and learned that the department was on an annual sabbatical in Buellton, 40 minutes south of Santa Maria. I spoke with Scott that afternoon. The judge approved withdrawing services from the mother after she chose from two options: stay in jail—her home since the last August night with her children—or be deported. She declined an attorney and chose deport.

"There is bad news," Scott said. "A great-aunt in southern California appeared at the hearing to say she wants the children. She's been around before, but was turned away the first time because of a child abuse charge she admitted to. I also have a problem with relatives showing up now, six months after the kids went into foster care."

Scott's job was to place children with their blood family, if possible. He didn't have to find relatives with superior parenting skills. However, waiting so long to call, whatever parenting skills the great aunt had, speed wasn't one of them. Instead of causing Scott relief, she made him worry about a late night rendezvous with the true parents and the kids in the trunk motoring down Highway 101, going south to their past.

"I'll check it out," he said. "Don't worry about it."

I worried about it. I did not want them to pull my children back down the drain.

"Let's meet tomorrow and talk about logistics," he said. "I'd like to meet you, too."

We met at lunchtime in the ground-floor café of the county building. His straight hair fell to his waist. I felt a kinship with him at once. When I was in junior high, I wore my red hair long, and his helping me sneak in Christmas gifts made him a fellow free-thinker. I offered to buy Scott lunch but, as I suspected, he was not a lunch person. He drank water and ate fruit.

"How are things going?"

"This is the greatest thing I've ever done. It's a blast."

"I've heard they're good kids."

"Do you have files on them, anything I can read to learn about them?"

"Not today. We're not there yet. I'll give you what I get when I get it." He was calm and professional. I knew he wondered who I was and if I'd make it. Ours was an unusual relationship: a man giving children he didn't know to a man he just met, both under pressure, sitting in a county café, eating fruit. At a clerical level, we had to trust each other, and we did, but over time and many phone calls the trust he gave me and I gave him evolved from a gift to each other to a determination we shared.

"Let's talk about money. Foster parents get paid for taking care of children. Depending on the ages and the needs of the children, payments range from $400 to $600 per child, per month. You'll be paid about $1,350 a month until the kids are adopted."

"Okay." I didn't know how much kids cost, but that sounded good.

"You also get a $10,100 federal tax credit."

"My tax rate is so high it will only be worth about $6,000."

"You don't understand. A tax credit is not subtracted from your income before you pay taxes; it's subtracted from what you owe in taxes. It's $10,100 in your pocket. Per child. It's an incentive."[6]

"That's a lot."

"I can't believe you didn't know about that."

"I had no idea."

"Your licensing trainers didn't mention it?"

"Maybe that was the class I missed."

"You'll also get $500 every six months for clothes."

I knew that if kids were difficult to place in homes they were designated Special Needs kids, and the federal Adoption Assistance Program guaranteed the monthly care payments until they turned 18. Children were designated Special Needs if they suffered mental or physical health problems, or if they met any one of these four criteria: part of a sibling group, over two years old, minorities, or having parents with an adverse background (like felons). My three Snickers bars, older than two and fathered by fellas with their own wing at San Quentin had it all. It was a Cinderella story. The trick was that you had to fight for it.

"I want the payments to continue until the kids are 18 under the federal Adoption Assistance Program. My kids are Special Needs kids,

---

6  States offer various incentives. Massachusetts, Maine, Kentucky, Maryland, Oregon, Texas, Virginia, and Florida offer free in-state college tuition to children adopted through Social Services.

right?"

"I'll say. They'll get free health care until they're 18, too."

"Okay."

The payments and tax credits totaled $310,000. I'd never purchased health care for children but at, say, $100 per month each (for up to 16 years for Craig), that was nearly $54,000 more. The feds would pay me $364,000 to change the path of three sweet little people.

They had their reasons.

If the children remained in foster care until 18 years of age, within four years of exiting the system we'd have a high school graduate on public assistance, a junior-high school dropout picking strawberries, and a prisoner.[7] If I am modestly successful, I'll raise a high school graduate, a college graduate, and a post-grad. Here's the value of the federal investment in me:

The high school graduate, paying $5,278 per year[8] in federal income tax, Social Security and Medicare payments on income of $26,000 per year[9], is a federal tax revenue gain of $237,510 from 20 to 65 years old.

Let's say the junior-high dropout spends half his/her life on welfare at $400 per month and half earning a typical drop-out salary of $17,000 per year, paying $2,601 per year in taxes. It's a net loss of $49,477.

A California prisoner costs the state $45,000 per year.[10] If he/she does 10 years for robbing banks the old fashioned way, that's $450,000 in today's dollars. After release, he/she might have the earning capacity of a high-school drop-out. Working half of the years until 65 years old and half on welfare is a net loss of $488,482.

Trio summary: a net loss of $300,450.

The flip side: The high school graduate pays in $90,000. The

7   California Foster Children and Education Report, 2008.
8   Estimated by a real CPA.
9   Alliance for Education. The High Cost of High School Dropouts, 2007.
10  National Institute of Corrections, 2009.

college graduate earns $52,000 per year and pays $10,956 in taxes, Social Security, and Medicare—a 41 year gain (four years in college) of $449,196. The post grad pays $23,475 for 39 years (six years in college) on $75,000 income, a gain of $915,525. The total income tax, Social Security, and Medicare revenue is $1,602,231. The swing from losing $300,450 to gaining $1,602,231 is $1,902,681, or 5.2 times more than the $364,000 invested in me. Then, if you add my $1.9 million to the other guys out there adopting three children abandoned by fieldworkers and felons you get...$1.9 million.

If two of my children complete graduate school or one strikes it big, robbing banks the Goldman Sachs way,[11] for example, tax revenues will soar.

The ripple effect of my children raising children with the same opportunity they now have adds, at three children each, millions in tax revenue per generation. California, with 154,000 high-school dropouts per year, foregoes $40 billion per year in personal income from people whose income would be just $9,000 higher if they graduate from high school.[12]

If they graduate from college, the $40 billion triples to $120 billion.

I have no idea how my children will turn out. At 13, Javier is old enough to drop out of junior high, join the 53%[13] of field workers with less than an eighth grade education, and work in the fields picking lettuce. That's legal in California. Instead, his current report card has six grades, all A's. He is probably better educated than his possible parents and for sure he's read more books and speaks and writes English better

11  Matt Taibbi, Rolling Stone, 2010, comparing Goldman Sachs to "a great vampire squid wrapped around the face of humanity, relentlessly jamming its blood funnel into anything that smells like money."
12  Alliance for Education. The High Cost of High School Dropouts, 2007.
13  Immigration Reform and U.S. Agriculture; Demographics Characteristics of Fieldworkers. University of California, 1995.

than any of those that might have been. This is not to criticize his parents. If they gave up selling Chiclets in Tijuana and came here for honest opportunities not available back home, they did what I'm doing, providing for their children. It's an instinct older than the Nile River.

Scott continued: "Here's the plan. Assuming I can get past the aunt, you get to see the kids again. I want you to spend evenings and weekends with them for a month to practice."

"Practice what?"

"Being a family. We also need to write a communications plan to tell the kids you want to adopt them. We do that in case they get scared. Some don't want to leave their foster home."

"How long will that take?"

"Just a couple of weeks. By the time the month is over we will have told the kids."

"They'll be fine."

"I'm sure they will. I'm concerned about me. One lady in the office told me I was crazy."

That was the third time Scott had warned me. I tried to imagine the rationale: 1) he's in it for the money, 2) single people should not adopt, 3) men should not adopt, 4) he wants to hurt the kids, 5) parents and children should be of the same ethnicity, 6) he's too old, or 7) he's gay—not that there's anything wrong with that—unless you live in Florida, Mississippi, or Iran.[14] However, with the kids in my heart, a new town, a new job, and the lawsuit, I didn't have time to contemplate the anxiety of strangers. I refused to imagine an opponent acting on prejudice. I was wrong. My list was one short. The lady who told Scott he was crazy for giving me my children wasn't opposed to me, she was opposed to them,

14  Gays can't be foster parents in Mississippi, adopt in Florida, or be alive in Iran.

the children. We'd meet soon.

"When can I see the kids?"

"I checked on the aunt. I'm not going to choose her over you. But I told her she has until Thursday to give me her best shot. I'll call and let you know. Then you can go over and see the kids."

"Okay."

"Don't do anything until I tell you."

I got a bigger house in a new development peppered with Hispanics. It was a three-bedroom, two-bath with a fireplace, and a separate one-bedroom, one-bath nanny quarters. I'd have Maureen Dowd in there on weekends and a slender, bi-lingual, Canadian nursing student working Monday through Friday. The house was surrounded by a six foot tall wall so the children could not run away. Flowering plants grew inside the wall in a dirt bed laced with irrigation hose. I imagined Craig pulling the hose out foot by foot. I didn't have a key yet, so I peered through the windows and saw that the living room, dining room, and kitchen were one big room and that was good. I'd be able to see the kids at all times. I looked through the bedroom windows and imagined the kids' beds in there. I decided to not show them the house until it was ready with our furnishings inside. I'd be across town now, my commute tripling from four minutes to twelve.

On Thursday I was thrilled beyond compare. After work, I'd see the kids for the first time in five weeks. I wanted to play with them. My cell phone rang. It was Scott.

"I have bad news. We received a call from a nephew. He wants to take the kids."

"Who is he?"

"I didn't talk to him. Someone else did and gave me their notes. He's 20, and lives in a one-bedroom apartment in Los Angeles with his sister and brother-in-law. I can't imagine anything will come of it. Where has he been? But I have to check it out. I'm sorry."

"How long will it take?"

"I just left him a message, but he hasn't returned my call."

"Are you thinking a 20 year old will be better able to take care of the kids than me?"

"No. But I have to talk to him. I think I can figure him out with one conversation. I have to do it, but I also know that after six months, this guy, like the great aunt, is slow. I know you're excited about tonight and I want tonight to go as planned. I'll give him a few hours. I'll call you at 4 p.m. when the coast is clear."

"I left them looking out the window five weeks ago, wondering if I'd come back."

"I know."

At 4 p.m. I opened my Palm Pilot to get Scott's number. As I reached to hit the first digit, the phone rang. "It's me," Scott said. "Tonight is off. He never called back, but I can't just give him a few hours. We have to wait until next week. I'll give him until next Thursday."

I wanted to rip his face off. "I respect your work," I said. "You need time to do your job."

"I know you're mad."

"I'll be all right." That night I drove to the new house and looked in the windows. I saw where we'd put the piano to sing songs. If I had a piano, songs and children.

I made the same frustrating phone calls I'd made for over a year. My mother didn't answer and my older sister, Diana, was on a business trip. My little sister, Joy, was home and cheered me up when she said that instead of joining Diana for a Disneyland trip after the kids moved in, she'd come out before I got the kids to help me prepare. I suspected she thought I had just two or three towels for the four of us. I was wrong—she thought I had one. I needed more towels, and she had an impressive list of ideas: girl things for Adriana, and food, paper plates, etc.

We laughed when we imagined the kids' reaction when the first dinner I made was frosted Pop Tarts with a side of Vienna sausage. I was excited about her coming and knew she'd be an immense help. I stayed up late packing boxes. When I packed Craig's bedding, I wrote "Kids' Bedding" on the box and wondered how many people without kids wrote "Kids' Bedding" on a box.

The next day I talked to Diana.

"I can't believe these people," she said. "I want to complain. Is there someone I can write a letter to?"

"I don't think so. Scott is just doing his job."

My mother called to tell me that when I got the kids I'd need lots of rags. "Today is your father's 70th birthday." She'd called me every January 31 since I left home thirty years ago to remind me of the date.

I thought of my father nearly every day, usually for just seconds. I don't believe in heaven, but I know he'd be proud of me if he were alive. He was the Hispanic father of pale kids. I was the pale father of Hispanic kids. We were a human anagram.

I packed more boxes and went to the house and looked in the windows again. Worried that the kids might escape through the five inch wide spaces between the wrought-iron bars on the front gate, I bought black, plastic mesh to match and fit the gate. An apparition couldn't slip through. It was this kind of cleverness that separated me from the other men out there adopting three children.


The Super Bowl was Sunday and I watched a few plays. I went to the new house and walked outside the bedroom, 12 steps heel to toe. A key would come in handy here. I went home and walked the current bedroom, also 12 steps heel to toe. The beds will fit.

Scott called on Monday. "I'm frustrated and embarrassed that people are raising their hands now, six months after I contacted family members and asked them to take the kids."

"What did the nephew say?"

"He hasn't called me back. The deadline is Thursday. Five o'clock. After I place the kids in your home it will be nearly impossible for anyone to interrupt it. But I have to make sure there is no genuine interest from a suitable family member. It's what I do."

"Assuming we don't hear from him, when can I see the kids, and how often?"

"I know you're busy," Scott said. "How often do you want to see them?"

"What's the maximum?"

"Well, I guess Monday, Wednesday, and Friday evenings. And weekends."

"That's what I want. Then they can move in full-time? I have a business trip to Las Vegas. I'll be back on February 27."

"If that's what you want and all goes well, we have a deal."

I told people at work what I was doing. Some nearly fell over, and I'm not kidding. Quietly, slowly, I learned that several colleagues were adopted and that several had adopted their kids. Instead of adoption being grand, it was a source of shame, a scar covered by long sleeves. I didn't get it. During my classes I learned that in the United States, 2.1 million people, one in 150, are adopted. That's about one per block. Moreover, with 2.1 million adoptions, there are (usually) two parents and a child affected. And aunts, uncles, grandparents, and cousins. The one in 150 people affected evolves into 10 in 150, meaning adoption impacts 20 million people.

People asked me if I'd tell my kids they're adopted. Well, I'm white with red hair. They're young and chocolate. I had no problem telling my children, it was a good story, but there was a reticence in the world. Over the years, seeing me with the kids, several people have said, "Your wife must be really, really dark." Adriana, on one of our walks when she was five years old, told me that she wanted to dye her hair red so people would not think she's adopted.

A lady who retired the week I started my job was back, nearly a year later, standing in my office with tears in her eyes. We hardly spoke when she retired and I didn't remember her name, but I knew why she was there.

"I heard what you are doing," she said. "It's wonderful. I'm adopted."

"They're great kids," I said. I walked around my desk and hugged her. On Thursday afternoon, Scott called.

"What happened?" I said.

"He never called back."

"Are we free?"

"You're free."

After work I went to Toys R Us and found a clerk to help me select three car seats. You got your boosters and your car seats and your convertibles and your travel systems. I didn't know the difference or the law. Plus, there were separate seats for infants. Was Craig an infant? I stayed up late adjusting car seat straps— trying to remember the leg width of children I'd known for 90 minutes.

## 5. Family Practice

On Friday, February 6, 2004 my life's miscues and excuses vanished with footsteps coming down the hall, keys jangling. The door to my future was unlocked—I couldn't wait to go. I changed into jeans after work and drove to Mimosa's at 6:15 p.m. The house was low lit and quiet. Then I saw Adriana through the window, waiting. Her smile when she saw me made me dream. Seven kids greeted me at the door.

"Daddy's here," Mimosa said to Adriana.

"Daddy's here!" Adriana said to Craig.

Javier knew Daddy wasn't there, but was sweet nonetheless. All three gave me hugs and kisses. I soared on high, unafraid. I didn't waver; no one would stop me. I sat on the couch. Craig hopped onto my lap and blew a wad of snot on my hand. Adriana rushed for a Kleenex. Javier was back at the table eating dinner, a piece of bread with peanut butter.

"Do you want to go to McDonald's?" I asked.

Three cheers!

Adriana held a little sweater. "Daddy, I have a sweater for Craig. It's mine, but he doesn't have a coat."

Adriana and Javier had coats, each with the name of someone else sewn inside the collar. Adriana's pants were blue and baggy. Javier's khaki pants were big enough to fit both legs in one side. She wore her long hair in a ponytail, held tight with a rubber band. He had a Hawaiian shirt Mimosa probably bought for a quarter. They looked like porch kids in the Grapes of Wrath.

Adriana constantly stood by me, squirming when I touched her shoulder. Javier stood by, watching. He'd been around.

"Can we go to the park?" Adriana asked.

"Yes, sweetie, Sunday, when the sun is up."

She beamed. "Can I have a Barbie doll?"

"Yes, sweetie."

"Can I have a bike?" I bent down low and whispered, "Yes," into her little ear. If she asked for a chandelier she'd get one. We loaded up. Some of the car seat straps were loose, others tight. My head was spinning. Mimosa rushed to the car and handed me a Pamper.

"Javier," I said. "Do you like school?"

"Yeah. I get A's and stars." He sat next to me on a booster seat up front; Adriana and Craig sat in the back.

"That's good."

We held hands across the parking lot. It was a great buzz, like the elation I felt 25 years earlier after my first skydive and wow…

Inside McDonald's, Craig stood next to the toy display. He touched the Plexiglas, trying to feel the toys. His pants were baggy with a patch over a knee and they were too short, barely covering his shins. His pockets were empty and his cheeks were chubby. He was a baby, but bigger.

I ordered three Happy Meals.

"What kind of Happy Meals?" the lady asked me.

"What kinds are there?"

Thus began a year's worth of long, blank stares from people figuring as I stood before them that I didn't know what I was doing. Was there anyone on earth with three kids, she must have thought, who didn't know there were chicken nugget, hamburger, and cheeseburger Happy Meals? Anyone at all?

"Daddy?" Adriana said.

"Yes, love."

"Can I get the ketchup?"

"Thank you."

She squirted ketchup into four white paper containers, picked a table with round seats and arranged the containers. I noticed that most people with children sat inside the play area. Was that the general rule?

"Daddy?" She liked that word. I did too.

"Yes."

"I love worms."

"You love worms? What are you talking about?"

She giggled.

"Daddy?" Javier said.

"Yes, love."

"I'm counting double-digits in school. Do you want me to show you?"

"Sure."

"Twelve plus twelve is twenty-four."

"That's great. You're smart."

After eating we moved into the tube room. Craig sat on my lap still eating French fries, one at a time. People stared.

After playing Javier rushed over. "Am I sweating?" he asked. I rubbed his head. "You are!"

Neither Javier nor Adriana let thirty seconds pass without checking on the whereabouts of each other, Craig, or me. With slight extensions in time, from thirty seconds to one minute and then two, but no more, this searching would go on for the next year and a half. They had to know where I was. If I was in the garage, taking out the trash, or in the bathroom, I would soon see three little ducklings lined up looking for me. The front gate mesh money was money wasted. They weren't going anywhere.

When Craig was on my lap, I noticed he wasn't wearing a diaper. That was why Mimosa gave me one. My head was confused trying to figure out how to get things done…the changing, the watching. How do I/we/us go to the bathroom? Do I go with them? Do I leave the rest outside? Alone? This must have been mentioned in the class I missed.

When Javier and Adriana were in the playroom tubes, Craig and I snuck to the car to grab the Pamper. Big mistake. Before we were back in the building, Adriana and Javier were out of the tubes and standing inside the door, waiting.

Did I learn my lesson? No.

Nervous, Craig would go in his pants. We snuck into the bathroom after Javier and Adriana resumed playing. I pulled the changing shelf down. It went past flat. Craig slid towards me. Was I working it wrong? Jeez, what a disaster. How do you raise three kids if you can't work a changing board? I stripped him quick and threw his shoes on the floor, worried that I had two more kids out there. We flew out of the bathroom with him under an arm and his shoes in my other hand. His pants were down near his knees. I'm lucky no one called the police.

Outside the door, Javier and Adriana stood and waited.

Did I learn my lesson? No.

When Javier and Adriana resumed playing, Craig and I snuck out to the car and grabbed the camera. Once again, Javier and Adriana caught me. I'd been parenting only 45 minutes so far and I'd sneaked away three times. I didn't see any other parents sneaking around so I knew it wasn't normal. Adriana saw the camera and organized Javier and Craig for a pose. I asked a customer to take our picture. He captured four big smiles.

I worried they'd scream or cry when it was time to leave so I gave them five minutes' notice. In 15 seconds, Adriana and Javier were tying their shoes. As we departed, I noticed a member of McDonald's staff posting a photo of us next to the photos of people who wrote bad checks. We'd probably get Special Certificates the next time we visited.

We held hands in the parking lot.

"I'll be back on Sunday," I said.

Javier held up two fingers and whispered to himself, "Two days."

"Javier, have you ever had any pets?"

"I was bit by a dog," Adriana said. "He chased me."

"At our real house," Javier said, "we had a rabbit, but the cat ate his head."

They referred to their "real house" on rare occasions. They never asked to go back, or had anything pleasant to say about it. It was a reference point. If I asked a question around the house—Did you have a bike, or a yard, for example—they referred to their "real house." Other than that, nothing. That wasn't healthy and I worried about them and what they knew, or heard, or felt or saw. When I got them full-time we'd head straight for a therapist. After our first session she'd call her husband and tell him to put a down payment on that place in Tahoe they always wanted.

"Daddy?" Adriana said.

"Yes, sweetie."

"I had fun."

"Me, too," Javier added.

I left them at Mimosa's, left the camera with the drug store one hour lady, drove to Walmart and wow, what a difference. When I walked in I felt 10 feet tall. I had children. I was a member of society, free to go wherever I wanted—little clothing, shoes, toys, the whole world was different. Other than some stock room employees, I bet I was the first person to get high in Walmart.

I needed diapers and a diaper bag. In the children's acre I spotted diapers, but as I zeroed in I realized it was just the end of the display. Rounding the corner I was astounded to see a wall of diapers ten feet tall and forty feet long. How many types were there? I saw Pampers, Plumpers, and Pull-ups. What the hell was the difference? Worse, the sizes were in kilograms. How would I know how many kilograms Craig weighed? I wasn't sure I knew his name. I called my sister Diana and asked her what to do, but I felt awkward waiting so I picked a package with a Hispanic boy on front. Maybe that was how they did it.

Diapers bags were pink with flowers or, if you were tougher, pink with butterflies. There was not a manly bag on the shelf so I bought a duffle bag in sporting goods. I learned two things that night: 1) Parenting was not really considered a guy thing, and 2) I went in to Walmart imagining there were some things, like diapers, that society hadn't fractured into commercial options. I came out different.

I got my one one-hour photo on a CD, drove to work to get the truck I borrowed to move, went home, and called my sister Diana.

"I've worked out where the kids should sleep," she said. "Craig and Javier should sleep in the same room."

"Okay. What time do they go to bed?"

"Well, I think 8:30 at the latest."

"How often do they take baths?"

"Hmmm. Every other day should work. You'll need to help them. You'll need to wash Adriana's hair."

While we talked I e-mailed the picture. I imagined friends and family looking at the fuzzy snapshot. Like a Bigfoot photo, they'd say, "Is it really him? David Marin? He has that familiar gait, but with children?"

After moving into the new house I went to Walmart to buy an automatic coffee maker, a present to myself for earning a $20,000 annual bonus. I found one for $19.95, but rang up $190 at the register. I had snacks. I replaced my adult, boring bathroom ensemble with a bright red and yellow, flowery kid set-up with neon red rugs. I bought bright blue towels for the boys and yellow towels for Adriana and washed them together so they'd be soft. They were soft, all right, and they shed all over each other, ruining the set. Our towels were off-yellow and off-blue. I arranged Adriana's room and then the boys' room and I was happy and then I assembled my bed and crashed at midnight.

In the morning I had fresh brewed coffee. The children were waiting for me. I arrived while they were eating breakfast: toasted bread dipped in a cup of warm chocolate milk. Adriana wore baggy pants and a fake fur coat, lined in polar bear. I'm thinking seventy-five cents. Javier had a tight little jacket with cartoon characters on front. I could barely see Craig tucked into a mini sports lettermen jacket over a little blue, collared dress shirt. The unbuttoned wrists stuck out two inches. He carried around a little green sippy cup. I'd never seen one before. I decided to get some. At home, Javier and Craig did somersaults on the race car bed while Adriana was in her room opening empty drawers.

Life was good.

Having waited 25 years for children and with three in my house, I had no toys. What was I thinking? I panicked and called my mother.

"They're here, but I don't have any toys."

"Do you have any cardboard boxes from moving?"

"Yeah."

"Put one in the living room floor, that's a toy. If you say it's a toy, it's a toy."

They loved it. We went out to buy the gifts I'd promised: a Barbie doll for Adriana and a toy for Jeremiah. I aimed for Walmart, but drove by in panic, wondering how I'd tell Scott I lost a child in its valleys of aisles. I drove to the smaller Kmart and placed all three kids in a cart I parked next to. For the next fifteen years I'll specialize in parking next to carts. It's a gift, like flying an F-18 next to a re-fueling tanker.

We stormed in. Craig and Adriana picked coloring books and Adriana found the Cinderella doll she dreamed about. Javier picked a math book. I got crayons (for them) and then we went for movies. After some negotiation, Adriana placed two movies in the cart: Shrek and Spirit.

On the way home we visited McDonald's and got two Happy Meals instead of three, saving $1.79. I did that because when we ordered three there was food left over. I regretted my decision—this time the kids ate everything and wanted more. Worse, we only had two toys. I went to the counter to get a third toy, but no. You don't get a free third toy, no, sir.

Craig and Adriana colored at the table. Javier cranked out 20 problems in the math book. I gave him stars when he got problems right, but noticed he was looking at the back of the book for answers. I told him to think first, and then he did problems without peeking.

In the car, Javier said, "Can we come live with you?"

"What do you think of that?"

"I want to. I want to live with my bed."

"I think that will happen someday."

They had no idea what was happening and barely understood adoptions. Only weeks earlier, after saying good-bye to Jeremiah and Flora they watched the sad siblings return to Mimosa's foster home after their new forever family sent them back.

We found a park, surrounded by yellow police tape. I got on Highway 101 without a clue where to find another park. What single guy paid attention to that? I spotted an elementary school playground, exited, and stopped at a store for bottled water. As I got out of the car, Javier pointed down the road and said to Adriana, "That's where our real house was."

She didn't respond. Did they wonder if their family still lived in their "real house?" I did. Months later, using an address from a Social Services report, I drove by. A front yard oak covered the house in shadow. Flowering vines draped the Highway 101 sound barrier in the back yard. I imagined the children hunting for bugs. I imagined a game of tag or the robbers taking them away. In a poor area, the house was worth about $250,000, the bottom of the coastal California market, with a rental value around $800 per month. Their mother may have rented the house. She may have rented the garage. She was a mirage with a name and a birthday I saw on court records. A year after I got the kids I saw her handwriting at the dentist office. I stared at it and wondered why they had 16 cavities and I thought about her and them and what it was like. I imagined she was pretty.

The files I had said nothing about their mother's background, where she was from, or what she did for a living, if anything. I asked Scott about her once; he said her records were criminal files I was not allowed to see. I'm guessing the parents didn't settle in Santa Maria for a life of crime— it only had two jewelry stores. Most came to pick strawberries, "la fruta del Diablo"—the fruit of the devil—difficult and painful to pick, by hand and low. Many local fieldworkers were Mixtec Indians from Mexico's Atlantic coast. Despised and broke, they clawed their way north; fathers to California to get paid by the box; mothers and children left behind in Tijuana to sell Chiclets to tourists.[15]

Only Javier mentioned a father. He said he got sick when he went in the car with his dad. However, according to Scott, no one knew the identity of his father. After my father died, and my friends got in trouble, I pretended the scoldings their fathers gave them were for me. That's how I learned right from wrong. Maybe Javier adopted a father like I did. That was one reason I adopted kids: To live the father-child experience I'd missed. In the early days I spent with the children I often heard "Daddy?" followed by a muffed question or a giggle. They loved saying Daddy and I loved hearing it. I never asked, but I assumed Mimosa was behind it, telling them to call me "Daddy." Mimosa was English illiterate (like I'm Japanese illiterate), but wise to the world. She could look out the window at a man in a suit with a Rolex and a Mercedes and say, "That's your daddy..."

At the playground the children laughed out loud and pushed each other on the swings. Back home we colored. Adriana sat next to me. I rubbed her back as she colored Cinderella's hair black. I wanted to show

---

15  Eric Schlosser. Atlantic Monthly, 1995. "In the Strawberry Fields." He writes about fieldworkers in Guadalupe, a town next to Santa Maria.

them affection and touch them and hold them, all the while knowing from my training that many foster children had boundary issues; affection was blurry, often dark. I saw nothing inappropriate with my three except for Craig: When I changed his diaper, he'd lie on his back, throw his legs up in the air and over his head, and grab his crotch, like you'd see at a Super Bowl half-time show. I soon realized Craig was just moving his diaper out of the way.

I took them back to foster on time.

"I'll be back in two days, on Tuesday. We're going to a restaurant to eat spaghetti!"

I went home, put their coloring books and dolls in their rooms, and closed the doors. I did not want the doors open if they weren't there. I didn't want to assume I'd get to keep them and I didn't want a reminder that they still really lived in a foster home.

A few days later we went to Target to replace six dirty, worn out tennis shoes. When I looked inside the old shoes for the size I saw the name of the child who wore it new. We eased into a cart I parked next to and we moved along the parking lot at dusk. Twenty feet inside the store, a lady of about 50 rushed towards us.

"Are they triplets?"

I was startled and didn't respond. Ten second later another lady, also about 50, said, "Are those your kids?" I pushed on, perplexed. I didn't think people would rush at me. We made it to the shoe area and I let them out. Not one traveled far. I found Craig's shoe size using my hand for measurement. I didn't understand the size rules and I don't understand them now. And I didn't notice until months later that if you look down you can see a pad with shoe sizes on it

"Will you buy me pink slippers?" Adriana asked.

"Not now, sweetie. Maybe later." I hadn't thought of her asking me for different shoes. Anything unexpected, like the ladies coming at me, confused me. I made a mental note to look up more.

"Let's go get some spaghetti." I said. If I had a guardian angel she would have grabbed my shirt collar, twisted it, and said, "Hey, what are you, stupid? You're taking three little Mexican kids to eat spaghetti at a restaurant? Have you seen them use a fork? Do you have extra clothes in case they spill something? What if they don't like spaghetti? Spaghetti is not Mexican! Think."

I was ashamed to find myself driving the long way to Giavanni's Italian Restaurant, worried about what people would say when they saw us. Fortunately, only three tables were occupied and Craig was asleep. I put him in the free stroller I got at Toys R Us for spending a fortune on car seats. We ordered three spaghettis and drinks. Javier and Adriana were polite, thoughtful, and helped each other. I was proud, until they used their forks, holding them like a killer wields a knife for the final blow. Were they raised in a cave? I showed them how to use a fork and I cut their pasta. The few people stared, but who cared?

The next day, I called Scott and gave him my weekend report.

"You need to tell me if something goes wrong. You can always change your mind."

"Scott, I've been waiting for 25 years. A kid spilling ketchup on me isn't going to make me change my mind."

"If you are going to go through with this I want you to consider one thing."

"What?"

"We like to keep contact between biological parents and kids. It would be great if you could send the mother pictures once in a while."

"Sure. Why not?"

She'd change my mind later.

I called Willie to meet and get a license at my new address. He asked me if I had three beds for the kids. I did, but one was a race car bed and the other two were a matching set of antique walnut single beds – one was in Adriana's room and the other in the guest house. He told me the county had an extra crib for Craig. I didn't know if a two year old was supposed to sleep in a crib, but Willie was offering and he probably knew and this would be a good time for me to just say, yes, thanks, like Bev told me to do, instead of analyzing every god-damned thing like a political science professor.

For our next practice session, we went to Toys R Us to purchase crib bedding. The kids had never been there. I eased the three into a cart I parked next to and kept them there so I wouldn't lose one. I asked Javier and Adriana to select bedding for Craig (Winnie the Pooh, a farm scene, etc.). Craig could point, but not talk. They stared in wonder at the toys, like we were wandering around Santa's North Pole workshop. None of the children asked for anything. It was like a dream to them.

We had fun, laughing, and playing. At the checkout stand, Adriana turned to me. She was at eye level in the cart, a foot away.

"Daddy, are you going to adoct us?"

I was stunned, but managed to say, "Yes, love."

Her smile was so big it hardly fit on her face. Javier was listening. I wondered if her question was his idea. I was warmed to toast and felt good about my decision to let them tell me what they wanted, instead of me telling them I was going to adopt them, or waiting for a bureaucratic communication plan.

Outside, Adriana asked me the same question, "Daddy, are you going to adoct us?"

"Yes, love."

"When, now?"

"We're in the parking lot, princess; I can't adopt you in the parking lot. It's too dark. I'll adopt you soon." It would take about six months, or so I thought.

Willie came to the house on Thursday, crib in hand.

"You won't believe what happened," he said. "The kid's social worker is named Melinda. She is, or was, preparing the communications plan. When she called Mimosa to tell her she was making the plan for the kids, to warn them and help them pack, Mimosa said, 'You're wasting your time. The kids love David and can't wait to be with him.'

"She told Melinda that she wished Social Services would find more people like you."

That made me feel good, but I was still cautious. I'd lost a $100,000 a year job, waited months to meet my children, and I still knew almost nothing about them. This was far from over. I didn't suspect Willie, but I remembered Scott warning me there were people in Social Services opposed to me getting my kids.

I talked with Scott the next day and we decided that all went well during family practice. The day I got back from my Pulitzer Newspapers corporate meeting I'd get my kids full-time, all the time. My sisters would be there and then my mother.

I told more people at work and showed them pictures. They were dumbfounded.

"Huh?"

"Three?"

"On your own?"

A lady said, "People see you differently now." I believed her. I'd noticed a change, too. Hauling children around by myself I realized a significant other to share this with would be amazing. But, with no time to find her, it would only happen if she appeared from nowhere.

## 6. Sealed in the Chamber

Craig's life was a cartoon. He was the prey, running away, like Jerry, the TV animated mouse escaping from Tom the cat or in a different cartoon, the Roadrunner chased by Wile E. Coyote. Just two years old, he was neither clever like Jerry, nor fast like the Roadrunner, so in real life he probably whimpered and moaned when the predators, his mother and her boyfriends, laid into him or took his food. When I first held him to smell his baby hair—my dumbbells weighed more than he did—he just held on, waiting for the drop or the throw. With no momentum of his own, he trailed behind us as we moved through life, turning the way we turned, a human shadow with a sippy cup. He didn't speak; he pointed and grunted. When I told people he didn't talk, they'd ask me his age. After I said he was almost two and a half, they'd turn away. That's not good, the turning away.

He put his clothes on backwards and he had a hard time keeping up on walks to the Santa Maria river levee, so he rode in the stroller. If we walked for long or went to an air show, and his little legs grew tired, I'd hoist him onto my shoulders. We perfected a fun take-down maneuver. I'd place my hand in his armpit and he'd jump and spin as I reeled him in like an elephant grabbing a peanut. He liked heights and a breeze in his face and when I pushed him in the swing he wanted to go higher than the clouds, into the stratosphere and away from it all. He fearlessly climbed the bars on the jungle gym at the park, but if a dog came near him he ran towards me, until he saw it was a squirrel the dog chased, not him.

Nothing was smaller than Craig. He was like a guinea pig, the most helpless animal, always looking around; there was danger ahead and behind, and with hawks, above. He could not communicate the truths of his early life to me. I knew nothing about him. He was one of three siblings and he loved to snuggle. If I blew kisses on his belly he laughed. He loved balloons for the height and float. Flying kites at the park, he gazed at his until he let go because he was thirsty. I had no records or files about him—they didn't even know his name. He just came along with the group, and he was such a joy and so sweet that had I learned that Social Services threw him in at the last minute—"Pssst, tell him he's their brother and we'll make our quota"—it wouldn't have mattered.

The children rarely asked for anything at stores, like they'd never been shopping or didn't know that we trade money for goods. I often got little treats at the corner market, hiding a pack of gum in my pocket or two packages of Twinkies behind my back. Craig always noticed first and laughed in delight, pointing at me to alert Javier and Adriana. I waited until he saw me and then turned away, looked back at him and then quickly away again, our signal that something sweet was near. His body shook with joy.

I worried because he was so frail and ill. During Family Practice, a social worker called me.

"Hi, David. You're taking the three kids, right?"

Caution light.

"We spend time together. I like them. I hope so."

"Has anyone told you that you have to wake up Chris every night?"

"No. His name is Craig."

"Craig?"

"We call him Craig."

"Okay. Well, anyway, you have to wake him up every two hours to see if his nose is bleeding. He has bad nosebleeds."

My adventure was like a real birth. First, I was harassed at work for contemplating a family. Then, I waited months to see if I was going to get girls or boys. I labored, waiting months to see the kids, waiting for them to come out. Now, like a nursing mother, I got to wake up every two hours. I was game, but ill-prepared. I had a Better Homes & Garden New Baby Book, a book about kids in trouble, and They Cage the Animals at Night, a book about life in an orphanage. I'd been hauling all three books around for 20 years. None prepared me to find Craig one morning lying in a pool of blood in his bed, like he'd been stabbed to death. The doctor said Craig's fingernails could be shorter and maybe he was picking at something. I felt ashamed because as a real parent it was my job to notice that. After we left the doctor's office, I drove to 7-Eleven because it was closer than home and I bought nail clippers. I looked around to see if there were any other parents trimming little fingernails in the 7-Eleven parking lot. But it was just me.

On the day after I brought the children home for good, Craig had a fever. I didn't know what to do and neither did Joy, my childless sister. This was the opportunity to evolve that Bev told me to seize. I called my boss.

"He's really hot."

"How do you know?"

"I'm touching him."

"Do you have a thermometer?"

"No."

"Buy a digital one. And get some Pedialyte."

"Pedialyte?"

"It's a medicine. In tubes. You can buy it frozen. It prevents dehydration. Then, take him to the doctor."

I took Craig to the emergency room. He was so weak his head bobbed like a toy doll. His eyes were dim. The admitting nurse said, "What have you given him?"

"What do you mean?" I wasn't sick. Whatever he got it wasn't from me.

"Medicine, what medicines have you given him?" A few nurses drew closer.

"Nothing. I don't have any medicine."

"You're supposed to give sick kids medicine," she announced through a 45 watt ThunderPower 1000 bullhorn. The circle drew in. *Should we call Social Services? Who is this idiot?*

"I just got him yesterday. I didn't think he'd be sick. I have two more at home."

I took Craig to the doctor many times over the next few months. He was constantly feverish. When he was ill he slept with me at night so I could make sure he was still living. I felt like I was lying next to a hot water bottle, the kind my mom used to put under my ear when I had an earache. I wanted to hold him but his body was a heaving chest, no larger than a snow crab and half as strong. I worried if I put my arm around him, or on him, I'd make it hard for him to inhale. He breathed like he'd just run the 220 meter hurdles. It would slow and then off to the races. I moved Craig's county crib into my bedroom. We'd wait it out in there until he was sturdier.

In the meantime, people at work told me that their two year olds could calculate the square root of 169 or design relay stations for the electric company. Craig was behind, let's say. I decided to teach him numbers and letters. How hard could that be? I drew a 2.

"Draw this."

He drew a crooked dash.

*Oh, no.*

I drew a C, the first letter of his name.

He drew two crooked dashes. His brain was scattered. Special Ed. He communicated in Morse code like a seaman on the Lusitania, oblivious to his fate, unaware of the torpedoes society shot at children like him, sealed in the chamber his mother built. I worried about his future after me. Should I work harder to go higher in the corporate world and make more money to get Craig lifelong help?

Scott told me I didn't have to take Craig. He said he could find a place for him if three were too many. I owned potted plants healthier than Craig, but I never considered returning him. I could not imagine giving him back and seeing him watch us through the window of a white county van, his plump cheeks trembling with fear, hauled away by the robbers into another breathless nightmare. He was one of us and that's how it would be. He grew to trust me and I carried him wherever we went, like a kangaroo with a fieldworker in her pouch. We bonded in the length of days and at night in our room. He learned that if he was thirsty I'd get him water and that if he was hurt from a fall or banged a shin, I'd be there to hold him. He couldn't say anything, but I know I mattered.

In my arms, he'd stare at me. What was he thinking?—*What's with the white guy?*—and then he'd lunge at me, wrapping his arms around my neck, giving me a hug or a kiss or trying to lick my face like a chocolate Lab puppy adopted by an Irish setter.

And then, a breakthrough. At the grocery store—all three kids in the cart so I wouldn't lose one—Craig made a noise and pointed to something he wanted.

I said, "Not now."

Good news! He said his very first two words!

Bad news! They were, "Fuck you."

I felt like someone punched me in the jaw. I said, "You're welcome," and kept pushing the cart, hoping he'd confuse "Fuck you" with "Thank you." It worked. He never said it again. Besides, counting those words, he was now a member of civil society, not counting those words. A few weeks later, in my arms at Disneyland, overlooking a pond while we waited for the train, Craig pointed to the water and said, "Two ducks."

He'd be okay.

He hadn't spoken before because he'd been beaten into silence or trained by his siblings to be quiet and not draw attention. Like a stealth submarine, he was sheathed in anechoic tiles to avoid detection. He actually knew a lot of words. Within weeks he was talking more and once, too much. Denied a snack before dinner, he ran away crying, found Adriana and Javier, and said, "Daddy hit me." Bev had told us in class that foster children were clever that way, but she didn't say toddlers would try it. I followed him and the four of us discussed what he said. I knew that he/she/they are hitting me was likely the best way for foster kids to get an audience and relief and that's why they did it. I told Craig and his siblings it was wrong to lie, especially like that, and it never happened again.

I knew that Craig emerging from his shell had something to do with me, a safe house, and his siblings not hiding him in cabinets. But the figure who inspired the left behind to become a boy was a green, solitary, swamp-dwelling ogre turned movie star named Shrek. He became Craig's hero at once. Shrek's loneliness, his leave-me-alone attitude and his inclination to defend himself were powerful images in Craig's eyes. Craig's favorite part was Shrek taking great leaps, belly flopping onto the knights, the police, the robbers, wrestling them into submission with head butts and body throws. He sat alone in the front of the TV, playing that scene over and over again to great joy, learning how to use the remote before he learned how to spell his name or count to five. He became Shrek, the ogre and hero, asked us to call him that and why not? When I ordered Monterey Bay Aquarium membership cards the young man on the phone found his name puzzling.

"Shrek?"

"Well, we call him that."

"What the heck, you're right, who cares?"

Shrek Marin remains on Craig's card today.

In my brain's recess, playing kickball with plans to save more money and rotate the tires, I wondered how to potty-train Craig. I consulted Google, my co-parent and digital spouse, and found videos and books. You got your timelines and you got your theories. Instead, I called Craig into my room and asked him if he wanted to wear "chonies," the kids' Spanish slang for underwear. He was thrilled.

"I'm going to wear chonies! I'm going to wear chonies!"

He ran around showing them to his siblings. It had never occurred to me to try earlier. He did great with a few exceptions, like the puddle in between his feet a lady at the haircutting salon noticed as he was about to climb into the chair.

I often arrived early to pick him up from preschool and watched him outside playing with children, trying to figure out if he'd become a Republican: "That's my toy!", or a Democrat: "Here, Billy, you can have Tom's toy." You couldn't tell by looking at him or people like him. Half of the 11.9 million illegals lived in four states. Texas and Florida were reliably Republican; California and New York were not.

Craig got along with everyone except with the boy who taunted him for not having a mother. "I have a mother," I heard Craig say, not knowing I was behind him. "She's in foster."

Craig loved to sing. On the drive to school we took turns picking songs. Adriana's favorite was "She'll Be Coming Around the Mountain," learned from a children's CD. At the end she added, "We'll be eating chicken nuggets when she comes, we'll be eating chicken nuggets when she comes." Javier's favorite was "This Land is Your Land," learned at school. I often played the Springsteen version at home. Craig had two favorites. The first was "Twinkle, Twinkle, Little Star" IF the rest of us raised our hands and wiggled our fingers like a twinkling star. One day, distracted by driving, I rested my elbow on the armrest and wiggled my fingers from there. Craig yelled, "Daddy, get your twinkles up!" and I did. His other favorite, learned at school or made up—who knew?—he called "our thankful song." We sang it before dinner. "We are thankful, we are thankful, for our food, for our food. We are very thankful…"

After spending time with Craig I learned that his intellectual challenges were temporary. Like a stream with the damming log removed, he learned to sing, count, and write his name. I taught him how to play catch and how to move in the swing to take himself higher. Like every new parent, I imagined if I exposed him to music he'd be a prodigy and we'd have recitals for a select group of people, but nothing too exploitive, of course, because he was just a child.

I began Craig's music training in the Land Rover bought special, driving from preschool to pick up Adriana and Javier at the YMCA after-school program. We began with the Rolling Stones' Sympathy for the Devil. As an example of beat, I moved my right hand up and down and left and right. It was a compact lesson on an important topic. If it worked I'd use the same method with Adriana and Javier. As we drove I complimented myself. This was what separated me from the other men out there adopting three siblings. How many parents taught music while driving to the YMCA after-school program? The next song, She's a Rainbow, was a symphony of piano. My hand moved like a wand. Craig was mesmerized. We finished with Wild Horses.

Childhood living, it's easy to do.
The things you wanted,
I bought them for you.

The lesson ended.
"Daddy," he said. Did he want a piano? I'd buy a little one with a mushroom stool. Maybe he wanted a violin. If he asked for drums I'd take him home and play Springsteen's New York City Serenade, re-routing him back to piano.

"Daddy," he said again.

"Yes, love."

"Does Tarzan live in the jungle?"

I sucked my cheeks into my mouth and took a deep breath. What a moron, thinking I could teach music on the way to pre-school. I made a note to not share any of my ingenious child raising strategies without peer review in a respected child rearing journal or at least an indication that my children were listening.

"Yes," I said. "He lives in the jungle. He lives with apes. He's in foster."

Because he was the baby, Craig's main chore was turning off the TV at dinnertime. One night, after I announced dinner was ready, he ran full bore to the TV and tripped over a two foot long, blown up sword he'd gotten at Burger King. I heard a loud bang as his head slammed against the (real) wooden pirate chest in the living room and then he was crying, holding his head. It was a gusher, a Panhandle bleeder, a three-quarter-inch gash above his left ear. I turned off the stove, wrapped Craig's head in a towel and told the older kids to get in the car. I drove to the emergency room, holding the towel with gentle pressure against Craig's head with the other. His injury required immediate attention.

"Sit down," the lady said. "It will be two hours."

"Can I have a phone book?"

I called Domino's and ordered a pizza with pepperoni and pineapple. "We'll need lots of napkins."

Javier said, "This is just like a restaurant."

The ER doctor had a big needle. I held Craig tight as the doctor stuck his head to numb him. Then the doctor took a staple gun, remarkably similar to one at, well, Staples, for example, and he put four, half-inch wide staples in his head to close the wound. We got home tired at 10:30 p.m.

At 1 a.m. I heard Craig crying in his room. The painkiller wore off. I brought him to my bed, but he couldn't sleep because he liked to sleep on the side with the staples in it. At 2 a.m. he said, "Daddy, I'm hungry and thirsty." Before our snack, tired, stapled, and with dried blood on his ear, he said, "I want to sing my thankful song." We sang We Are Thankful, ate applesauce, and went back to bed.

The human shadow, the boy without momentum, has his own forward motion now. Craig is easily the most curious child of the three. He wants to know why the moon doesn't fall and how ropes hold the Golden Gate Bridge. He's the one who makes me want a non-digital spouse the most. Other than seeing me with a girlfriend and watching us interact with something special between us, my children had no idea what a normal male-female relationship looked like. To Craig, the unattached adult was the typical adult. To him, I was the mom and the dad and there was nothing wrong with that. When he was five, he told me that he wanted to be an unmarried astronaut and adopt kids.

Today he makes friends easily. He loves the attention good grades bring, and he wants to learn more. Like a sponge he soaks up and processes everything into his little whole. Other than a sniffle now and then, he has not been ill, or hot, in many years and he's never missed a day of school. He's a sturdy and inquisitive boy, the opposite of what he used to be. Once or twice a year he looks around the house and tells me if he sees a way the robbers might come in. But he knows they'll never return and if they do... Bam and into the river.

In the beginning, if I'd dismissed adopting a diapered child because it was too hard I would have made a huge mistake. I learned from Craig, about him and about myself and I miss his youth and having a baby in my home. I could have done much better had I known more about parenting. Watching him grow up makes me want to have another baby, so I can keep feeling how it was to reel him in like a peanut or smell his baby hair. But for now, I take his old baby sandal with me when I go on business trips, and I look at pictures. I'm amazed that we did it. He emerged from his chamber and became a boy. I emerged from mine and became a father.

# 7. Beaked Shadow

Scott called me at work. "Can you come over? I have something to show you."

"What is it?"

"I want to show you the kids' history. I have some files."

"What do they say?"

"You need to come over and read them. Now. I'm not supposed to show you this, but you need to know what the kids have been through. You need to know before you make a commitment."

*I made a commitment the day I met them.*

"I'm on my way."

I arrived at the Social Services building at lunchtime. A receptionist showed me the elevator. I followed Scott through the department. People peered over cubicles. That's. The. Guy. Scott took me to a small, windowless room with a conference table and six chairs.

"You're not supposed to see these files until the kids are in adoptive placement. Since we haven't even severed the rights of the parents yet, the adoptive placement could be next year. But you need to see these. You need to know. Having read the files myself, I can only imagine the parents' rights will be severed. I might as well show you now."

I was afraid something would ruin everything. After my brief childhood and life challenges, I fancied myself with a stomach made of Milwaukee steel. This day would test that.

Scott left me alone. He returned with a pile of files. The word abuse hung in the air. I was ready to read about a long last night of cries, boots through the window, and blood on the floor. I was not prepared to read about Social Services knowing about cries, boots, and blood for longer than my children had been alive, and, in a collective collapse, permitting, even causing, more of the same. My children's lives were not the endless summers of youth.

Scott handed me a Disposition Report summarizing the children's history with Social Services. Social workers prepared the report for a judge to review when the county lawyer went to court to win permission, granted the previous week, to stop working with the mother. The report contained an important note: Social Services wanted the judge to know that they'd found a "family" interested in adopting the kids. It was me. I'd meet them two months later.

The report began with a list of the children's names and birthdays. I learned how to spell Adriana. I thought it had two N's. I saw the mother's name—Benedetta. The report tried to name the fathers. Emine and Maribel, my kids' older sisters, had different, real fathers. Javier had an "alleged" father—mother's best guess—whereabouts unknown. Adriana's and Craig's fathers were established by default, meaning the guys the county sued to prove paternity didn't show up in court. Whereabouts unknown. Three whereabouts unknown was a lot. It was more of a gnarled root than a family tree. I bet they had great tattoos.

Next was a chronological Incidents section, each entry a few sentences. Scott told me when we first spoke that the kids were placed in foster care in August, two months before he called me. I imagined the trouble began that summer, or in the spring. Instead, the first entry was November 1993, ten years earlier. I bit the inside of my lip. The local hospital called Social Services to report severe neglect to an unborn baby—the mother was four months pregnant with Maribel. Social Services went to the hospital and learned that the mother used to drink eighteen beers a week, but that she didn't drink anymore. She told Social Services that she drank when she was pregnant with her first child, Emine, born eighteen months ago, and she came out fine. Social Services gave her a brochure about birth defects and wrote that the allegation of severe neglect to an unborn baby was, "unfounded due to the child not being born."

On April 25, 1994, the day after Maribel, the "unborn baby" was born, someone called Social Services alleging physical abuse on Emine. The "referral" stated that the mother and Emine tested positive for cocaine and alcohol at the time of Emine's birth. The name of the person making the referral was absent. The mother said she didn't use drugs and only drank two beers. The newborn, Maribel, was detained (what did that mean?) and the mother entered into a three month monitoring program. The program ended after the mother told Social Services she didn't need it anymore.

In August 1994, someone called Social Services and said the mother drank a lot and could not care for her children. The social worker closed the case because the family could not be found. In September 1996, someone called Social Services to report drug abuse and that the mother and a boyfriend were beating two-year-old Emine. Social Services sent a team to the scene, found the mother pregnant, and advised her of her duty to protect her unborn child. They wrote that the allegations were inconclusive after the mother said she didn't use drugs or abuse the children. The unborn child she had a duty to protect was my son, Javier.

I was curious who wrote the reports.

Six months later, on March 24, 1997, seven weeks after Javier was born, someone called Social Services to report the mother for physically abusing her children and not fixing them food when she was drunk. The mother denied everything so Social Services called the report unsubstantiated. The March 24 incident was the only one in the nine-page report that mentioned the kids not having food. I suspected there were more occasions.

Javier gave me the following stories when he was in the second grade, seven years later:

The Magic Shoes by Javier Marin

One fine day a kid went to but some shoes. At the store but they ran out of shoes. They only had Magic Shoes and the kid bought them. On his way home he began to get hungry then he said I'm hungry and with a blink of an eye the magic shoes gave him food.

Dragon Get's By by Javier Marin

Dragon's cupbord was bare. Dragon needed to go shopping the store was at the top of a steep hill. Dragon was a wise sopper. When dragon was done the food would't fit in his car then he ate all of the food then he could't fit in his car. Then he got an idea he pushed his car home. When he got home his cupbord was bare then said time to go shopping.

On August 13, 1998—five years before I'd meet my children—someone called Social Services to report lice, beatings, severe neglect, drinking, and drug abuse. Social Services wrote that the allegation was "evaluated out" because a social worker saw the kids recently and didn't see bruises. Lice? The report didn't mention that. Severe neglect? No mention. Drinking? Nada. Drug abuse? Zip.

Six days later someone called Social Services to report drinking and abuse of three children, including Javier. Social Services sent a reading team to the scene, advised the mother of the definitions of child abuse and left, calling the allegations inconclusive after the mother told them she didn't drink.

Scott sat next to me. I said nothing. He said nothing. I clenched my jaw and inhaled through my nose. More came in than out. I used the rest like a panting dog to keep myself cool.

Two days later, a babysitter called and told Social Services that the mother left the kids with her six weeks ago and hadn't returned. If the August 13 report was true, the social worker who hadn't seen any bruises made that observation while the kids were at the babysitter, but the worker didn't learn from the babysitter that the kids had been there six weeks. Or, more likely, the social worker didn't see any bruises because he didn't see the children at all. The mother explained to Social Services that she left the kids at the babysitter for only 20 days, but it was too late. Five years after the first allegation, Social Services went to juvenile court and obtained "a plan for family maintenance," meaning the mother was on notice that Social Services, instead of waiting to be called by someone before they acted, so to speak, could initiate home visits on their own. The plan would last two years. Emine and Javier were placed in foster care. Mom had visitation rights.

On March 18, 1999, seven months into the two-year maintenance program, my daughter Adriana was born. She weighed more than six pounds, but was premature and sick. Five days later, after five-year-old Maribel was returned to her mother, the mother was arrested for disturbing the peace and Maribel went to foster care. Six months later, after five-year-old Maribel was returned home, her mother was reported for neglect. In November 1999 Emine told Social Services her mother was hurting her. They called her complaint inconclusive. The two-year maintenance plan expired in August 2000 with the children returned to their mother.

A May, 2001 referral alleged that Emine, Maribel and Javier were being abused.

The beaked shadow haunting my youth was coming to get them all.

Social Services leapt into action, sending eight-year-old Emine to counseling and the mother to parenting classes.

On September 16, 2001 Craig was born. Nine months later, someone called to report neglect, abuse, and abandonment. Social Services, high on spray paint fumes, entered the mother into another family maintenance plan that ended when she told social workers said she didn't need "additional services."

That was the end of the incidents section. The report kindly invited the court to peruse the criminal files of the mother and fathers. The entire time I was reading, Scott never left my side.

"Tell the mother she'll never receive pictures from me."

"I understand. You don't have to."

"We'll be moving on."

The file was a disaster. Worse, the reports ended nine months before the kids were removed from their home permanently. I imagined something really bad happened, but what? I'd spend the next year trying to find out.

I went outside, sat in my car, and looked through the window of Adriana and Craig's preschool. In a few hours, they'd be there, waiting like they did every day, two noses pressed against the glass looking for daddy. The partnership I formed with Social Services to insure the well-being of my children changed right there. Instead of seeing Social Services as allies, I saw them as foes. Scott's warning that social workers were opposed to me providing a safe home for my children magnified my frustration. Did those opposed read these reports? Did they write them? My Kafka transition from an observer on the wall to a fighter on the floor took just a few moments—I would protect my kids, not with Social Services, but from them.

It was amazing the children showed any signs of life or joy. The ultimate impact of their journey through the darkness may never be known. The effects of alcohol and drugs on fetuses are well documented, but the long-term results of that research are not plain. The brain is a mystery, and people prove resilient, tough and adaptable. The heart? I wondered and worried, but what could I do? The children were sweet and innocent. Later, I was comforted to read the boys' birth records. Their official newborn tests were normal (but oops, Craig's name really was

Chris. Sorry, everybody!).

I knew my children were happy and healthy after spending ten minutes with them. Each time we went home—not sometimes, but each time—Adriana opened the door first and skipped down the hall. She skips through our house today.

As for future psychological issues, nightmares, children gone bad, what parent knew how their children would turn out? Who knew why one was in college while another slept in a crack house? My own family was a perfect case study: CFO with a Masters degree (older sister Diana), me, my brother the homeless heroin addict, my brother the homeless alcoholic, and my younger sister Joy, an engineer with a Masters degree. Someday I'll share the truth with my children and help them sort through their lives the way the rest of us sort through ours.

Roaring through the reports like a freight train was the wretched lack of accountability of anyone in "Child Welfare" Services. There were lots of contacts with the children and lots of writing, but the names of social workers were never mentioned. No one took responsibility for anything. They acted like highway weigh station workers, noting the weight of a truck and then nodding, watching another pull in as the first pulled away. Nowhere did it say, "And I, Mr. Johnson, decided that Emine was telling the truth," or "And I, Ms. Johnson, decided that thirteen complaints of abuse, if spread out over ten years, isn't that many, really." Social Services would argue that they needed to protect the identity of their employees. With shabby work like that, putting my children in the talons of the beaked shadow, I'd want my identity hidden, too.

The result of their work is that my children see them as robbers.

What was Social Services' thinking over the endless decade? Edward Tufte's book Visual Explanations, a favorite of mine, demonstrated that if people stopped and looked at evidence, charted it and thought, they could see great things. London's 1854 Cholera epidemic, for example, would have been solved sooner if deaths were plotted on a grid of London so investigators could see that the dying lived near a water pump, suggesting water as the transmitter. The Space Shuttle Challenger would not have launched the day it exploded had the failure rate of o-rings been charted vs. temperature. Mr. Tufte did it later. It'd be great if Santa Barbara County made a chart, or had a person monitoring cases, one person with the perspective to look at an entire file and make decisions. Well, he existed. In a manner both cruel and bizarre, I'd meet him. My transition from Social Services friend to Social Services foe would soon be complete.

## 8. This Case: A Child Raised by Children

To celebrate Adriana's birth at Santa Barbara's Cottage Hospital, her mother went out drinking. She never returned. After treatment for a lung infection, Adriana went from the maternity ward to a foster home. That was all I knew. I may learn more because in 2005 her social worker left a note telling me she had more information on "This Case." I hope to see it soon.

From other court reports, I learned that Social Services eventually placed "This Case" with her mother, took her away, gave her back, took her and gave her. Re-gifted. Four foster homes for the four-year-old. "This Case" spent more time in foster than with her mother and in the end her mother committed assault and battery on her.

"This Case" did not like the robbers. She was a dimpled delight, a talented little forger, and when she was hungry and ate grass she threw up, she told me.

Pavarotti didn't sing when she walked by.

One day, Adriana came into my room.

"Daddy, what's a signature?"

Fun! I showed her how to draw a big A, and a D like in Daddy, an R, a dotted I, and how to engage an N with an A. And here's what my signature looks like. She left to practice. How sweet. This was the essence of parenting. A few weeks later, I found a note from school informing me that Adriana talked too much. As required, it had my signature. Big trouble for Adriana? Not really. I admired her creativity. If becoming a princess didn't work out she could work for Goldman Sachs.

Like Javier, Adriana obsessed over food. Her concern was not quantity, but permission. At an average of five times per day in our first two years, led by Adriana, the children said, "Daddy, can I have a snack?"

about 3,650 times. I'm not kidding. It wasn't about me—they were welcome to snacks, except near dinnertime. Her actions bespoke fear, punished by the old regime for eating too much or out of turn. I let it go and did nothing.

Adriana did not disguise her fears—attached like tattoos. Instead of hiding she announced them and stood tall.

"Daddy," Adriana said, after we'd been in our new house for one hour.

"Yes, sweetie."

"Craig went potty in his pants."

After the McDonald's diaper fiasco and my wimpy diaper bag shopping trip, I'd rebounded with a kit made special: a new Pamper, Pull-up, or Plumper, whatever the hell they called it, baby powder (I'd seen a girlfriend use baby powder five years earlier), wipes, a changing pad and a towel. I laid Craig on my bed. When I returned, four-year-old Adriana and six-year-old Javier stood dead calm, shoulder-to-shoulder between me and Craig.

"He's just a baby," Adriana said.

They expected me to be mad.

"It's okay if he goes in his diaper," Javier said.

They wondered if I'd hurt him.

"I'll change him," Adriana said.

"It's okay," I said. "I'll do it."

They stood aside and watched me have a great time baby talking to Craig and 'oops' you don't unscrew the baby powder top. A year later, when I obtained the files of their final days with their mother, I learned Adriana was beaten for "messing her diaper." Instead of Adriana waiting to see if I did to Craig what her mother did to her, she stood with her big brother and blocked me, protecting Craig like he was a little bird. Their efforts were pointless in our home; I was the proud dad of a baby and changing a diaper was part of my deal. Moreover, learning in classes that foster children might have potty issues coupled with my experience as a bed-wetter away from home when I was 16, and the ridicule that followed, I'd made a commitment to myself before I even met my children that my patience with that issue would last forever. And it does.

Adriana was a child raised by children. She had no filter, no sense of right and wrong, no civilizing force to distinguish between good and evil. Walking through the airport after Aunt Joy's three-day provisioning trip, the children and I passed an African-American woman. Adriana said, "Hey, a nigger."

No one in my adoption class mentioned this. I was fearful about our future. What else would they say? I told the kids it was a dirty word and never, ever, ever say it again. And they didn't. Mimosa must have heard children in her home use bad words, so she left a parting gift on Adriana's shoulder. One morning on the way to school, out in the free world, Adriana had a question for me. She always started sentences with "And," like everything we talked about followed what we talked about before.

"And, Daddy, is there a devil on my shoulder?"

"Huh?"

Javier jumped in. "There's a devil on your shoulder. It's there in case you do anything bad."

*Anything?*

"Is it true, Daddy?" Adriana asked, eager to lighten her load.

"Who told you that?"

"Mimosa."

"Mimosa," Javier repeated.

"No, it's not true. There are no devils on your shoulder. There are no devils in the world. People make that up to scare people. Don't worry about it."

Adriana grinned and looked at Javier. He thought twice: *this changes everything.*

Mimosa impacted our young family in another way. After dinner, Adriana wanted to help do dishes. Her desire to bond touched me so I bought her a white two-step ladder to reach the sink. A few weeks later I took the kids to Mimosa's house to say hello so they wouldn't think that when new people came into their lives the old people disappeared like fog. As we said goodbye I understood Mimosa telling Adriana in Spanish to remember to help me in the kitchen. That night, as Adriana climbed the two-step, I said, "Adriana, it's sweet of you to offer to help me with the dishes, but you don't have to. If you want to play instead… Adriana?…hello?", but she was gone, joining her brothers outside playing. She never did dishes again (we had a dishwasher, anyway), although she often volunteered to help cook, for fun. Especially brownies.

Our evenings were quiet with reading time before baths. While he sat in the tub next to Javier I washed Craig's hair, hurrying to get to Adriana. She did not like to be alone and she did not like to be out of bubbles. I'm not one to come running. I go at my pace. Hearing, "Daddy, I need more bubbles!" changed that. The children bathed in Ivory Liquid dish soap because a lady at work told me the chemicals in shampoos were bad for girls. We often wiped out a stores supply of Ivory Liquid, and no, it didn't occur to me what a detergent that cuts through grease and crust might do to a girl's body. I needed advice, got it, and used it. Had someone told me that Drano was fine for gargling I might have tried that, too. While washing Adriana's hair, we'd sing songs she learned at preschool, like "Where is Thumpkin?" Or "Benny Bear." I tried to remember nursery rhymes from my youth but couldn't.

Before going to sleep, Adriana wanted 100 kisses on her little brown cheek. I did it once, but got tired; my mouth dried out and leaning hurt my neck. In a clever maneuver, I changed the count. I'd get up to "27, 28, 29," and then seamlessly switch to, "90, 91, 92, 93, 94, 95, 96, 97, 98, 99, 100!" She never caught on.

Adriana had challenges. One was me, having no idea how to raise a little girl. When she asked me to braid her hair I Googled braiding instructions I could not master even after practicing with tennis shoe laces. I fumbled again when her fifth birthday approached. I'd never thrown a birthday party for anyone, but I'd learned that if you're a parent and something big was happening, you had to go to Walmart. My Parental Advisory Board—the ladies in accounting at work—told me I needed a "theme." I not only didn't have a theme, I didn't know what that meant. A slogan? A concept? That night I consulted with Google, who I'll call Brittany, and learned that birthday theme means that plates must match the cups, napkins, and invitations. And who would I invite? I didn't know Adriana's preschool friends. Did I hand invitations directly to kids? And I needed activities and entertainment. How about golf? Oh, well. I was ignorant, but not dumb. I managed to have a shiny new pink Princess bicycle with training wheels and a basket in front and a bell on the handlebars.

At least that agony was in private. When Adriana showed me a birthday party invitation she got from a preschool colleague, I was confused. Do I drop her off? I didn't know the people. Should I wait outside? Check references? How long would it last? Did I go? The boys? We could make or break any party. I decided all of us would go and that was okay until I found myself at age 45 standing in a kitchen with four 25 year old mothers discussing TV shows I'd never seen and music I'd never heard. I drifted into the backyard, me and their dog, and watched the kids play in a jump house rented special.

That experience was helpful in one regard. Adriana had been asking me to paint her nails. I had no idea how, or if it was even allowed on a five-year-old. At the party, looking at other girls' fingers and toes, I learned it was permitted. However, I didn't know I could take her to a nail salon and do it for $10. How would I know that? That week Adriana had to visit the elementary school to have her skills tested. I wanted her to look normal so I went to the drug store for nail polish. I didn't know they had removable nail polish for little girls. I picked up a tiny paintbrush in the craft area because I wasn't certain there was one in the jar. That night, as I zeroed in on a practice toe, my vision got blurry when things got close. She giggled. I was nervous.

"It tickles," she wiggled.

"Hold your feet still. Don't move your feet."

"You're spilling it. It's on my feet."

"I can wash that off," I said. I wiped her feet with water on a Kleenex.

"It's not coming off. People at preschool will see my feet."

"Time for bed!" I yelled to the boys.

"Let's do this tomorrow night," I begged.

The next day I went to the drug store for turpentine to remove the polish. I asked around and found a solution. I also found kids' nail polish. In a burst of competency, I bought it.

"Adriana, let's paint your toenails!"

"Are you going to spill it on me again?"

That night, wearing nine dollar glasses I bought at the drug store I painted, er, polished the cutest, happiest little finger and toenails this side of the Sierras. She wiggled and giggled the whole time.

The elementary school assessment test made me nervous. How to prepare? We spent evenings studying letters, numbers, colors, and major philosophers like Hume, Santayana, and Charlie Brown. On the way to the test, I recalled my admissions interview at my night law school. To prepare, I'd read important cases and reviewed early American legal history, especially about separation of powers. If I had lived near the Black Hills I would have visited Mt. Rushmore for inspiration. The Dean and I met in a little room. I was nervous. What if I botched an amendment?

He was friendly and easy to talk to. At the end he said, "David, let me ask you a question."

*Here it comes! Brown vs. Board of Education! Thomas Paine! Commerce Clause! Miranda!*

"David, how do you expect to pay for this?"

"I have a good job. I'm going to write you a check every month."

"Okay."

When Adriana and I arrived for the assessment test a little girl was leaving. We were next. The ladies there had heard of me. They said, "It's nice that you've adopted three kids." I thanked them and surveyed their ring fingers. They measured Adriana's height and weight. I met Mrs. W., who told me she'd be Adriana's teacher. She escorted us into the library for the test and sat with Adriana. I sat nearby.

"Adriana, do you know your address?"

"Cesar Chavez," she beamed. That was our street.

"2443," I added calmly. It was all about teamwork, really.

"This is to assess her skills, not yours," Mrs. W. said. "You can wait outside."

The library had a glass door so I could watch and see that Adriana was having fun with Mrs. W. Our time slot was nearly over. I went back inside in time to hear Mrs. W. ask Adriana to count as high as she could. Off she went. She got up to 20, 21, 22 when I had a bad feeling. We did some counting, before bedtime, when she got her kisses.

"23, 24, 25, 26," she continued.

*What if she…no, I just skipped ahead because I was tired.*

"27, 28, 29, 90!"

I slipped into unconsciousness.

Mrs. W. was puzzled. "29 is pretty good," she said. Adriana got a free pencil.

Adriana's past posed other challenges for us. One night, with bewildered sad eyes, she showed me her homework assignment—fill out a chart showing her mother's name along with aunts, uncles, and grandparents from mom's side of the family. I told her to go to her room to get her scissors for another project, took her homework out of the packet, wadded it up, and threw it away.

At a local burger joint with our friend Carmen, two Hispanic ladies, twins, worked the counter. Well, what do you know? The ladies recognized the kids.

"Oh my gosh, how are you?" They used to be neighbors and that was nice. I was hungry and ordering and there was a line behind me. Carmen and the kids sat at a table. One of the cashier twins hurled a spear through me, landing a direct hit on Adriana.

"Adriana," she yelled across the restaurant, "is your mom still in jail?"

Adriana looked at me and lowered her eyes to the floor. I'd brought her to the lion's den. Her shoulders sagged. Carmen spun around, glared at the twin and turned her into stone.

"We have a new life now," I said.

"Oh."

"This is another reason to leave Santa Maria," Carmen said after I sat down. I agreed. In town, I'd noticed Adriana staring out the car window, remembering this or that house, this or that street, this or that whipping. When we left town for a day trip she changed. She played with her brothers, enjoyed spelling words I asked the kids, or played I Spy. It was different and better. The only way to fix Santa Maria was to put it in our rearview mirror.

While adults hurled spears, little people flung arrows. Adriana could not get away. One night she said, "And, Daddy?"

"Yes, love."

"A girl at school told me I was ugly."

"Adriana. Do you remember the princesses at Disneyland?"

"Yeth."

"You are prettier than all the princesses in Disneyland."

"All the princesses?"

"Yes, love. All of the princesses."

Waiting outside McDonald's for a McTeacher McFundraiser for the McSchoolsystem running out of McMoney, a girl recognized Adriana.

"Where's your mom?" she asked.

Adriana was confused and speechless, but her big brother came to her rescue.

"Is Carmen coming?" Javier said, loud enough for all to hear. Hearing that and seeing me confused the girl. She faded into the crowd. At home in bed after eating a McCherry pie, I saw Adriana staring into the McDarkness. I asked her about the girl.

"You didn't know what to say, did you?"

She shook her head no. The corners of her mouth formed a melancholy, hopeless crescent. My heart climbed from my chest and lay next to her.

"The next time that happens you say, 'I'm here with my Daddy.'"

She smiled. "That's a good idea."

"Let's practice."

"I'm here with my Daddy."

"Again."

"I'm here with my Daddy."

"Perfect."

Within minutes I heard her muffled, sweet snore.

A child raised by children, Adriana had no interest being with children when she could be with adults friendly to her. When I drove by school to see my babies, I'd see a hundred children playing, and four teachers huddled and talking with Adriana standing among them looking up. Her teachers told me that during lunchtime, Adriana walked alone door-to-door, looking for erasers to clean, or papers to hand out, or guinea pigs to feed. After school she walked the blind child from the classroom to the parent area.

Over time Adriana grew to trust me. And she gained confidence. "Helping" with her homework, I teased her for not knowing how to make a four.

"You are four," I said.

While I was outside with the boys launching balsa airplanes onto the roofs of our neighbors, Adriana wrote "44" on ten yellow sticky notes and placed them all over the house.

"Forty-four," she said, "is my favorite number."

Adriana didn't need support; she needed a stand of redwoods. I was happy to oblige. Adriana's ability to shed her past depended on me shedding my ignorance about raising a little girl and learning to treat her like a little person instead of a toy. I respected her fears and her dreams and she knew I would stand by her no matter what. She did no wrong. It was unconditional love and I found it there, taped to my bedroom walls, in the thirty drawings Adriana made for me, all with the same message: "Daddy, I love you. Adriana."

It all came together at a Santa Maria pond on Huck Finn Fishing Day. The YMCA supplied poles, bait, hooks, fish, and people helping. We were the first kids there. We got the first free pancakes off the outdoor griddle and we shivered in the morning fog. When the sun topped the trees, we stood in line with other kids near the pond filled with catfish brought special. The pond was circled by a temporary fence so you couldn't fish without waiting in line because fishing without waiting was the kind of thing that pissed off the YMCA. Two volunteers, seeing me with three, offered to help. They didn't realize I was watching them to see if they put the marshmallow on the hook after the worm, or before. Within two minutes Craig and his volunteer had a fish. Craig stopped fishing to play with the bait. Javier and his volunteer caught two. Javier squirmed in delight, his mouth in full grin, because he'd never caught a fish before, or even been fishing. A man with the megaphone told everyone there were five minutes left, but no one cared because almost everyone had a fish. Most were posing for pictures taken by the lady who gave you her card and said, "Go online and download the photo and you can just pay me there."

Time was up. Only Adriana didn't have a fish. She was sad and I was heartsick watching her watch kids celebrating with their fish. It was a terrible day. The man told everyone to leave. I was 45 years old. I had wanted children my whole life to help them, to teach them. I needed to say something profound. I needed to seize this opportunity to teach Adriana a life lesson. Instead, when megaphone man turned away, I seized the opportunity to re-load the hook. I grabbed a gob of wriggling worms and marshmallows and squeezed it into a wad the size of a spinning nickel. I stuck it on the hook and threw it into the water. The splash was so loud I was surprised the man didn't notice. Had the wad landed on a fish it might have crushed its skull, but it was too late. It was time to go. The life lesson had to be about the hard side of life. Something like that. It was important, I was going to say, to experience all of life's emotions to the fullest, even that sadness worn on her face like make-up.

We needed to reel in the bait. It was the entirety of the emotions, to know pleasure you must know pain (a Chinese proverb, I'd note), that contributed to the overall knowing, the understanding of depths. Sadness, I'd say, was just as important, in this realm, as joy. It was a great lesson except it was mostly bullshit, and when I started to speak I looked at her shivering, watching kids running out of the fenced area with their dead fish and people taking pictures. That sadness on her face crushed me. I panicked. All I could think of was a line from a Rolling Stones song, "You can't always get want you want, but if you try sometime, you just might find you get what you need." I'd waited 45 years to teach lessons and this was all I had? She didn't even know Mick Jagger. Still, we could not quit on sorrow; that was a lesson. I handed her the pole so I could speak freely and gesture. As she placed her sad brown hands on the pole I felt a tug. A three-pound catfish kind of tug. I set the hook, nearly pulling it through the fish's ears. My princess, stunned and happy, reeled it in.

Daddy, the failed philosopher, watched and encouraged every turn. In the cool Santa Maria morning I realized that I'd be more helpful if I avoided philosophy and focused on the day-to-day joys and challenges. That was okay by me. After the photographer took our picture we put our four catfish in a bag of ice. As we walked through the park, all holding hands, Adriana said, "Everything makes me happy."

At home I transitioned into my World Famous Chef garb. It isn't easy being a World Famous Chef, but I did what I must. It is not easy being a World Famous Chef and doing what you must and, you know, if I saw through this particular area of the catfish I'll saw right through my finger. That's what I did, including the fingernail. The World Famous Loser had a gusher and three children watching TV. We went to the emergency room—our third trip in six months—and the kids watched the doctor clean catfish guts from the cut.

"When was the last time you had a tetanus shot?" the doctor asked.

*About 25 years ago.* "Um, maybe last year."

He didn't call me a liar in front of the kids as he prepped the needle. "That was a big one," Javier said.

We went to McDonald's. The other fish went into the trash with the butchered fish. We never went fishing again, although I wouldn't mind, knowing all about it like I do.

The next week I met Adriana's super kindergarten teacher, Mrs. W., for our conference. As always, she was smiling. Adriana adored her and the feeling was mutual. Mrs. W. was excited to tell me how well Adriana was doing. I told her the 29...90! story.

"She's ready to read," she told me. "She's ready to read right now. I'm going to give you two books for her. Bring them back. Her grades are perfect. Adriana and her big brother will go to college."

I signed the report card below a handwritten note from Mrs. W.: "Adriana has shown tremendous growth academically and socially. Her willingness to help others has continued to shine in her daily. Thank you for all your support and Adriana is a wonderful reflection of her father."

I understand that a report card wasn't about the dad, but why not? While Adriana grew from behaving like the grand-daughter of a Klansman, I evolved from the loner in the song "Desperado" to a father who read to his daughter until both fell asleep, her on my lap. We did this most evenings, she holding me tighter than I held her, though not by much. We grew up together, the dimpled forger and the iconoclast, she joining the civilized, and me—possibly the only single Caucasian man in America adopting three minority strangers[16]—becoming a family man, not the dreamer, but the one who tried each day to feed children and clothe them and cut fingernails and fill bellies. It wasn't like my previous adventures: skydiving, water skiing on the Caribbean, rescuing olive ridley turtles in the Costa Rican surf, or trying to join Lech Walesa's 1981 anti-communist revolution in Poland, and it would not get me the Hinckley sloop I always wanted or the house by the beach, but it was a path to a place I'd never been. Taking it with Adriana is an everlasting joy.

My prior life communication skills—grunts or sports analogies, telling employees to 'stand tall', or listening to a friend but adding little— were not sufficient with a little girl. It's hard to stand tall when you need a two-step ladder to reach the sink and the world scares you even if you could. I learned to listen, and say, "How did that make you feel?" When

16  In 2005, according to U.S. Health & Human Services, only 8,000 children were adopted from Social Services by people without a previous relationship with the children. Just 2%, or 160, entered the home of a single male.

89

she told me, it worked. We grew together.

Adriana's fear of the robbers eased with my help. I taught her what police normally did. We said hello to officers at community events and fairs. She refused at first; plain scared and who could blame her? She felt better over time. Graduation came in our driveway. We'd been in the house together for a year. The neighborhood was quiet and the neighbors, um, quiet. We actually hadn't met any of them. The neighbor north of us had a goat for a few days. Another came over for a little while, but he was running from his parole officer, someone Adriana and I met when we went outside to mail a letter. He was standing in our driveway in plain clothes, holding his pistol ear high.

"How are you?" I said.

"Good."

I didn't want Adriana to panic.

"A neighbor, living three doors away, ran off when we were doing a parole check. He went through your side gate."

Adriana held my hand tight.

"I can never get that gate open," I said. "I always have to yank on the cord."

"He had no trouble at all."

"I have three little kids here. Can you check the garage and make sure he's not in there?"

"Okay." After he checked our garage he left, so we had two people come by, him and the man he chased, and Adriana was not afraid of either one. Adriana, so sweet, the beauty queen who gave us fashion shows and smiles and laughter, is now the young woman in our house. We're blessed with her energy and effort to help those around her. She changed my life more than the boys, not because of anything they didn't do, but because I had so much further to travel to join her. I was a stranger meeting a young traveler on the open road when we joined hands and went forward, and it was good. Considering her life, the beatings, the re-giftings and the robbers, Adriana embracing an adult she didn't know was astonishing.

I still listen to Bob Dylan's "Tangled Up in Blue" and look back at what my life might have been, but now I let it go when the song is over and know that no matter what happens from here I did good and something better happened to me.

# 9. Homecoming

After returning from a Pulitzer Newspapers corporate meeting in Las Vegas, I'd be a Dad. The children knew about the trip, but didn't like it because a foster care stable mate told them that children were in foster care because their parents were on business trips.

Like a town new to air travel, Santa Maria had one airline, United, flying one way, to Los Angeles. The twin engine prop plane had thirty seats; half were occupied. A young lady was the flight attendant. A man and woman handled the controls in the morning rain. At about 70 miles-per-hour on our way to a 100 miles-per-hour takeoff, we heard a loud bang. The plane fishtailed violently to the left. We went right. I worried I'd never see the kids again and wondered what they'd think. I didn't have a will. I was waiting for the final adoption. The plane fishtailed right, throwing us left. The pilots regained control. The attendant was still. Her mouth wide open, she stared like the Buddha. Do we run for our lives? Were we going to burn? She did nothing. If this job didn't work out she could work for Social Services. We drifted to the side of the runway. She sat. We waited. Soon the pilot was on the intercom, "Uh, sorry about that. We'll try again in a minute."

Home safe, I arrived at Mimosa's at 6 p.m. The social worker assigned to meet me with paperwork waited in a white county car. I introduced myself to Murray and we shook hands. He was thin, 40-something and melancholy, like someone stole his dog.

Through the front window I saw my children smiling and giggling. I was high again, like someone opened my cranium and poured adrenalin inside.

Murray said, "I've known the kids for many, many years."

The kids ran out to greet me with big hugs and happy kisses.

"Hi, Adriana," he said. "I remember when you were born."

She didn't answer. Did Murray know about the years of Social Services reports? Did he write them?

"Javier. How are you?" he said.

Javier didn't answer. He hugged me and went around me so I was between him and Murray. Javier knew him. He was one of the robbers.

I walked into Mimosa's house with a disposable camera in my pocket. She'd prepared three garbage bags filled with used clothing and broken toys. I saw holes in the clothes through holes in the bags. The clothing allowance she received made no distinction between new and used. I wanted to capture the joy on film for the ages, but Murray, carrying the weight of the world, was lethargic and meandering so I left the camera in my pocket. I decided to get out as soon as possible. Our party would start later.

We sat at the table. He had a six inch tall pile of files, two inches per child, mostly medical consent forms, with the county turning over primary care responsibilities to me.

"Sign here, and here," he said. He knew I wasn't reading anything but the headlines. He didn't care, and robotically replaced a signed form with a new form. "And, here."

The county could have sent a tape recorder instead.

"Daddy," Adriana said, bursting with joy, "Are you going to adoct us?"

"Yes, love."

"Hooray!" she yelled. "We're getting adocted! We're getting adocted!"

"Daddy, can I sit on your lap?"

"Yes, sweetie."

"We're getting adocted!" she told Javier and both erupted in sweet chorus, "No more foster! No more foster!" Mimosa was not offended. She understood.

Craig sat on my other leg. I had to reach around two kids to sign.

No problemo.

"This is so sad," Murray said. Why did Social Services send him to our celebration? It was cruel and unusual. Did he remember Adriana's mom leaving her at the hospital like a pound stray? Did he drive Adriana from the nursery to foster?

I ignored him and signed. After a few minutes, me draped in children he'd known for many, many years, he said, "This is such a disappointment; we really tried to work with the mother."

Murray was at least a co-conspirator in a decade-long series of miscues that began with a mother abusing a child not yet born. How it ends I won't know for years. I wanted to grab Murray by the collar, pull him in slow and close, drill holes into his retinas, and say, "Murray, is this the right forum for that; is this the right time? Do you remember the spring of '97?" I couldn't believe Social Services sent him. They could have sent a card, or balloons. But no, they sent the beaked shadow himself.

He scared the kids. I thought about asking him to step aside for a minute; maybe he saw something... I'd ask him if he'd ever eaten grass, rubbed food on his lips, or been in a rabbit cage. But I wanted my children to be happy. My signature morphed into initials for the speed that was in it.

At the end, I told the kids to say, "Thank you, Mimosa, for taking care of us."

Javier and Adriana reported in unison. Craig made noises. Mimosa was happy and sad. With Javier's help, I told her that we'd invite her and her girls to Adriana's birthday in a few weeks. We dragged the trash bags into the driveway. My sedan was too small. Murray offered to put some things in his car. I agreed, because I didn't want to offend Mimosa by leaving the belongings she organized in a heap. I also wanted Murray to see that my $575,000 house wasn't a good place to buy crack.

When we got home my sister Joy was inside. She'd arrived that day from Phoenix to rummage through Costco buying supplies for my fifteen year long camping trip. She got giant sizes of detergent, wipes, pull-ups, dishwasher soap, Kleenex, toilet paper, and trash bags. The trash bags lasted the longest—one and a half years. She decorated the house with balloons to surprise the kids with an adoction party. My job was to take pictures and not panic.

"Aunt Joy is inside," I said. They ran to meet her.

Murray was so drab I didn't invite him in. I wanted to explain, but I decided to let him contemplate the irony over the years and work it out himself. I said good-bye in the driveway, leaving the garbage bags next to his car. He didn't look up; he didn't look in. The kids were long gone and soon so was he. We'd never see or hear from him again. His part was over, but my challenges with Social Services were just beginning. Others would take his place: robbers-to-be, working their way up from petty theft. One would threaten to take my children from me.

The children spent most of the first weekend in the kitchen opening cabinets bursting with food. The 'cupbord' was not bare. They were happy and played. No more shouts out the door; no more hiding. I felt like a magician who changed four lives with the wave of a wand. We ate cake and laughed and took pictures and baths and oh my, what had I done?

It was a mind-bending experience of blissful joy.

Night time was different. Their closed eyelids were like projection screens, amplifying the memories. They didn't bring their mother or the robbers with them per se—as in real life those arrived after midnight—in nightmares sparked by an unknown light or a noise in the yard near the gate. They were afraid to be alone so we made a slumber party camp on the floor near my bed like we did during Family Practice. We were so close we could have lived in a van. Surrounded by new pillows, warm blankets, and stuffed animals they slept soundly, wrapped in each other like strands of DNA.

Our first weeks together were a blur. Adriana and Javier were long gone from my room at night, driven away by my snoring. They weren't that scared, but they did miss each other, so they made a camp in the living room under a comforter tent; lit by the dull glow of a nightlight. They enjoyed camping out more than anything and still do.

Craig was so fragile I wondered how I'd manage work and the other kids. Thankfully, Mimosa agreed to watch them when they were sick. She watched Craig often. I paid her. One day though, after preschool called to tell me Adriana was sick, I couldn't find Mimosa and stayed home. That was the only day of work I missed because of sick kids. My boss, a divorced and dedicated mother of one, didn't tell my peers I quit to raise a family somewhere else. She asked if she could help.

Like tag team wrestlers, Grandma arrived as Aunt Joy departed. She stayed for two weeks and taught me how to poach eggs. She could not watch three children all day, so I arranged child care at the YMCA preschool for Shrek and Adriana. A van would pick up Javier after school and take him to their program. I called Curtis, the YMCA director, faxed the applications, and worked out finances. I was his biggest customer. After we spoke I imagined him calling the asphalt people and ordering the new parking lot he always wanted. I took my checkbook to the Y and told the lady I was there to pay thirteen sixty-two. She found the paperwork for one child—$454 per month—and sympathetically whispered, "Are you just making a small payment? Thirteen dollars and sixty-two cents?"

"No, I'm paying one thousand, three hundred, and sixty-two dollars. There are three of them." I learned that the preschool program, Stepping Stones, was not at the Y, next door to my newspaper, but across town, on the bottom floor of the Social Services building. No harm there, right?

On Sunday, we took my mother to the end of the 1,370 foot long Pismo Beach pier built in 1924 for the little train to carry fish inland for processing. Now it was an old, rickety calamity of a walkway. We strolled past old men gutting surf perch at the public fresh-water table. Seagulls hovered in the breeze like giant hummingbirds. The shadows of 400 pound sea lions floated like storm clouds under the water, waiting for scraps. We bought three crabs and shrimp. Raised in Missouri, my Mom and I tried to figure out what part of the crab to eat. It turned out that crab, like wine, was mostly for show. It was more fun to tell people you had crab, "We went to the pier and got some crab," than it was to eat the crab. We got a bite each.

My mother was a calming presence, having gone through much worse than I did to become a single parent. When I thought about parenting three children by myself, I thought of her. What I did was not unusual. Single parenting was my experience. She was my role model.

With blonde hair, the daughter of a Missouri dentist, she looked the opposite of my Puerto Rican father. She had two sisters. When they were in high school, their father bought them a Dairy Queen so he'd know where they were after school. She met my father at the University of Missouri, where she graduated with a degree in Home Economics; a pre-wed major. After my father died, we moved from a Milwaukee suburb (where he had worked for a defense contractor; she stayed home) to Maryville and into a room. That's what $5,000 in life insurance bought you in 1967.

She was devastated to find herself a single parent with five children under ten. Every day she went to the church on the hill. The nuns at the convent, we were told, were helping her get ready for a job. In fact, I learned much later, she had tried to commit suicide. She was there getting counseling. People tried to help her. One of the people was the local priest, Father Tim. He was a great guy. He got us a pig to keep in the basement (gone after two weeks), and he taught us how to shoot cans off a fence post with a .22 rifle. He drove a Thunderbird, and he fell in love with her and she with him, and we all liked him, but the Catholic Church frowned on indiscretion so they transferred him away.

I lost my second father figure in a year, and I wondered why God kept wrecking our lives. My family never spoke about how that felt, or about the greater pain of my father's death. We had a silver box full of slides we watched in silence, the six of us, one by one leaving the room in tears, led away by our broken hearts.

We moved 90 miles south to Kansas City. My mom got a job teaching home economics at an all-black junior high school across the river in Kansas City, Kansas. She was one of two white people in the school. The other was also a teacher. At night, my mother attended school, earning a Master's degree in Marriage and Family Counseling. When I went to night law school, on top of working 50 to 60 hours per week at the Monterey County Herald newspaper, I often came home exhausted. After reading cases my eyes stung. But I recalled her doing the same thing and coming home to five kids and I found inspiration in that.

Now, she was leaving. That was okay; I had to see how I'd do on my own.

Our daily routine was a free-fall. I got up at 6:04. I set the clock on 04 because there were four of us. I drank coffee, read the newspaper, made three lunches and woke the kids at 6:30. They dressed while I showered. Breakfast was on the table at 6:45 and at 7:05 I told them to wash up while I helped Shrek get dressed. We were out the door at 7:15 so Javier was at school by 7:30. We were never late. Fortunately, the kids loved preschool and Javier loved first grade, so the routine was pleasant. They were thrilled to put on their new backpacks, even Craig, though his was usually empty. He never looked inside. Javier and Adriana wanted to put toys or crayons in their backpacks to show other kids they had things.

The children each had one Disney character plate, fork, spoon and cup I washed every night because it didn't occur to me to use adultware.

Their mouths were too small for regular forks. We frequently ate out because an early meal, baked scallops (I'd swear I heard someone say "booger balls"), was disgusting. Going out was easier. They soon learned I needed only the slightest provocation to go out to eat: good report card, good day, good new restaurant, or good cash-flow.

McDonald's was a favorite, me reading the Wall Street Journal while they played in the cubes. Or we got take-out from El Toro, a fieldworker deli serving mouth-watering carnitas, perfect rice, and fresh tortillas made while I stood there, at five-foot-ten the tallest person in line, next to workers from the fields across the street. I wore a light starch Brooks Brothers shirt and they wore rubber boots, but for those moments in line we were in the same place and that was good.

We practiced manners at dinner. No standing on the table, no toys on the table, no talking with your mouth full, etc. Or we played the adoption game, naming famous adopted people, like Superman, Snow White, and Spiderman. And my contributions: Malcolm X, Aristotle, John Lennon, and Nelson Mandela.

"Are we famous?" Craig asked.

"To me you are."

I had three rules for me when the kids moved in: Always wear a collared shirt as a civilizing emblem, keep alcohol out of the house, and never let the kids see me drink alcohol.

When foster care kids moved, the law required a doctor's checkup. I called the pediatrician's office where the kids had been going for years to schedule appointments. Files were misplaced. Who the heck are you?

Each trip was the first time I was alone with each child. I realized I'd been acting as conductor, or referee, when I was with all three. It would be good to get to know them. Shrek was first. His outfit matched in the morning. I was anxious because the doctor report went to Social Services. When I arrived at preschool to get Craig I found him alone in the toddler room eating a peanut butter and jelly sandwich. He wore both ear to ear. He was also wet, shirtless, and painted green. It was "paint frogs green day," they said. I cleaned him up except for the green part. I couldn't get it off. When we arrived for our appointment, the receptionist had news for me.

"We're not going to perform the examination."

"Why not?"

"According to the file, the kids had a checkup six months ago. We only get reimbursed for one check-up per year."

"Then why did you make the appointment?"

"I didn't make it, someone else did."

"This is different. I'm adopting the kids. They're changing residences, so I have to bring them in."

Like the emergency room trip with Craig, a posse gathered. I hadn't planned on drawing the attention of small groups.

"They just had a checkup," she said. "Haven't you seen the file?" This elicited grins and chuckles from her peers, amused I knew so little.

"Seen the file? I barely know their names. Can I have the file?"

"No."

"Who is in charge here?"

"Our office manager."

"Can you ask her to come here?" She made a phone call and said, "She won't come, but you can go see her, she's downstairs."

My lunch hour slipped away. I carried the green kid downstairs. The office manager told me the same thing—they already had a checkup and won't get another one.

"Call Social Services," I said, "and ask them if your policy trumps the law. The law doesn't say the kids need to have a checkup when they switch residences if they haven't had a checkup lately. It says, when they move, they need a checkup."

"I know the law," she said.

"Would it be helpful if I called Social Services and recommend they not send patients here if you're not going to do what they ask you to do? One of us should call, since we disagree. Can I use your phone?"

After phoning Social Services she called upstairs to tell the grinners and chucklers I was returning, but when we arrived everyone was gone. After a few minutes a doctor came to the waiting room and invited us in for the exam. He looked at Craig and tilted his head.

"It's paint frogs green day," I said, pretending it was no big deal.

"I've heard of that," he said.

I would visit this practice often and interact with the most thoughtful and patient doctors I'd ever seen. A white father and son headlined the team, along with a Hispanic doctor who wore blue jeans, cool shoes and worked weekends. I trusted them and did everything they said, but I had one big problem: Each time I checked in, I was given an emergency notification and contact form to review and initial. It contained names and addresses from the old regime. I refused to initial it. "Things are different now." They refused to change the information. A simple phone call to Social Services, six blocks away? Hey, there's a guy here with children you used to have. He seems to be slowly kidnapping them, but he never misses an appointment, so...

Each time I went, three times, five times, seven, ten, they gave me the old form. Each time I said it was wrong and each time they refused to take my information. I wondered if the practice sent out appointment reminders and worried they might send one to the old regime.

At night before bed I thought about what I'd do if an old regime war party came through my door looking for my children. I got the chance to wonder for real the night a shadow came over the fence and into the courtyard. Standing in the living room in the dark watching a Santa Maria police officer sneak into the courtyard with his revolver drawn made me consider buying a weapon.

After a couple of weeks on our own, my older sister, Diana, arrived with Jane, her youngest daughter, for a trip to Disneyland. Diana arranged for a private $170 dinner with Goofy at the Disneyland Hotel. The next morning, we went to the Magic Kingdom, the Happiest Place on Earth, and bought $260 in tickets. After we rode in some teacups, Adriana found Tigger and asked him if she could pull his tail. He said yes. I would have tipped him, but he didn't have any pockets. Our trip was one of the great joys of life, three kids in a magic kingdom and one man in a dream world.

Until the adoption was final, Social Services had the right to check on us, appearing unannounced if they chose. However, we agreed they'd let me know when they were coming because it was more civilized.

"It's Melinda," the voicemail said. "I'm the kids' social worker. I need to see them for my report. I'll just go find them at school and preschool."

That night, I told the kids. They were afraid. "What does she want?" Javier asked.

"She wants to know if we need anything."

"I don't want her to talk to us," Adriana said.

"Don't worry," I replied. "She's a nice lady and wants to help."

Melinda never appeared at school, but soon called. "Can I come over right now? I'm on deadline."

We sat at the kitchen table while the kids and Aunt Diner—the kids' pronunciation of Aunt Diana—watched TV on the sofa 15 feet away.

"How are you?" Melinda whispered, like I was intubated in intensive care.

"We're good. We just got back from Disneyland."

"I don't really have anything to do here," she said. "I can leave quickly."

"Okay."

"I do need to know if you've taken the kids to the doctor."

"All three."

"I need to know the dates."

I told her.

"Have they seen a dentist?" she asked.

"Not with me."

"I'll send you the name of their dentist. They have one."

She took no notes. I didn't expect her to call with the dentist's name and she didn't.

"How does this work from here?" I asked.

"Well, the next step is to sever the rights of the parents, which I organize."

"When will it happen?"

"I think we can get it done in late April, early May. We hold the severance hearing and then I notify all of the parents. They have six months to respond."

"You give them notice after the hearing? Don't people get notice before a hearing?"

"No," she said. "Don't worry."

"Have you done this before?"

"Not really."

"So how does it work again?"

"After the hearing, I have to find all of the parents, or people who could have been parents. If I have to, I'll run ads in newspapers in the towns where we last located them. It's because it takes so long for me to do my work that adoptions take a long time."

I didn't go to Harvard, but…the process, any noticed process, worked the opposite of the way Melinda described.

The next day I called Scott. "She said she provides notice after the hearing," I said.

"People get notice BEFORE a hearing, not AFTER."

Melinda was friendly, but overworked, over employed, or under trained. Or two out of three. Or all three. She was not managed properly, if at all. I had to monitor Melinda's work or I'd be one of those people on TV crying in the yard as a van pulled away with my children because the adoption was botched.

"I assume she was just confused," Scott said. "I'm glad you called. You're going to get three checks for $1,889 as your first foster care payments and clothing allowance." The next day I received five checks for $1,100. I called Scott and he said, "Oh, the bureaucracy. You'll get one more check for $789." The next day I received two more checks for $222.

Scott called a few weeks later. "I need to tell you a couple of things. First, Melinda missed the deadline to publish legal notices in newspapers before the hearing; there is no hearing. Maybe this summer. Second, the cousin who called in late February to say he wanted the kids to live with him and his roommates in their one bedroom apartment in Los Angeles sent me a letter. He wants the kids to live with him in Los Angeles in a two bedroom apartment. There are eight other people living there."

With the kids, it would be twelve. Perhaps they slept in shifts. Or perhaps it was all bullshit and when the cousin got the kids he'd call their mother and she'd wade across the Rio Grande River and take the Greyhound to Santa Maria, make a boyfriend and steal a car and my kids and drive to Mexico, stopping for beer and, if there was extra money, food.

"Since he's family," Scott said, "I have to check."

I'll say this about the cousin: He didn't need much room and he knew Scott's address. I never heard about him again. I wasn't indifferent to a family member wanting the kids. However, the timing would have been better if the letter to Scott arrived five years earlier, or ten. Even five months ago, or ten, would have made a huge difference in their lives. I never would have met the kids. However, they were mine now and my resolve to protect them grew up and around them like a trumpet vine.

I called Aunt Diner to tell her the news. She was smart, a Michigan MBA, familiar with the ways of the world. "I wonder if she failed to notify the parents on purpose," she said. "Maybe she's on the same page as that guy you met the night you got the kids for good."

Signing Adriana and Craig out at pre-school I saw two notes above the form. The first was a warning, telling parents that starting Monday the staff would list the junk food parents brought for their kids' lunch with the name of the parent next to each item. That weekend, I switched from giving my kids Twinkies and chocolate milk (I worried they wouldn't eat regular food) to vegetables and fruit and the note went away.

The second note asked parents to bring hard-boiled eggs for kids to decorate. Without that note, I might have missed Easter. I bought and boiled a dozen eggs for ten minutes and placed them in the car so I wouldn't forget to loan them to preschool. I asked the Advisory Board how to decorate Easter eggs we'd do at home. I wanted us to be normal and that's what normal people did. Was painting still the best way? Had anyone developed a spray? Had the technology changed? Go to Kmart and buy a kit, they said. You put an egg and ink in a plastic bag and smush it around.

The Easter Bunny, also shopping at Kmart apparently, left baskets for the kids, dolls for the princess, and a soccer ball and a basketball for the boys. "I wanted a ball, too," Adriana said. This was the last time I, er, the Easter Bunny, the sexist jerk, bought girl toys for Adriana and boys' toys for the, um, boys.

Wanting to meld into the Santa Maria community we went to the local Easter egg hunt at the new high school. We parked and held hands on the sidewalk. There was a jump house. An exotic pet store brought dragons, turtles, and snakes. We ate hamburgers near the ball field. I wanted to show the kids how not to litter but the wind blew our trash away.

The hunt was divided into roped areas separating children by age. I sent Javier to the seven to ten pen. Adriana, Craig and I stood next to the toddler pen. I felt an instant kinship with fellow parents.

A lady yelled instructions through a hand-held megaphone. "DO NOT ENTER THE AREA UNTIL I HAVE SOUNDED THE HORN."

Parents moved closer to me. I wondered if they noticed the yellow bow I put in Adriana's hair. It was crooked but it matched her socks.

"DO NOT TAKE THE EGGS UNTIL I HAVE SOUNDED THE HORN."

After the hunt, I'd chat with fellow parents and we'd count the eggs our kids got. Maybe one would invite us over for hot chocolate. If I said yes and began bonding, I'd send Bev an e-mail telling her this was the third time in four weeks I used her 'it takes a village' advice.

"DO NOT TAKE MORE THAN SIX EGGS."

She repeated the rules. It was a lot for children to remember.

I'd stay outside the ropes with other parents and take pictures of our first hunt. How did a little kid hold six eggs anyway?

The horn sounded! Parents rushed under the ropes, past startled kids and stuffed eggs into their pockets. Some kids got in, but it was too late. There were only a few eggs left. I found Craig on his back, screaming. A kid was stealing a red egg from his tiny, trembled hand. Adriana was in tears, looking for me. I spun around and saw Javier alone in his pen. Adriana saw me and opened her hand. She had a blue egg. She gave it to Craig. I found Javier. He had a green egg.

That night we held a special family meeting. After reviewing the day's events we decided not to socialize with people anymore.

# 10. Ricochet

If a pill made a person invisible, Javier would overdose. If he remade the world it would be two-dimensional so he could hide by turning. Javier didn't ease into my life; he escaped in, rumpled and running, gasping for breath, scared. When I introduced the children to co-workers Javier stood in the corner of my office, saying nothing, staring at his shoes. He was a silent crystal figurine glazed in real life and if you ignored him that would be great. If his life was music it'd be the man on the knoll at Spanish Bay playing "Amazing Grace" on the bagpipes. Was I too late?

After a Family Practice outing we returned to Mimosa's empty, unlocked house. After stepping outside to wait for Mimosa to return, I went back in to find Javier guiding and folding Adriana and Craig into a kitchen cabinet to hide. They thought I was leaving. He took the outside position, the one that got pulled out first and whacked. He knew where to hide and when. He knew when to peek or stay. He knew where to hide food and when they fed the rabbit. When he got fed at his old house he'd save some for later, he told me, by rubbing food on his lips to taste when he wanted. His older sister taught him that and did the same. If people could regurgitate he'd try it. He wrote stories about being hungry and he told kids he was little because he didn't eat much with his old family. Two days after he moved into our house I found him with a piece of bread in his pocket.

After I bought things he'd quietly ask if we were running out of money. I learned that his mother did not allow the children outside except when she sent them to beg for quarters. I never figured out if he asked me if we were running out of money because he didn't want to go door-to-door or because he knew how to get some. At night, he said, his mother made him and his siblings wash their clothes in the kitchen sink.

I imagined Javier paying an ugly and heavy price for past wrongdoings, real or alleged. He had marks on his palms he said he got at "bad foster." When he was six years old, the robbers left him at a shelter without kitchen cabinets or rabbit food. He told me that at one foster home he slept in a box on the floor. He didn't trust a soul. He didn't believe in the inherent goodness of man or that people would help a scared boy. He didn't understand why he and his brother and sisters, and children like them were the last on our list, the left-behind, the wretched refuse.

He was tired, poor, and tempest-tost, but with the Statue of Liberty 3,000 miles away, there was no lamp by the golden door.

The result was a finely tuned ability stronger than instinct to deflect blame. With his experience who wouldn't lift the same shield? When I asked Javier if he left his toys outside, he'd ask Adriana if she left her toys outside. When I asked him if he left the light on in the bathroom, he'd ask Craig if he did. He was more ricochet than boy.

After Scott told me to visit Javier's school and introduce myself to his First Grade teacher so she'd know he was in a transition period (in case he hit someone or swiped their lunch money, like I did when I was his age), I asked Javier if he had any friends. "I have a lot of friends," he said. When he said, "Hi," to kids we wandered by, he watched me to see if I noticed his "friends." But the kids looked away like they'd never seen him before. I don't think they were being mean; they hardly knew him. According to Javier, this was his third first grade that year. Social Services played him like bumper pool. Nevertheless, I'd asked him if he wanted to stay at his school—there were just a few months left—and he did. In order to meet his teacher, I needed to know her name. I asked Javier.

"Mrs. A."

I needed more. "Can you spell her name?"

"M...R....S....A."

His public elementary school taught mostly field workers' children.[17] Across the street, three blocks from Mimosa's house, field workers had a yard bazaar of used clothing. I arrived around noon, the only 45-year-old white guy with a Mercedes in the parking lot. Mrs. A. was a delight. Javier found refuge in her classroom. When the year ended with Javier enrolled at the school near our home, I told Mrs. A that I would always give her credit for saving Javier.

"He could have gone in a different direction," I said. "You helped him."

During Family Practice, I took the children to see our new house. As we drove through the development of brand new four and five bedroom homes, Javier said, "Do you live in an apartment?"

"No, I live in a big house."

"Wow."

From the garage, we saw down the hall, past two bedroom doors on the left and a bathroom door on the right. My bedroom was at the end of the hall with a window to the back yard. Javier passed the first bedroom door.

"Javier," I said. "This is your room. When you come to visit me, this is your room."

He pushed the door open and stood stunned. He stared at the bright red race car bed and the Mandelburg polar bear print and a print of black horses. He didn't move or speak. I left him and escorted Adriana to her room.

"Snow White sheets!" she said. "And flowers."

"Look," I said. "You have a basket. And two bunnies."

17  In Plyler v. Doe, 1982, citing the Equal Protection Clause, the U.S. Supreme Court found that the children of illegal immigrants were "people," overturning a Texas law prohibiting their education. Texas's other argument—not educating illegals would save money—was dismissed when the court noted that not educating children would create a permanent underclass of illiterates, costing Texas even more.

Javier found us.

"There are six places to put my things." A boy with a spot at foster to put his things had counted surfaces, shelves and drawers. Now, if he only had six things.

"I want to live with the polar bears," he said.

In the living room, he saw the couch. "Who sleeps there?"

"No one. We use it to read or watch TV."

"Wow."

After surveying the home, Javier had a question.

"Daddy?"

"Yes, love."

"Where does Craig sleep?"

"I haven't decided yet."

"Craig sleeps with me because he gets scared."

"I'll get Craig his own bed so he can sleep next to you."

"Okay, but the beds have to be touching."

"When I get scared," he added, "I hug Kitty as tight as I can." He pulled Kitty from his jacket pocket. It was a pathetic, hand-sized gray stuffed cat with white ears and whiskers. It looked like a bulldozer backed over it. For the next two years of his life, and for the past however many, it was his prized possession: trips, naps, sleeping; they were one. I tried to imagine the horrors he'd heard, beatings, rapes, the robbers, fights, swearing, listening to other kids come into foster crying, sniveling in the darkness, not knowing who was lying next to him in the box. Will he hit me? Will he hate me? Kitty was his first and best friend.

Javier's life was more difficult than mine. His memories were deeper than those of his little sister and brother. His scars were longer and crooked. No matter where we were, he looked for an escape route. I watched him calculate. He never cried after spills or in frustration, except when we lost Kitty in the folds of hotel sheets taken away. After searching on his hands and knees under the bed, he quietly walked into the bathroom and shut the door. Craig, Adriana and I stood outside the door, listening to him weep. I gave Javier my favorite golf hat to make up for his loss, but it didn't work. After we left the hotel and I made several calls, I retrieved Kitty, washed and not grey, it turned out. I put him outside the front door, rang the doorbell and asked Javier to answer the door.

"There's no one here," he yelled. Then he looked down. He gasped in joy and called to his brother and sister. They danced and celebrated.

On the way home from visiting the new house, I asked Javier why he didn't live in his real house anymore. He couldn't answer, but he didn't have to. After my father died, leaving my mother alone to raise five kids— we were one, three, five, seven, and nine years old—she moved us to her parents' hometown, Maryville, Missouri, 100 miles north of Kansas City. We were broken and broke. We went from a two-story, three bedroom house with a playhouse in the back to a room on the second floor of her dad's dentist office. It had green slime growing on the walls. A bare bulb hung from the ceiling by its cord. I called it the "creepy compartment."

"Javier," I said. "I had a new real house (or room) when I was your age."

He looked at me and said thanks with his eyes. Javier was why I became a dad to children without one. I knew what it was like. Bev, the training social worker, was right—it was easy for me to relate to their loss and help them take a new path besides one of anger. Yet, with Javier, there was none of that. Besides hiding food and playing ricochet, he caused no trouble.

Shortly after the school year began, I got a call at work.

"Mr. Marin?"

"Yes."

"This is Carol Hutchins. I'm the assistant principal at Taylor Elementary."

"How are you?" Javier probably won an award. He was good at marbles.

"I have a question. Has Javier given you a slip to get signed for me?"

"No."

"I caught him throwing rocks over the fence on Monday. He threw them into the pond. That's against regulations. I gave him a discipline slip and told him to have you sign it. Did he give it to you?"

"No."

"I found him on Tuesday and asked him if he showed you the slip and he said he forgot. I found him on Wednesday and he said he forgot. Yesterday, he said he forgot. This morning…"

"Let me guess."

"He forgot. You need to sign the form."

"Okay. Thanks for calling."

What a nightmare! I left work and drove around wondering how I'd raise three children when the assistant principal said my son was a rock-throwing liar. What should I do? What if he got expelled? Who would watch him? What if he joined a gang? I needed room to breathe. I needed to call Scott and tell him this might not work.

During my drive I made several observations:

Every week I took the kids to a field near home, through the gate with the No Trespassing sign, and we threw rocks over the fence, trying to hit the water trough of a horse we named Spirit. Javier had the best arm.

When I was seven, I didn't throw rocks over a fence, no sir. I skipped school and walked across town to buy spurs. Later, with $20 for a bow and arrow, I bought a BB gun and shot a woodpecker. It hung from its tail upside down and died on the trunk.

When I was eight and living in Kansas City, a friend and I skipped school. We went to my house and, without inhaling, smoked cigarettes while we sat in the big chairs.

When I was 13, I was the functional equivalent of Chief Operating Officer in my gang of white suburban Kansas City jerks. We skipped school, egged teachers' homes, never did homework, rode our mini-bikes across school grounds while school was in session, and spent many days at the Electric Palace pool hall playing adults and winning their money. We practiced at night. We were very good.

Before I was 16, I'd been arrested three times. My brothers and I got caught stealing outdoor Christmas light bulbs we needed to pop in the cul-de-sac by the woods. I got nailed riding my mini-bike through town without a helmet and nabbed for being drunk in public at the drive-in theater. I threw up on a policeman after my first try at drinking. Home before my working mother, I intercepted all three juvenile court notices and threw them away.

By my sophomore year, I'd been expelled about 15 times.

When I was 18, I stole an entire box of scratch and win tickets from Safeway. I scratched, but didn't win.

In college, I stole food from Safeway,[18] or I hid a sandwich in the aisle and walked around and took bites.

I'd spent two nights in jail...both for not paying the same speeding ticket.

I lucked out of my adolescent troubles, rescued by books. My mom had a new bedroom made for me in the basement. One night, the light bulb in the adjoining utility room came on, and then off, and back on. I was terrified, thinking someone was in there. I walked into the room and tightened the loose bulb. In the corner, I saw boxes my alcoholic uncle left for us to keep while he wandered. The boxes were packed with books, many wet and moldy. There were books about astronomy, mathematics, history, and physics. There were works by Tennyson, Ralph

---

18  Nothing personal, Safeway! And I'm making it up to you now.

Waldo Emerson, Hemingway, Steinbeck, Thomas Paine, and Lincoln. I took the books out of the boxes, dried them near the heater and stacked them by category.

The books smelled; they smelled like freedom. I read them and resigned from my gang to pursue other interests. Off to prep school, I made Dean's List and became a member of the National Honor Society. I won a Daughters of the American Revolution Good Citizenship Award and a U.S. senator's nomination to the United States Naval Academy. And I got a haircut. Javier loved books, too. We had that in common. He always had one with him and loved to do math problems in his free time. Books were liberators, and I hoped Javier could learn from them, like I did, that there is a world older and different from our own where good things happen and people change their lives.

That night, I told Javier that the assistant principal called.

"Do you know why she called?" I asked.

"Yes."

"Did you do something wrong?" I wanted him to tell me. This was the big part of the lesson. And I wanted to hear if he lied.

"Yes."

"What did you do?"

"You know what I did."

Was he playing games with me? This was more severe than I thought. This was what Bev warned us about in training. I didn't want a smart-ass, like me. I wanted a sweet kid.

"How would I know what you did?"

"The assistant principal told you."

"How do you know that?"

"I was sitting in her office when she called you."

That night, I had Javier do 10 push-ups and I told him that in the future if he got in trouble I wanted to find out from him.

At a school open house, after the teacher told us about the year and asked for money for pencils and Kleenex, Javier and I stood next to his desk. His old name, Javier Fuentes, was in black block letters and taped to the desktop. I looked at him. He looked at me. I looked at the name. He looked at the name. I looked at the teacher who wasn't looking at us. Like a mama grizzly, I put my claw over his name, tore it off his desk, scrunched it and pitched it into the trash.

"You have a new name now," I said. He levitated. I told the teacher, who was happy to write a new name for my son.

At an honor roll ceremony Javier waited for other kids to line up so he was last. In his old life it was probably safer to have everything in front of him, but that was then. Afterwards, I told him that Marin children don't stand at the end of the line. We stand at the front.

People who saw us together told me that Javier did everything I did, like a mirror. On Father's Day he made a card for me at school: *For Dady from Javier Marin. Happy Day Dady.* Inside: *I love you Dady. I have never had a Dad like you.* It was a wonderful card and the first time I'd ever seen a kid write in italics. He was that good. Another card, made at school and given to me on Valentine's Day: "*Dear Dad, No matter what happens, when I'm in collige you'll always be my dad.*"

In spite of his past, he was kind to me and a thoughtful and helpful big brother. He did not let Craig out of his sight EVER and often helped get Adriana and Craig ready for a road trip. He was indeed bright, earning A's and stars and winning Student of the Month before other children in his class.

Before the parenting right-of-passage called the Parent-Teacher conference—the first time a stranger analyzed how a child fits into society, or not—I huddled with the Advisory Board. Do I bring anything? Do I take notes? What will happen?

"Your teacher will either say your kid is great, or a creep."

Javier's teacher was disappointed I didn't bring him and said I should have. I felt bad but I didn't know.

"Javier has been a good student, loves to spell, and is a talented little writer," she said. She took me to the new gymnasium/cafeteria and showed me the poems of five student winners selected from 900 entries in a contest inspired by the Peace Project. Javier's winning poem was brief: "No guns, no violence. Peace and quiet is good."

Back in the classroom, I said, "I am worried because Javier never gets mad. I wonder if he represses his feelings."

"Look at his life," his teacher said. "What does he have to be mad about compared to what it used to be? Let it go." A few weeks later a letter from the school district asked my permission for Javier to be tested for the Gifted and Talented Education Program. I'm guessing it was based on the safety tips he wrote for an assignment. 1) Do not walk with strangers, and 2) Do not stand near a panther.

As a reader might gather, there were a lot of things I didn't know when I adopted my children. I had no medicine or toys and I washed them like a set of frying pans. But the biggest surprise of all was my ignorance about the public school system. I had no idea how infrequently schools were in session and for not that many hours a day, or that they needed graham crackers and paper because they were out of money.

In an amazing coincidence, just weeks after the kids came into my home, I learned from Javier that the annual school fund-raiser was at hand. Javier needed to go door-to-door selling coupon books and won't we help, the flyer said, because the schools have run out of money. If he sold ten and gave his teacher the money he'd win miniature versions of the prizes in the brochure. This was a good time for Javier to learn a lesson. And I was less likely to end up in the ER, like on Huck Finn Day.

I, a trained businessman, demonstrated to Javier how to say hello, show, and tell. We practiced three times. He accepted my instruction with enthusiasm. Adriana and Craig joined us in baseball caps and sandals for our sales trip around the neighborhood. I was apprehensive because a few days earlier, as I got the mail, a lady walking across the street yelled, "Hey, you're the guy with the kids!" and I wondered if everyone knew I was the guy with the kids, and if they'd come at us. Regrettably, we soon learned that all of the houses had coupon books; some had a lot. No one wanted one of our coupon books except for the nice lady next door—she bought one. Then I bought four. Five to go.

I needed a place where it was unlikely kids had been selling coupon books. I'd never met them before, but you had to love the guys at the Harley Davidson dealership. In ten minutes, Javier sold them all. Rick, with a beard to his chest and tattooed arms, invited the trembling Javier and his siblings into the back shop where the guys bought all of his coupon books. Rick thought the kids were sweet so he gave each a dollar.

A few weeks later Javier was back with another school project and won't we help because the schools had run out of money. This time he was supposed to sell seeds and win more miniature prizes, but I could not imagine Rick needing legitimate seeds so we opted out. We were not going to sell seeds or vegetables and we weren't going to mow lawns or paint cars. What the hell happened to the nine percent California state income tax I paid?

On a cold, dreary day, I told Javier to get his jacket, but no, he'd lost it. In nine weeks of school, he'd "lost" five jackets, all brought home in garbage bags from Mimosa's foster home. How was that possible? The Lost and Found had nothing, he said. I wondered if he was giving them away to poorer kids, or if someone stole his coats, or if he was ashamed to wear coats with the name of another kid written inside. Whatever the case, five was all he had, so I left him at school in 55 degree weather wearing a short sleeve shirt. I often didn't have a coat when I was young and as I watched him walk away I thought he'd just have to learn a lesson.

It was only October, a long winter awaited him. How many more coats could I buy? Three. It rained all day and at 3 p.m. I stopped at Kmart. At home, I wrote Javier's name inside his coat so when the next kid got it he'd know who had it before.

Javier asked for nothing and was surprised when he got something. At Target, when I replaced the kids' mangled shoes, Javier picked a Spiderman pair, put them in the cart, and said, "I'll never wear them."

"Why not?"

"I want to keep them new. I've never had a pair of new shoes before."

"If they get dirty, we'll wash them. If they get old, we'll buy new ones."

Javier said, "Okay." He was impressed with upper management. Me? Not so much.

I made a mistake with Javier. Instead of seeing him as a wounded little boy, I treated him as the big brother, the leader and trailblazer, when he was more comfortable last in line. He was not the leader, I was, but I couldn't see that then. A few weeks after I got Javier I called my sister Diana and complained that while I wanted to play catch with the football, Javier just wanted to watch cartoons.

"Well," she said softly, "he's just a little boy."

I saw me in Javier and I didn't like it. I had rebelled against my early life by causing trouble and making mistakes. I didn't want Javier on that path so I held him to high standards, higher than he could achieve. Worse, not satisfied with him being better than me, I felt compelled to do what other parents did—make him stronger, smarter, and faster than the other kids—let's go kickboxing! I knew it was wrong but it was hard to resist. The lure of creating the perfect son was too strong. And no one was less qualified to do it than me.

I had to remind myself that he was just seven years old. I was living the death of my father through him, but I was not a father lost, I was a father gained, the opposite. When Javier started to excel on his skateboard and read chapter books I realized that the secret to his success was not for him to be like me but for him to be the opposite of me. It didn't take me a few sentences to figure that out, it took years. Looking back, he taught me more than I taught him.

Javier is more relaxed now and so am I. He is a thoughtful, growing boy still leery of attention, even if it's good, but he doesn't stand at the back of the line anymore. He's a star student, he goes to student dances with his friends, he's a loved and loving son, and he's an impressive athlete. Every so often, he wonders if we can take his mother some food.

# 11. Free Shrimp

We recovered from the Easter egg hunt ready to explore coastal California. Worried something might go wrong on our first trip, I picked the local Air Museum. I'd always loved planes and enjoyed the Salinas Air Show when I lived in Monterey. I had jumped out of planes twice, and I'd rented a few planes and pilots. I knew how to taxi, take off and fly, but not how to land. I packed the diaper bag with extra clothes for Craig, sun block, water, bananas, and snacks in case we got hungry during the six-mile trip. The night before, afraid the children might run away, I told my sister Joy on the phone that I'd seen parents with child leashes.

"I'm thinking about a triple bungee cord arrangement."

"That's the dumbest idea I've ever heard. If you're serious you're an idiot. They aren't pets."

The museum was built for the movie Rocketeers and then moved to the Santa Maria Airport grounds. A colored sign said Bigelow Aeronautical Corp. on the high wall. Two of the four walls were thick, heavy, wooden, sliding doors for planes. The ceiling was wood beamed and rounded, like an igloo. There were a lot of cars, meaning I'd made an excellent selection. We did not want to go to unpopular places. I parked and we practiced unloading procedures. I walked around the car opening three doors. Adriana and Javier got out and stood next to the car because of the parking lot. I untied Craig from his car seat and we held hands. Everything was perfect so far.

The entryway had a giant green World War II artillery shell. I didn't know if I had to pay, so we stood in the doorway and waited. A man wearing a suit and a woman in a long dress walked past us. We followed them and I immediately issued orders: don't touch anything, don't break anything, don't run off, and don't yell. The kids wondered why we were there.

On the right was a man wearing jeans and a plaid shirt. He stared, but said nothing. On the left were hats, shirts and model airplanes and a lot of glass cases and I thought of a new rule: Don't touch the glass. And don't steal anything, another rule and a good one. I wondered if other parents had six rules. We still held hands, but that didn't work in the narrow confines so I turned Javier loose to walk ahead. An old wooden plane had big open wheels. More little planes hung from the beams and there were photos of planes and pilots. I saw more people dressed well and I realized I'd been mistaken about Santa Maria. They had a certain style. I saw tables covered with white cloths and wine glasses on the tables and chairs going all the way out the heavy wooden door into the taxiway.

There weren't too many Mexican kids there, three actually, and people stared. I was busy watching all three and that's a lot. I didn't have the time or inclination to explain to everyone how we came to be. We weren't going to hide. Though it was tempting.

We strolled past an old plane, a flight suit, and a bowl of fresh, free shrimp. Then, on the tarmac in the sunshine, I spotted musicians setting up. A jazz show! On our first trip the kids were going to learn about planes, bombs, history, hangars, six rules, class, heavy rolling doors, free shrimp, and jazz. The downside was that no one had said hello. We floated through the room like ghosts. We were just an arm's length away from folks, but they were indifferent. We went out the door past the bomb and held hands across the parking lot. As we pulled away, a limousine arrived. Inside were a bride and groom. We'd crashed our first wedding.

Back at work, my new company just finished its best revenue month ever. We achieved our annual goal, $1 million more than the prior year, on May 15. My department won a corporate contest earning me a $500 award. I asked my boss to give it to two people who were instrumental in the project. She said no, take the money. I bought bikes for Javier and me.

Shrek got a bike seat that cost more than my bike. He ate cookies back there during rides. At least he said he was eating cookies.

Life was good. Walks on the Santa Maria levee, shopping at JCPenney, or going out for pie, everything we did made me proud. On weekends we made scrapbooks, one and then two and three. My life was so far from what it used to be. I learned how to be a parent and got better. Instead of acting like an executive, telling them what to do if they had a challenge at school or with another child, I learned how to say, "How did that make you feel?" That opened the door to a place they'd never been. For me, too.

We were turning into a butterfly, but we did not live in a cocoon. After days leaving voicemails, I found Melinda and asked her what happened with the severance hearing.

"I had to postpone it. I was supposed to notify the parents before the hearing, not after. Plus, the notice must be at least six weeks ahead of the hearing."

"I'm pretty sure that's how it works."

"I learned the name of another possible father, so I have to notify him, too."

"How did you learn his name?"

"It was in the file."

"This is important. People in my position want the process to move along."

"I'll make a note. I'll make a note for the file that says you would like this to proceed faster. I'm trying for July 1 now. I think I can do it."

"Thank you."

"The other thing I have to do is notify the mother by letter. I don't know where she is. Someone told me she moved to a new town in Mexico and someone else told me she's on her way back to Santa Maria."

"If you can't find her, why don't you just publish a legal notice like you're doing for the others?"

"I guess."

"It would be easier if the mother bothered to contact you."

"That's true."

"Part of the reason the mother doesn't have the kids anymore is because she drifts away."

"Whether I find her or not, it won't affect the July 1 date."

"So what do you know about her returning to Santa Maria?"

"Someone told me she might be coming back."

"Should I worry? Does she know where Javier goes to school?"

"I don't know. Let me look through the file and see." She looked. "I can't tell if the mother knows the name of the school. I'll find out and let you know."

I expected she wouldn't call and she didn't. Six weeks later I called Melinda for an update.

"Everything is on schedule for July 1," she said.

"Good work."

"I spoke with the mom."

"Where is she?"

"She's still in Mexico. She wants to talk with the kids. I think that's a bad idea."

"Scott said that if this came up, he would recommend that the mother write a letter to the kids. Less drama. They've never asked for her."

"I'll talk with my boss."

"Please just make sure I know what's happening in advance."

"I will."

A few days later, Melinda called my cell phone and left a message. "The mother wants to talk to the kids. I'll just go get them."

I called Melinda, who had never answered her phone in her career, and left a message.

"Hi, Melinda. I got your voicemail and I'm confused. I thought the plan was for Mom to write a letter to the kids. In any case, my kids aren't together except from 6:30 p.m. to 7:30 a.m. Also, why does the mother want to talk with the kids now? We're going on six months since they've spoken. If the call takes place I want to know when, rather than you 'just getting my kids,' so I can help them understand what it means."

The next day I called Melinda's voicemail to remind her I called the day before. I worried about her getting my kids. That sounded like robber talk to me. I called Melinda's boss, Jessica, and left a message. The next day I called Jessica to remind her I called the day before. I checked with the kids and nobody got them. The next day I called Social Services and asked to speak with Melinda, or Jessica.

"Hi, Jessica. This is David Marin. Do you know me?"

"I've heard of you."

"I'm adopting three little kids. I'm trying to find Melinda."

"Actually, I'm sitting here with Melinda. We're trying to figure out what to tell you. We have a judicial order that says we have to allow the mother to maintain contact with the kids. On the other hand, we know the kids are happy now. I don't want to upset the judge, although she just denied contact in a case similar to yours—the parent had ignored the child for quite some time. I was really surprised the judge ruled that way."

"Why don't you just make the same argument here?"

"I cannot imagine the judge doing it again."

"Well, try it. If the call with the mother occurs, can I listen in?"

"Sure."

"I'm not opposed to the call. I'm opposed to the kids being confused and I'm opposed to them having nightmares. And I'm opposed to Melinda getting my kids. Is the severance of parental rights hearing on schedule?"

"Yes, it is."

"Are you going?"

"No."

"Is anyone that knows me going?"

"No."

"Do you think I should go?"

"No. It won't make any difference."

I decided to go. No one would recognize me. Plus, the couple who took Jeremiah and his sister Flora from Mimosa's foster home told me they attended every proceeding, invited by the county, or not. We hung up with me not knowing the plan: Ask the judge to skip the phone call, or go ahead with me listening. The phone call with the mother never took place, as far as I knew. And what if their mother did show up? I decided to rely on Social Services. Instead, Scott will suggest I meet her, saying, "Hey, you never know…"

A few days later my attorney called to tell me that the company I sued wanted my old Alameda County adoption training records. Clearly, if I was lying about the classes, the first aid training, the fingerprinting, etc., they'd want to know that and win the lawsuit. But their maneuver made me wonder how far they would go. What if they tried to get the kids' records, or interfere with the adoption? Would they go that low?

Why, yes, they would.

Hunched in the shadows was the return of a woman who made our children beg for quarters; a Social Services department tip toeing through land mines they laid themselves; a faceless social worker, or workers, opposed to me adopting my children; and an Oakland Tribune defense attorney who'd ask me after learning in a deposition that I had children if they'd ever been injured in my home.

# 12. Walnut

Scott warned me for months, "There are people in Social Services opposed to you adopting the kids. I'm sticking my neck out for you."

Four months after the children joined me, a woman called to say she was replacing Melinda on Social Services' visit this month.

"It's just a coincidence," she said.

Really? What did her coming to our home coincide with? I imagined her working behind the scenes, trying to get to us. I don't know why and didn't ask, but my mama bear instinct linked her to Scott's warning.

At 7 p.m. sharp she knocked on the door. Her name was Sandy. She was about 50 years old. She tried to shake hands with the kids; they high-fived her. Handshake fail.

"And who are you?" she said to Javier.

"Javier."

"And you?"

"Adriana."

"Kids, let's gather around and have a little talk," she said, turning my living room into a scout camp.

Adriana looked at me. Javier squirmed. They'd been through this before. This wasn't their first "little talk." Their antennae detected a robber. I had removed people like Sandy from their lives. They looked at me like I was disappointing them. The sooner she left, the better. But the regulations required me to be nice.

"My sisters came to Santa Maria after the kids moved in," I said. "We took them to Disneyland."

"That's nice," she said.

"Adriana," I said. "Why don't you show Sandy the scrapbook Aunt Diner made for us?"

"Okay. Aunt Diner made us this scrapbook from Disneyland," Adriana said, sitting next to Sandy on the couch. Each time I appeared in a photo Adriana said, "That's my Daddy," and Sandy sank further into the cushions. I didn't want her to get comfy so I remained standing. After the Disneyland presentation, Sandy asked Adriana if she liked living in, "this house." Adriana crawled up the back of the couch like she'd spotted a water moccasin.

"Yeth."

"Is there anything I can do to make it better?" Adriana, all of five years old, saw this as a trick question. She looked at me and twisted. "No."

Sandy asked Javier the same question.

"I love this house."

Anything she could do? "No." He faded away, joining Adriana in her room.

The little talk ended with Javier and Adriana saying an average of three words each.

"Is there another one?"

"You mean my son, Craig?"

"Where is he?"

"He's taking a nap."

"I need to see him."

We walked to my bedroom door. A queen-size bed, leather topped library table, and wing chair were on the right. A cherry wood dresser was behind the door. The wall displayed my collection of three hole-in-one golf balls, a piece of Mike Smith art depicting the oceanside farm where I dreamed of living, my law degree, and my grandfather's 1933 Dental College degree. The master bath was in front of her.

"Is this his room?" she said.

"No."

She leaned in close to Craig, barely able to detect his little form tucked in the flannel sheets. She twisted her head and stared. She asked nothing about him. She couldn't make it better. I decided to give her a tour of the house, ending at the front door. She liked Adriana's furniture.

"I've always wanted a set like this."

"That's nice."

Adriana and Javier were watching us.

"I'd like to buy it."

"It's not for sale. Adriana likes it. She's never had her own room before."

"This is what I want. Does it have another single bed?"

"In the guest house."

"It's walnut, right?"

"Yes."

"I've been looking for a set like this for a long time."

"Sorry."

"If you change your mind, let me know."

In the boy's room I showed her Javier's race car bed and told her that I'd buy them bunk beds someday. We stopped in the dining room and I showed her the chart I used to measure the kids growth. After six months, each child was nearly two inches taller.

"Have the kids had their check-ups?"

"All three."

"And you? Taking these kids?"

Oh say can you see... Why would someone want them—Javier, Adriana and another one? She didn't oppose me, she opposed them, the kids no one wanted, the kids they had trouble finding homes for. They were just miniature field workers, the lowest common denominator. Subterranean.

She wasn't alone, I learned later. Some social workers opposed mixing races to preserve the identity of the children. The first multi-racial adoption of a minority by white parents was in Minnesota in 1948. As late as 1972, the National Association of Black Social Workers objected to blacks in white homes. The controversy ended in 1996, not counting Sandy Van Winkle, when a revision to the Multi-ethnic Placement Act prohibited agencies wanting federal funds from considering race.[19]

I didn't appreciate her intimating that my children were scrap metal, but my priority was to assist Sandy out the door, so I elected not to engage in conversation about the state of my mental health taking "these" children, my fountain of youth. Plus, I didn't know her status. Was she a nosy interloper or a high-level Social Services person? How much trouble could she cause? The night before Sandy landed on us, I talked with the woman who took Jeremiah and Flora out of Mimosa's foster home to live with her and her husband. She told me about the painful delays caused by Social Services. After my experience with Melinda, I was curious if Sandy had another perspective.

"How long do adoptions take?"

She turned at me with ears like a cropped Doberman. This was more than she hoped for! She came looking for news and what bigger news than, "He's taking the kids away! We have to stop him and thank God I was there!"

Breathless, she asked, "Are you leaving town?"

"People like me are curious about how long things take."

"The reason things are taking a long time lately," she explained as she glanced around the room, disappointed, talking to the walls, "is because there were new attorneys assigned to the parents and the files weren't transferred when the attorneys changed. These things take a long time, usually a year or more, because of the trials."

In the two years, two counties, ten classes, and countless conversations

19   for a really neat website, go to the University of Oregon Adoption History Project: http://pages.uoregon.edu/adoption/index.html.

since I began my adventure no one ever mentioned trials.

"I think my case will go smoothly."

"All cases end in trials."

"It took over two months for me to meet my kids," I said, thinking the miscue was something she could understand.

"Why did you wait so long? Why didn't you want to see the kids?" She sat down.

"The withdrawal of services hearing took forever and Scott told me to wait. One time it was cancelled because an attorney for the county had a cold. Maybe you know her. I basically met the kids by mistake. Then, after the hearing, in late January, I began seeing them again."

"I don't know why you would wait so long; we have a hard time placing kids like those."

O…kay. Let's change the subject. "I've been getting the information from the county." The county mailed a newsletter every month. I never read it; it was for people considering adoption. I didn't tell her I read it; I told her I got it. I wanted her to know I had it so she'd think I gave a shit about what her department thought about things.

"What are you talking about? Do you work for the county?"

She knew nothing about me, either. I was a single guy she knew nothing about adopting kids she didn't know.

"No, I don't work for the county."

She rose from the couch and took two steps towards me.

"How are you obtaining county information?"

"Social Services sends out newsletters to adopting parents."

"Oh." She stopped and stood, looking around.

"So, what do you do, anyway?"

"I'm an attorney by training and a vice-president of the company that owns the Santa Maria Times."

Bullseye.

"Well. It's time for me to go." She gave me her card.
"Call if you need anything."
*I will!*
"She's gone," I yelled to the kids.
I never saw her again. But she wasn't finished.

My admiration for Scott grew that day. I imagined him laboring in a cubicle alongside Sandy and others questioning his decision, defending me in meetings, pulling away from the pack.

## 13. Wishing Is What I Used To Do

Having exhausted Santa Maria's cultural activities, it was time to hit the road. I loved accelerating on a freeway entrance ramp, leaving troubles behind. I explored the West on a motorcycle when I was 18 and I wanted my children to know the joys of road trips. From Santa Maria, we could go west to the Guadalupe dunes; north to San Luis Obispo, Highway 1 and Big Sur; or south to Santa Ynez and Santa Barbara. There was nothing east except dirt. We went south first, to the green valleys of Santa Ynez still wet from the spring rain.

I packed enough supplies to feed a tanker crew. Our first stop was Flag Is Up Farms on the two-lane road to Solvang. A co-worker said if you pushed the button at the gate like you lived there the gate opened and you could go in. Owned and operated by Monty Roberts of Horse Whisperer fame, the farm had one hundred acres of deep grass watered by 50-foot long sprinklers like long leg spiders on wheels. Fences and trees separated the colts, stallions, and mares. Through the gate safely, we drove a paved lane lined with red roses blooming under an arched canopy of boughs and branches. One lane went in, another out, with yellow roses in between. We saw Quarter Horses and Thoroughbreds, Pintos and Appaloosas. Two draft horses the size of Caterpillar tractors stood near the fence line. A young, powerfully shouldered Clydesdale with marble columned hindquarters fed near a trough, eating yellow hay culled from the open field.

We drove alone down the lane and parked next to a building with a big barn near it. The lot was empty. There were no people. We may have trespassed, but we trespassed as a family. We held hands in the parking lot. A sign said, "Visitor Information." Under it was a life size poster of Monty Roberts in front of a brown horse with a white nose. I signed honor-system liability release forms I found on a table and put them in the envelope. We walked towards the 60-stall barn and watched a lady lead a horse. A worker from a nation north of Guatemala and south of the United States rode a brown Quarter-horse. We found a handsome three-year old Thoroughbred in a round pen. He was wingtip black with hind legs like a grasshopper. He trotted to us with his head high. His mane hung like a web in the wind. We petted his nose. He liked us.

"Daddy," Adriana said. "Can we take him home with us?"

"He won't fit in the car."

We walked to the end of the dirt path and saw half a dozen colts lounging in the tall grass next to deer, under the branches of the lone tree in the middle of the field. They stayed away from the edge where bushes and trees hid mountain lions. Two colts, more like jumping beans than horses, stood, ran, and played with each other. My mother bought me a pony when we moved to Missouri after my father died. I was eight. I named him Shadow. He was a Shetland pony, black and chubby. He loved to escape the fence and run across town to stand next to the real horses at the farm with the white house and the fence around it. Soon we moved and left Shadow behind. We returned for a visit a year later and Shadow had a big, big belly. Shadow was a girl.

The kids and I climbed the stairs of a giant round structure with a 20 foot radius and walls 10 feet high. We looked down and saw a young horse looking at us from the Horse Whisperer's studio. Students and spectators stood around the raised perimeter and watched him train horses famously without hurting them or breaking them. His secret was letting the horse come to you. If you then turned and walked without fear, you were the leader.

We saw young penned cattle near the road to the main house. We fed them spilled hay. They liked us, too. Adriana wanted to take one home but we couldn't because of the lease. It didn't say no cattle specifically, but she'd never know because she was just learning the alphabet. It went like this, by the way, to her: ABCDEFG, HIJK, I'm a little P, QRS, TUV, WXY and Z. I knew it wasn't right because of the casing, but I couldn't find it in my heart to tell her because I loved hearing her saying it. I wish she still said it that way, but a lady at preschool changed it. We left the farm, but often returned to show family or friends that if you pressed the button on the black gate like you lived there, you could drive down the lane with red and yellow roses and see grasshopper horses.

Across the highway and east was Ostrich Land, with emus in a separate pen near the road. The kids wanted to play with the ostriches but you couldn't go in the field because of the kicking. You could feed them though, for $5. In the store with ostrich feathers, steaks, and eggs, we watched a real cowboy buy a belt buckle. I gave the man $15. He gave us three scoopers. We walked outside and turned left, dragged the scoopers through a bin of grains and corn and we walked to the feeding area, a deck mounted three feet above the dirt pasture. Craig spilled his scooper and cried. I went back for more feed, wondering whether each scoop was $5 or if I'd rented the scooper for $5, entitling me to unlimited scoops.

We leaned over the deck rail, three feet high and six feet off the ground, and looked into the eyes of the ugliest, dumbest animals on earth, with brains the size of peach pits. A fist-sized head topped a neck longer than my arm attached to a body of feather covered racing wheels. Ostriches did not survive 15 million years on smarts. They survived on speed. Natural selection couldn't catch them.

I was a runner. I left home at sixteen for an East coast private school and I've been going ever since. Until now, when I have to stay grounded, because when you have kids you can't keep running. I knew my days of leaving without notice were over. I had responsibilities now and they made me happy.

The next week a golfing friend called. He was perplexed at my new tax status, but had an idea. He had just hired a woman who recently moved to Santa Maria with her 15-year-old daughter. If the daughter baby sat we could play golf. He told the mother I'd call, and I did. After I said I adopted three kids, and she said you and your wife have done a great thing, I said what wife? She wanted to meet the kids before her daughter did. That evening she knocked on the door. I opened it and saw white leather shoes with smooth pointed toes. Her ankles were like the narrow stems of champagne glasses and then I saw brown legs rising. I tried to speak. The brown legs rising ended at a black skirt and my ears were warm and I stood there, stuck like an Easter Island slab.

She had soft brown hands with opal colored nails. I was a peacock in the hills and my tail was spreading wider in green, purple, and blue. I circled around her making noises. Her shoulders were slender and her neck was made of Ghirardelli chocolate. We'd live in the jungle near the river and when it rained I'd hold palm fronds over her, letting a few drops seep through. Afterwards, we'd go out for some Canadian food. Her hair was an ink black waterfall. I rode over the side and paddled to the edge. I lifted myself from the water and stared into her brown eyes. I am the dreamer.

Her lips said enter here.

"Oh," I said.

"Hi. My name is Carmen."

Stepping on my tongue, she carried three little ice cream sundaes in to the living room. The children surrounded her in nanoseconds, watching and wondering. I was glad I'd kept my tie on. I can't remember anything that happened after that except we ended up in the guest house, all five of us, the kids climbing up my legs and stomach as I flipped them over like we were a circus act. She sat, watched, smiled, and ordered popcorn.

"We're going out to get some food," I said. "Will you go with us?"

She said no because she had to pick up her daughter at a friend's house. I told the kids to say good-bye but they just stared, mesmerized. Not one said a word. I was embarrassed and mortified and when I went to bed that night I realized that if the kids treated women like that I'd always be alone. That night was the low point of my parenthood. I lay in bed thinking this was the sacrifice I'd made. It wasn't playing golf seven times a year instead of seven times a month. It wasn't driving by a marina and watching sailors prep for a day sail. It wasn't taking the kids to see the Princess Bride movie, although that was close. It was being alone, crushed and graded like cheap gravel.

I called my sisters. They told me to quit complaining because kids acted like that all the time. Get over it, they said. I called Carmen, asked her to lunch on my birthday. I apologized to her and she said kids act like that all the time. Get over it. As the days passed, Carmen was on my mind. I wanted to see her but I had three children the law compelled me to watch. I called Scott.

"I want to find a babysitter so I can do other things."

"Doing other things is good."

"Some people at work have volunteered a son or daughter to baby sit."

"No problem. Just send me their names and the names of their parents."

"Why?"

"I'll need to do an FBI background check."

"An FBI background check?"

"Right. That's how we have to do it."

"Do you get a lot of requests from people like me to do FBI background checks on their friends?"

"Not really."

A few weeks later after talks and lunches, we picked up Carmen and went to the Mission near Lompoc. If Santa Maria was a sleeping pill, Lompoc was a keg of intravenous sedative. Being with Carmen was so exciting I drove through the Ranger Gate at the Mission without noticing the Ranger. She caught me in the parking lot and told me that since I ignored her, I should put the $5 fee in the book shop jar where people paid who didn't stop at the gate because they were too excited about Carmen. I couldn't find the jar so I left $5 on a bench.

The mission sat in the low hills east of Vandenberg Air Force Base. The hills were rain green and the grass was tall. A sign warned of mountain lions. The kids went potty and then we walked to a little wooden bridge in the trees. It spanned a creek with water in it. Next to the bridge a lady dressed to period sat knitting a doll. The kids thought she was real and she was. We crossed the bridge and walked into an open pasture. On the right was a fence made of six-foot tall sticks nailed to straight branches as the crossers. Inside, sheep grazed on the wet grass, pulling the roots for the water.

I held Carmen's hand.

Chicken hawks pecked at the ground and old plow horses fed in the field. An old lady wearing rags ran by and told us to be at the bell tower at noon, "The pirates are coming." We walked past the garden with corn and lettuce in rows. At the end was a pigsty with two huts, mud, and pigs in it. Circling back to the 70-yard long mission, we climbed the foot tall adobe step and entered the blacksmith's room. He was pounding. Back out the door I saw a uniformed ship captain standing alone near a table in the field. He was old, broken and tired and could barely lift his head for the picture I took. If my math was right, he'd been there for 175 years. A different lady told us to be at the bell tower at noon. "The pirates are coming."

We went through the mission into the back courtyard. Some ladies made soap and others made fresh tortillas. There was a priest. He didn't do anything. We each got a tortilla and then another and the kids went to the chicken coop and gave parts of their tortillas to the chickens when the ladies weren't looking. It was nearly noon. A crowd gathered at the bell tower.

The guards had muskets, goofy fur hats and old leather boots. The pirates were coming, and it was the guards' job not to capture the pirate but to shoot him. The bell rang twelve times. The guards were scurrying now; three fanned out and faced the pasture. In the tall golden grains, crawling to sneak up on us, but wearing a bright red bandana, was the dumbest pirate I'd ever seen and I'd seen plenty of pirates, trust me. His bandana gave him away. He was surrounded.

Adriana began to cry. "Are they going to kill him?" she yelled.

Shots rang out, but just to frighten the pirate, who stood up. The guards captured him without incident, brought him to the stockade, and placed his legs in irons and his hands through two holes cut in a large piece of long wood. The pirate asked to make a call but it wouldn't happen because of poor reception in the hills. On our way out, I slowed at the Ranger station and told the Ranger I left $5 on a bench. She said you were supposed to put it in the jar and I said, "What jar?"

Soon it was Father's Day. We went to Pismo Beach to meet Carmen and her two daughters—the sitter and her older sister, on summer break from Bryn Mawr College. I took the kids early to feel my first Father's Day sooner. It was amazing. I wished my brothers were there, too, or my father, and my mother and sisters, but wishing was what I used to do and now my life was real and I shouldn't complain when we're parking near sand so we can walk on it.

Adriana wore a fluffy pink birthday dress my boss gave her. Her hair was in pigtails I tied up after Brittany showed me how. Her little brown feet were in little white socks and she had shiny white shoes bought special. Craig wore a sweatshirt and khakis and Javier shorts and a t-shirt. I didn't tell my kids what to wear. They'd wear what they wanted. It was windy and they found swings. Javier could fly on his own so I pushed Craig and Adriana, who were just learning. The sand was warm but the wind blew our finely combed hair into messes. Javier looked like one of the Beatles, circa 1968, and Craig looked like a black mink had nested on his head. I hadn't brought a comb.

We met Carmen and her daughters for brunch. The waitress told us that she'd spent all day serving food to families pretending they were happy and that she enjoyed seeing a family that really was happy. After brunch we walked to the car show at Pismo Beach. I gave Carmen's youngest daughter $20 when no one was looking for her to buy something at the booths selling jewelry and trinkets. After our walk we had ice cream. It was a wonderful day, but all was not well. Adriana was sad. Several times, Carmen and I caught her staring and wondering at Carmen's daughters. We knew she was thinking about her two older sisters. She needed to know her sisters were safe and so did I.

I had their phone numbers and the names of their fathers. Ten-year-old Emine lived with her father in Nevada, according to the file. Eight-year-old Maribel lived with her dad in Santa Barbara, 70 miles away. Scott told me not to contact anyone from the old regime until Social Services severed the rights of the parents. I waited while Adriana wondered.

## 14. Waves From Japan

"I'm going to the severance of parental rights hearing next week," I told Scott.

"I don't think they'll let you in."

"After it's done, I'm going to call the kids' older sisters. Do you know how they're doing?"

"Well, we'd know about Maribel since she's still in Santa Barbara County. I haven't heard anything bad. We'd have no way of knowing about Emine in Nevada."

"Can you call Social Services there and ask them to call you if there's a problem?"

"Sure. Why do you want to know all of this?"

"I'd hate for them to be sent to foster care when their siblings are in a home with more room."

If I moved, I'd have more room.

"Okay. But if that's what you have in mind, the better way to accomplish it is for you to make contact, see how things are, and if it turns out you want the girls then negotiate that on your own. I'll follow up with the legalities."

Negotiate? I wondered how much they'd cost.

I called Melinda.

"Is the severance hearing on schedule?"

"Yes."

"I'm planning on going."

"The courtroom is tiny. Everyone will know you're there."

I worried. If just one of the alleged parents resisted I'd be in for a long haul. Worse, if they fought well and prevailed in the hearing, I'd lose my children that day. I went to bed curious about whether I'd soon have three kids, or none. I could be living in a giant house or a studio, and driving a van or a motorcycle. I could be blessed with a brood or mortally wounded, bleeding alone. I placed 100% of my future in the hands of Santa Barbara County attorneys I didn't know.

A few days before the Thursday severance hearing, Melinda called.

"Are you going?" she asked.

"Yes."

"I did everything right."

"Everyone was notified on time?"

"I'm sure of it. Everything should go smoothly."

"I'm sure everything will be fine." Was it possible she'd botched it again?

Carmen and I went to court at 1 p.m. If Melinda was right, the parents and the candidates were invited to attend. Had they come to Santa Maria? Would they arrive with mud on their boots? What if I liked them? Without planning, Carmen and I scanned the faces of everyone there. We looked for Craig, Javier, or Adriana in the drawn and haggard wear of the years and the lines and the mouth and the way it moved. Most of the people in the little waiting room were Hispanic, but we saw no matches. There was a couple with a lawyer, but after eavesdropping on their Spanish conversation, Carmen told me not to worry.

A case was called and then another and I wondered if I had the right day and place. Carmen noticed a sheet on the wall listing the cases that day. Three of the kids on the list were mine. I went out for a breath. When I returned I asked the guard if there was a place to get water. He pointed to a vending machine behind me. I read the case roster again. We were near the beginning of the list. The first cases dragged on for 90 minutes. I worried. I started to think something was wrong. There was no one left but us, sitting alone, holding hands. I looked out the front door and saw Melinda running towards the building, carrying a bundle of papers.

"Has your case been called yet?" She was out of breath.

"No."

"They can't do it without these papers. I think you're going to win."

"We'll see."

Finally, the last names of my children were called. We entered a small room, about 24 feet by 24 feet. Next to the right wall, the bailiff sat at her desk. The judge, a Caucasian woman about 50 years old, sat in the back behind a large brown counter. She looked serious. Five females sat in chairs backed against the left wall. The wall facing the judge had five chairs with five lawyers, I supposed.

Carmen guided me to sit two chairs from the door, leaving her the seat next to the door. The lawyers were to my immediate left. I looked at the women by the wall. They smiled at me. I had no idea who they were. The lawyer for the county passed out two sheets of paper to the other lawyers, the judge and me. One was Javier's report card. It had 40 categories. He received the highest possible score in all 40. He was never late and hadn't missed a day. I had received the report card in the mail 48 hours earlier. I didn't know how they got it. The other paper was a letter his teacher wrote me. How did they get that?

The letter read:

Dear David,

Javier is a remarkably capable student. I know he has found most of our work boring, and for this I apologize. He has nonetheless accepted my instruction with pleasant participation. You have a wonderful boy in Javier and his joy in having you as a father is happily apparent!

The best to you and your new family!

Sincerely,

Mrs. A

Thank you, Mrs. A.

The judge announced the case number. She asked the attorneys to introduce themselves. Four represented fathers. Craig's alleged father's lawyer was a beautiful blonde; she must have been from out of town. An attorney for the mother, who wasn't there, told the judge he was representing the real attorney for the mother, who wasn't there either. A county attorney I'd never met stood and said, "We have a guest. I'd like to introduce David Marin." How she knew me I didn't know, although in the tiny room, Melinda was right, it was me.

"Welcome," the judge said.

"Thank you."

The judge reviewed the paperwork. "All of the parties have been served. None of the parents have attempted to contact the children in six months."

The judge asked Craig's alleged father's attorney what she had to say on behalf of her client.

"I know the kids are being adopted. I am thrilled they will be together. We submit."

That meant she gave up without a fight. The women next to the wall smiled at me. The judge asked the attorney for the attorney for the mother his thoughts.

"I can see a good thing happening. We submit."

I was stunned. There was no confrontation. The wall women continued to smile. I looked at Carmen and smiled. The judge queried the other lawyers. All submitted. The judge, pleased that something decent was happening, talked slowly to dramatize her announcement.

"All rights are severed. It is remarkable the kids will get to stay together." She smiled at me.

This was the step, the severance of legal rights, that social workers strongly suggested occur before meeting kids you wanted to adopt. I was way past that. Bringing the children into my home had been a flat out risk. I knew it when I took it because I trusted Scott and I wanted my children the minute I met them. The severance hearing ended my risk, assuming everyone was notified. The ghost of running Melinda lingered. All of the attorneys congratulated me. I wanted to run out of the room before something bad happened. I'd entered the courtroom thinking about packing the kid's stuff into pillow cases in case I had to give them back.

"Can we go?" I asked the bailiff.

"Do you want to say anything?"

"No. Thank you." I blew it. One of my main rules was 'always be prepared for success' and here I was looking like a dope with nothing to say. I went to bed the night before wondering whether I'd soon have three kids or nothing but a ceramic bunny, a basket, and three cardboard boxes I called toys. I had a lot to say, like thank you for saving four lives, five with Carmen.

Carmen and I got up.

"So," the judge said. "What is a lawyer doing in the newspaper business?"

"Uh, I'm a vice-president."

"That's a good job," she said. Everyone in the courtroom nodded and mouthed, "That's a good job, that's a good job." I was half way out the door, looked back in and said to everyone, "We are happy. Thank you."

Carmen and I got in the car and drove around in shock. I called my mother and my sisters and they were happy. Carmen was driving to L.A. that night to see her sister, so I got the kids and we went for ice cream. They didn't know why. We'd had an adoction party in February and you can't have two if you have to explain to children that their Dad fibbed the first time. After ice cream we played at the park. We bought batteries for Javier's flashlight ring and following preschool directions on a note hung at eye-level, I bought cookies for the little kids' preschool Fourth of July party.

After the children went to sleep, I removed a page from a report I was not supposed to have. It had contact information for their older sisters, Emine, the oldest, in Nevada, and Maribel in Santa Barbara. I had Emine's father's name, phone, and address. A girl answered the phone.

"Hi, is this Emine?"

"Yes, it is."

"Hi, Emine. My name is David. How are you?"

"Good."

"Emine, I'm adopting your brothers and sister, Craig, Javier and Adriana. We live in Santa Maria."

"Who are you?"

"Well, I work at a newspaper. I met the kids last year and they've been in my house since February. Would you like us to send you pictures? Or a letter?"

"Yes. Can I talk to them?" She was soft spoken, kind.

"The kids are asleep now. Let me speak with your dad, we'll arrange for you to talk with them later."

"Okay. Thank you for calling me. I wondered where they were. I worry about them. I miss them."

"You're welcome. They are happy and healthy."

Emine was 11 years-old. The next time I'd hear her voice she'd be 16.

"Hello?" her father said.

"Hi. My name is David. How are you?"

"Fine."

"I'm adopting Emine's younger brothers and sister. I called to say hello and see if we can get the kids talking again."

"Have you adopted them?"

"Well. That's the plan."

"But have you adopted them, has it gone through?"

*Warning. Warning.*

"We're making progress."

"Where do you work? What is your address?"

"I'm calling to see if we can set up a phone call."

"I don't know, I'll think about it."

"Okay. I have your address from the court papers. I told Emine we'd send photos and letters."

We sent her a package, using Scott's Social Services address as our return address (his idea), but we never heard from Emine. Soon, their phone was disconnected. I imagined that her father ended up in jail because that's a good reason people disappear and I was right.

After speaking with Emine, I called Maribel. I spoke Spanish badly to an adult woman, but managed to ask for Maribel.

"Hello?"

"Hi. Is this Maribel?"

"Yeth." Already sweet.

"Hi, Maribel. My name is David. Your little brothers and sister live with me in Santa Maria. I'm adopting them."

"Can I see them on Saturday?" I saw her through the phone, long black hair, puppy brown eyes.

"Yes, sweetie. Saturday would be great. But can you let me talk to an adult first? Do any adults there speak English?"

"My step-brother."

"Can I speak with him?"

"Yeth."

"Maribel. Your brothers and sister are fine. They miss you and will be very happy to see you. Let me talk to your step-brother, please. What's his name?"

"Miguel."

"Thank you, Maribel."

"What time Saturday?"

"I'll talk with Miguel and we'll figure it out, okay?"

"Okay."

Miguel was friendly. He asked no questions about me or the kids. He agreed to tell Maribel's Spanish speaking father, who was in the shower, that I'd call back in an hour to get permission to see Maribel Saturday. The joy I felt reuniting the children with their sister trumped my concern that I'd be revealed, or trapped. I called back in an hour and all was well. We arranged to meet at 9 a.m. Saturday morning at a McDonald's near their home. I told Miguel I'd call to confirm before we left. Then I'd tell the kids. I didn't want to re-break their hearts by telling them too soon. On Saturday morning I called Miguel and told him we were leaving in a few minutes for the 70-mile drive. He said he and his wife would bring Maribel to McDonald's.

My children were in the living room.

"We're going to the beach," I said.

"Which one?" Javier asked.

"In Santa Barbara. We're going to the beach in Santa Barbara with Maribel. We're going to see her today." Javier and Adriana stood stunned, mouths wide open.

"How do you know about Maribel!" Adriana asked.

"You tell me about her all the time."

"How did you know where she is?"

"Daddy knows everything."

"Does she know we're coming?"

"I spoke to her Thursday night. The first thing she said was, 'Can I see my brothers and sister on Saturday?'"

Adriana and Javier trampolined through the air in joy. It was the most brilliant thing I'd ever done. A perfect spiral. We drove through the hills north of Santa Barbara, past the grey donkey guarding llamas from mountain lions. We passed acres of wine vines leafed and green and tied to stakes. Near Goleta and the railway ties where the ocean first appeared on the right heading south, the hills were black and gray from another huge Santa Barbara fire. Freed from roots, dirt rolled down the hills to chain link fences installed to stop stones from hitting cars. The stones at the fence were burned. It was a moonscape. In the strip between the lanes wild yellow mustard bloomed bellybutton high.

Adriana said, "Smokey the Bear came to preschool. He got burned."

"What happened?" I asked.

"He climbed in a tree to get away from the fire. His feet and fur were burned."

"Is he better now?"

"Yeth."

We exited Highway 101. As we neared McDonald's I saw a man, a woman, and a little girl standing outside the front door.

"There she is!"

"Where?" Adriana and Javier said in unison.

"Right there, by the door."

"No, that's not her," Adriana said. Javier agreed.

We waited until the oncoming lane was clear to turn left and entered the parking lot. The couple and the girl were 20 feet away.

"Are you sure that's not her?" I asked.

"No, it's not her."

It had to be her. She waited with two adults. I waved to the man as we parked and he waved back.

Looking right through them, Adriana said, "Where is she?"

I was mighty confused. I got out of the car and said to the man, "Hi, Miguel. How are you?" He nodded his head and waved. I got the kids out of the car. We assembled and held hands.

"There she is!" I said, trying to be happy.

"That's not her," Adriana said.

Maribel watched, but said nothing. My expectation of a supernova reunion collapsed into a black hole. I'd made a big mistake. I should have let things be. We walked towards the three. There was no emotion, no reaction whatsoever from Maribel. She did not recognize her siblings, nor they her.

"Hi, Miguel," I said, walking ten, then five feet away. None of the children reacted. There was a nastiness to the world. There was a place where nothing made sense and there was no way out and we were in it. I shook Miguel's hand. The kids were now inches away from each other. Nothing.

"Kids, this is Maribel." Nothing.

"What are their names?" Maribel asked me.

"This is Craig, and Javier and Adriana."

Nothing. My kids stared at her. It'd only been eight months since the robbers took them away. Maybe she thought Craig was Chris.

"What are their birthdays?" Maribel asked me.

"Adriana's is March 18." I had to think to remember. "Craig's is in September. Javier's is in February."

"That's them." She reached into her little coat and removed three cards she made for the kids. She handed one to each.

"Are you Maribel?" Adriana asked.

"Yeth."

"Daddy, I want a cheesebooger," Craig said.

Adriana and Javier hugged Maribel. She took three one dollar bills from her pocket and gave one each to the kids. I realized as I stood there why the kids did not recognize each other. When I lost my father I froze my last memory of him forever and all time. He never changed his shirt, he never needed a shave, and he was still smiling. He remains unchanged today, fixed and formed like a suit of shining armor. I imagined the kids taking a last glimpse of each other as the robbers took them away and burning that memory into their minds like a cattle brand. A new shirt would throw them off. And now, bigger kids; and Adriana's hair cut short and Craig talking... It was the fog of war except for the killing.

I told Miguel we'd go to the beach and return in three hours. He was friendly and calm. His wife, Lupe, was quiet and curious about me.

"We've been calling the county," he said. "We tried to get your name and phone number to call you. They wouldn't give us any information."

"Well, now you have my name and number. Thanks for meeting us."

As we walked across the parking lot holding hands, Maribel pointed to her father and his wife arriving in an old car. They got out and we shook hands. She was suspicious, with eyes like a mine shaft. In Spanish, I asked her if she knew my kids. She nodded. Maribel's father was calm and looked me in the eye. He appeared about 50 years old, but was probably younger inside. Working in the fields added 10 years to a man. The support they gave Maribel impressed me. Four people to see her off illustrated a difference between our two cultures. The percentage of illegal immigrants living in two parent families was more than double the percentage of U.S. born households.[20] As Latinos become a larger part of the U.S. population, this characteristic will make American culture evolve for the better, with less emphasis on work and money and more on family, feelings and the things that make us human. I wished border wall advocates Lou Dobbs and Patrick Buchanan could see this. Clash of civilizations? Please. This was the brotherhood of man.

Maribel sat in the front seat. "The police were at my house yesterday."

"Why?"

"A man with a gun was looking for drugs. He said he'd kill us if we

20  Pew Research 2009 Portrait of Unauthorized Immigrants in the U.S.

didn't have any."

"So, how do you like school?"

"I like my school. I have a good teacher."

"Do you like living in Santa Barbara?"

"It's okay. Is Brianna in kindergarten?"

"She's in preschool," Javier answered.

"Who's Brianna?" I asked.

"Right behind you, my sister," Maribel answered.

"Adriana?" I said.

"Who's Adriana?"

"We call her Adriana."

"Oh," she said, staring out the window.

"Why do you call her Brianna?" I asked.

She paused. "I can't remember."

I had no idea what was happening. Were we going to the beach with a stranger? Adriana's birth certificate and hospital records read Adriana. Was this a Rain Man re-enactment? Did Brianna sound like Adriana, like Rain Man sounded like Raymond? Two years later the kids and I encountered a little girl at a mall. She saw Adriana and said, "Hi, Brianna."

"Maribel," said Javier. "Do you remember our old house?"

"Yes."

"We had a rabbit," Adriana said.

"The cat ate its head," Maribel said.

Bingo! She was one of them. My worries were over. As the day progressed, Maribel often referred to Adriana as Brianna. As we gently corrected her, she came around.

"Javier," Maribel said. "Do you like school?"

"I get A's and stars."

"Javier is very smart," I said. "Adriana, too. Adriana has a new bike."

"I have a new bike," Adriana said.

We drove to the beach and the kids talked and laughed and they knew it was true: they used to be in the same family and they used to hide together. I asked Maribel about her older sister, Emine. She said she spoke with her often and that she had a cold. She told me again that she liked Santa Barbara and school, but there was no kid left in her. She was a nine-year-old adult.

We parked in a 90-minute spot off State Street, put Craig in the stroller, and walked towards the water. We were hungry. I spotted Rusty's pizza shop fronting the beach, across the street from artists displaying paintings and crafts. Brianna, er, Adriana rode piggy-back on Maribel's back. Javier skipped beside us. Life was good. I found myself surprisingly at ease with four children, but I soon realized there was a part of me interviewing Maribel, watching her mannerisms and interactions with her siblings. I was assessing her to see if everything would be okay if she ever came to live with us.

The kids played video games while I ordered. Maribel put a $10 bill into a change machine. She divided 40 quarters amongst the kids. The weight in his pockets made Craig's pants slip below his hips like he was in the music business. As we ate, he began to cry. After a few guesses, he nodded his head when Maribel asked if his tummy hurt. Maribel stopped eating, left her food, and took him away to the sit down near the video games. When I got my kids, Javier and Adriana did the same thing. If Craig started to cry they took him out of my sight. It was a defense strategy that reminded me of biologist Konrad Lorenz's observation that if an injured goose drew attention, the others would kill it to keep predators from noticing the commotion. Lorenz compared people to geese. My geese, and Maribel, soon learned that Craig was safe. Not all adults were predators.

After lunch, we crossed State Street near the dolphin fountain. The sky was blue. We got the usual stares. A young lady in her 30's grabbed her man's arm, swung him around and pointed at us, as if to show him, "Look, look, that's what it looks like adopting kids!" She had a big smile. We got on the wood pier walkway and looked over the railing. On the sand, with the marina in the background, we saw small white crosses planted in long, straight rows. There were nearly 900, according to the sign, one for each dead American soldier in Iraq.

Some Santa Barbara homeless lived under the pier. They put jars or bowls on the sand, six feet below the elevated walkway. Next to the containers were signs that said "Make a Wish" and coins lying around the containers from people who could wish, but not aim. Like a long brown caterpillar with a white head, we walked to the end of the pier, past shops and bins of fish and a restaurant serving live crab and lobster pulled from tanks visible through the window.

After our stroll, we went to the beach and took off our shoes and played in the sand. Craig found a stick. Adriana chased seagulls in our path as we walked to the cold water's edge. A lifeguard stood at his mount watching a wet-suited teenager playing on the waves. People played volleyball. Maribel went in the water first, to the awe of her siblings who watched their big, brave sister. She went in to her shins. I rolled up the kids' pant legs. The water thrilled them. A large wave reached us. When it pulled back it left sparkling sand on the toes of the children next to me. It was time to go. Maribel went to the water, deeper where it was clear. Cupping her hands, she scooped clean salt water. She did this three times. She scooped the water and she brought it to us. She brought it to us, and, one by one, she got on her knees and washed the feet of her brothers and sister.

We stood and watched waves from Japan blend with sand. We inhaled the sweet salt and watched pelicans flying in formation ten inches off the water and this is why you adopted three children even if you didn't know what you were doing because they stood next to you on the beach watching pelicans. It didn't matter how we got there or where we were from or what color they were or I am. We were five people together for a moment in time deeper than the ocean before us. No one bothered us. No one said you can't be who you are. I was grateful for that.

We arrived at McDonald's on time.

"Did you have fun?" I asked Maribel.

"Yes. I had a lot of fun."

"Me, too," Javier said

"Me, too," Adriana said.

"And, Daddy," Adriana said. "Can we have Maribel for a sleep-over?"

"That would be fun, wouldn't it?"

"Yeah." Adriana often sighed when speaking, making everything she said a dreamy, breathless wonder.

Miguel and his wife were waiting for us.

"Maribel," I said. "You have our phone number in case you want to call and say hello."

"Okay. I will."

"Do you have any pictures of when you were little?" I wanted something from my children's past. Anything. A relic. A pulled tooth. An old shoe. They appeared from nowhere, like the three obelisks in 2001: A Space Odyssey.

"I have one."

"Can you show it to us the next time we meet? I'll make a copy for the kids."

"Okay. I'll bring it. But you have to give it back."

"I will."

On the way home Craig fell asleep. I told Adriana to close her eyes and sleep.

"I'm going to dream about Maribel," she said. In a minute, she was snoring.

Javier and I drove the hills. On the eastern crests we saw the bent, blackened branches of dead, burned trees. The wind sucked the ashes into a grey, aerial whirlpool twenty, then forty feet tall. On top of the low mountains we saw white smoke rising and a plane spotting for flames. On the ocean side, tall tilted utility poles were black at the bottom, too weak for wire. Burned railroad ties needed to be replaced before the Coast Starlight train came from Salinas. There was some green grass on the ocean side, a living bush, and five birds near it.

I told Javier that in the summers before and after my first year of college I fought forest fires on a U. S. Forest Service helicopter hotshot crew stationed in Southern California. This was a good time for Javier and me to learn more about each other. It's hard to be one-on-one with each child when you have three. I told him it was dangerous, tough work and people got burned and we had to hike after the helicopter left us on the mountains above water, hoses, hydrants and reporters. Even though it appeared that everything was dead and all was lost there were seeds underground, like Javier and his siblings. It was an important lesson for Javier to learn and I'm sure he would have agreed had he heard it. His head had fallen with his mouth open. He slept against the window, dreaming of Maribel.

## 15. I Saw What You Did

Before I left Oakland for Santa Maria, I e-mailed Oakland Tribune colleagues to explain my departure. Months later, several said the Tribune became family-friendly fast, and that was good. After Kevin left the company I was fine with settling the lawsuit, leaving the fiasco behind me like skid marks. He was done harassing people like me, or the newly pregnant manager who "resigned" after Kevin drove to her site for a chat, or Martha, the woman who inspired me to adopt. Kevin called her when she was on adoption leave and told her to read Bay Area newspapers to see if they had advertisements we didn't have.

Instead of settling, the company defended Kevin. Kevin told me he had dirt on them and I imagine they discussed that. Years earlier, he'd told me, they gave millions of dollars of advertising to customers to settle allegations of circulation fraud. That was Kevin's topsoil. Then, Mark, my attorney, obtained a letter from Martha that someone placed in my personnel file after she learned of the e-mail I sent to colleagues. She was in Denver, having transferred away four months after returning from adoption leave to work for Kevin. In the letter, she praised him as being a superhero supporter of woman with children and, by the way, she didn't like me. She left out the part where she promoted me three times. And she mentioned that she was an upstanding person in case anyone was curious.

Mark was curious. After we discussed Martha's career and the phone calls she made the week I lost my job, Martha was added as a defendant next to Kevin. We didn't want to settle with creeps. They needed another lesson.

Like a lot of newspapers, the Tribune published a special edition every year with the results of a reader poll naming the Best Italian Restaurant,

Best Sporting Goods Store, etc. The sales staff sold ads to businesses to run alongside ballots printed in the newspaper, and then sold more ads into a special section announcing the winners. After I joined the Tribune in 2001 (Kevin and Martha argued about who should get credit for hiring me), Martha, the vice-president of advertising, called me with poll results. She asked me to make a list of names of advertisers to name as winners, or businesses we didn't like, so she could remove their names from the list. I declined. She said she'd handle it. After she left and I was promoted and took over the contest, a lady in Marketing called not to congratulate me, but to ask, breathless with excitement, if we would run an honest contest from now on. We would. A year later, at a deposition, she forgot that conversation.

Mark's paperwork adding Martha as a defendant, and his explanation, got the media's attention. The lawsuit was covered by several large California newspapers. One story quoted an Oakland barber shop owner who complained that after years of winning the reader contest he lost after he declined to run ads next to the ballots. "How can a four chair shop beat a 12 chair shop?" he complained. Indeed.

For sport, I contacted a muckraking writer at Denver's Westword magazine in Martha's new hometown. He wrote a column about the fraud and printed a picture of me and the children at the Monterey marina. The ripples went further. Scott, my social worker, on a trip to Tennessee, called me.

"David. It's me, Scott. I'm in Tennessee, driving through the woods. I just heard your name on the radio, on NPR. They have a story about a contest and they mentioned your name."

I assumed Scott wanted me to hash the details for him, but instead he laughed and made me feel bad for my industry because he wasn't surprised by the news. After I explained how I got to Santa Maria I think he admired the riposte.

The Attorney for The Firm defending Kevin had a few questions for me. Carmen watched the kids when I drove north to meet Mark at his office in Half Moon Bay, an oasis south of San Francisco. We'd never met—we spoke over the phone after I hired him on the recommendation of an adoption attorney. He was friendly and open.

"I want to thank you for your help the week I lost my job," I said. He'd told me to take the Santa Maria job and get my life together. Revenge would come later. "It's hard to imagine what it would have been like without you."

"My pleasure. I apologize for taking so long to file the lawsuit. I had a tough summer. My father died."

We traded pictures of our children.

After he explained how depositions work—mine was scheduled for all day Friday and Saturday—I drove to Oakland over the Bay Bridge. Each time I crossed it, 220 feet over the water, I imagined it collapsing and me hanging onto a 526 foot tall tower, awaiting rescue. I got on the western span and rose above the water and then down through the largest bore tunnel in the world under Yerba Buena Island. There was no chance of falling here, but there was a chance of being crushed by millions of pounds of rocks in an earthquake so I hurried through and emerged on the rising eastern span to Oakland. I hurried to escape the shake and fall, relieved to be in Oakland where I'd be safe except for the murders. Like riding a roller coaster I rose above the poor, criminal neighborhoods of West Oakland. You were in a tough area if you had a fence around your front yard and your address was spray-painted on the roof.

From the window of the downtown Marriott I saw the Oakland Tribune tower with the high clock on it. I was restless and drove to The Firm to avoid getting lost when I walked in the morning. I drove by the Essex where Bev had interviewed me and recalled watching the Berkeley crew team row on Lake Merritt in the early morning, led by a voice in the fog. Across the lake was Merritt Bakery with fresh cookies, cakes, and pies. I was home. I got up early the next day and walked within 100 yards of the Tribune but I didn't see anyone I knew. Across the street from The Firm, I stopped for coffee.

It was scary knowing that you were about to face a person who wanted to destroy you. I steeled myself. Mark was outside talking on his cell phone. We shook hands and rode the elevator. The Firm was a big, fancy one with wide halls and no one in it. Mark told me not to be surprised if Kevin was there so I wasn't when I saw the back of his white head at a table in a room with a view.

"That's him," I said.

"Welcome to the party, Kevin." Mark responded.

We met Stu, the lawyer for The Firm. He was small enough to bench-press, but wore a Fu Manchu in case you tried it. His files and boxes were already on one side of the table, signaling us to sit on the other side. I walked in and shook Stu's hand. I walked around the table past Kevin. He didn't get up. He didn't look at me as I looked at him. He sat quietly, the opposite of what he was. A former colleague, a potential witness, told me that he'd seen Kevin recently and that he was startled when Kevin tried to hug him. Part of the defense strategy was that Kevin was a humble, harmless man. In his former capacity Kevin would tell Stu to get him the fuck out of there so he could play golf, but not today. Throughout the deposition he communicated with Stu in whispers.

"You're normally on this side of the table," Stu said to Mark. Mark did not usually represent plaintiffs like me. Stu wanted Mark to know he knew. "What are you doing over there?"

"I adopted four children," Mark answered. "This is personal."

I was sworn in. I had nothing to look at besides Stu so I pretended the court reporter was the jury. I addressed my answers to her.

Stu's primary objective was to devise a strategy to defend his client.

He also needed to evaluate my character and viability as a witness, and he'd need to know what damages I suffered to assist with settlement calculations. In lawsuits that large, settlement conferences were mandatory. He worked from a box loaded with files. He had a legal pad with handwritten questions and he worked methodically through the box, front to back. A good file with promise he put back in the box. A bad file he tossed to the floor, in between him and the court reporter.

Stu began with a friendly chat about the rules. Don't interrupt was a big rule, unless he didn't like an answer. Second, he stressed the importance of not answering a question until he was done asking it unless he liked the answer, then it was cool. In the end, as he tired, he answered questions for me. Stu began with the easiest questions, asking me what efforts I'd made to find a job prior to my departure from the Tribune. Kevin told people I'd quit to "raise a family somewhere else" and the investigation by the Human Resources department, conducted without talking to me, confirmed what Kevin said. I denied that and sued for wrongful termination, so finding out that I'd planned on leaving would prove them right and me wrong.

"Do you have any documents anywhere in your possession, custody or control at home that would reflect any efforts you made to obtain employment?"

"Kevin found a job for me. That was the only job I applied for, and I got it."

The file went to the floor. Next, he asked me to name every person from the company I'd communicated with since I left. He'd probably make a list and call them. The conversation might go like this: "Hi. This is Stu Hamilton. I'm defending us against David Marin's outrageous allegation that he lost his job because he wanted to adopt kids. I want you to know that David can add anyone to the lawsuit at anytime, and if that happens, I'll be there for you. Make sure you let me know if they call you." Since nearly everyone still worked at the company and taking a principled risk for a guy you knew is problematic, he'd prevail.

Then he plowed through my resume. Mark said it was easy to discredit someone with a resume because most people fibbed or exaggerated. I was no exception. Mark said he normally spent half a day on a resume. Stu spent about an hour. He got excited about my resume showing that I worked at a law firm for two years when it was only a few months. I should not have done that, but I didn't want employers to know that after graduating from law school I groveled, missed several meals, studied for the bar exam, ran out of money, and started a failed business.

Stu learned that I left a lot of jobs off my resume: dishwasher at the Holiday Inn, selling Kirby vacuum cleaners (lasted one day), selling greeting cards door-to-door, pig farm poop scooper, bakery truck driver, x-ray scanner, waiter, library book shelver, pathology lab gopher, bus boy, forest fire fighter, sink fabricator, house painter, landscaper, gas station attendant, dog kennel cage cleaner, and sports analyst. I put the jobs I thought mattered to the reader on and left the others off.

"Have you ever been fired from a job?"

"Yes."

"What happened?'

"I got caught reading Sports Illustrated in the bathroom at a dog kennel." The manager told me I had a lot to learn.

Next, we reviewed a handful of letters that appeared in my personnel file after I was gone. We knew about the letters because we got copies prior to the deposition. Mark said he was certain Stu would discuss the letters at the deposition, but it was highly unlikely the letters would make it to trial because it was blatant character assassination. And what an amazing chain of events for my file to have no negative letters before I left and then several afterwards. And for what purpose if I was gone? No judge would allow that, Mark said.

Stu asked about a woman who said I was sexist. When I told Stu that on the first day we met she asked me if I was looking at her butt and that she accused other men of the same, her file went to the floor. We discussed a letter from a woman who said she was afraid of me. When I told Stu she was afraid of a lot of people and that she often worked late at night with her husband asleep under her office desk because she was scared, her file went to the floor.

Next, Stu wanted to explore the counseling sessions Martha and Kevin told him they had with me. When he learned there were none, and no write-ups or follow-though, and that the official investigation done by the HR department never mentioned any performance issues, the file went to the floor. The court reporter was getting uncomfortable; she had no room to move her feet.

Stu asked me about a woman who, I told Stu, called to tell me Kevin was fishing for dirt on me the week I lost my job. The file went to the floor.

Another approach, soon to fizzle, was that I wasn't serious about adopting kids anyway and was I really going to get my license the day after I lost my job? I guided Stu through the process: classes, fingerprinting, references, etc. Nine times he asked me to prove that I was to get a license the day after I lost my job. Eventually, he relented; file to the floor.

It occurred to me that he didn't know I had children. I'd wondered if the friends I'd kept in touch with told Stu about me having kids. One, who wrote in an e-mail that she wanted a front row seat at Kevin's trial, sent gifts for the kids.

"And so," Stu said, "you never did get your license to adopt, correct?"

"Not here."

"Have you subsequently received a license to adopt anywhere?"

"Yes."

"Where?"

"Santa Barbara County."

"When did you receive that license?"

"August of last year."

"So you received a license to adopt from Santa Barbara County in August of 2003, correct?"

"Right."

He stuttered. "And... have you since... had a child placed with you for adoption or foster care?" A huge defense option was detonating. I decided to play the word game Bill Murray played in the movie Stripes. When an Army recruiter asked him if he'd ever been convicted of a felony, Murray responded, "Convicted?" and then grinning, "No, never convicted."

"A child? No."

His ears turned red. "More than one child?"

"Three."

Kevin squirmed.

"And," gulp, "were those three children placed with you in your house?"

"That's right."

He couldn't comprehend. Lost in space, he returned to questioning me about whether or not I was serious about adopting children. From the report Bev wrote recommending that I have children placed with me, he kept referring to her sentence that said I'd need help, a support structure. Ignoring the fact that I had children—he had his list of questions and he was determined to use it—he wanted to talk about whether placing children with me was a good idea or not, and whether I was capable of raising them. Nine times I told him it didn't matter now because I already had children and then, plop, the file went to the floor. Next, the man who didn't know I had children when the deposition began, said, "Have any of the three of them had any physical type of injuries since being under your care?"

"No." (Craig's panhandle gusher occurred after the deposition). I'd remember that question when I later told Mark how much to demand at settlement.

After reviewing the letter my best friend Greg wrote for my file after I left the company, Stu tossed his file on the floor when I told him that Greg was one of my adoption references, filling out a multi-page form attesting to my character and fitness to be a parent.

We discussed the phone conversation I had with Martha 90 minutes before I lost my job—the one where she warned me that I did not know what was going to happen. She'd begun that conversation asking me about some of our recent accomplishments at work. I told Stu I thought I was being interviewed. Perhaps she wanted me to come to Denver and work there. The story amused him and brought him back to life, nourished by the treachery. He was proud, like a coach watching his team execute the perfect play.

We chatted briefly about the Vice President of Finance saying, "You must have really made Kevin mad," after Kevin announced I'd quit. The court reporter shifted her feet. With the exception of my resume folder, all of the files were down there. Down there was bigger than up here and the deposition would not last two days.

"What was your pay in Santa Maria?"

"Seventy-five."

"$75,000 a year?"

"Right."

"And did you have any incentive or bonus plan?"

"Yes."

"What was your incentive or bonus plan?"

"It's a 20% bonus worth $15,000. It goes up to $20,000 if you do real well."

"And did you receive any bonus for last year?"

"$20,000."

I made $90,000 at the Tribune, plus a 20% bonus worth $18,000. Kevin made my bonus calculation so convoluted I earned none of it. Adding the $20,000 bonus I made at the Santa Maria Times to my $75,000 salary exceeded what I made at the Tribune. In our legal system, damages must be foreseeable (by the person who might have to pay them), unavoidable (people have an obligation to try to improve their condition), and certain (possible to calculate). In law school we called it FUC. Since I got a higher paying job without missing a paycheck and I didn't wear a neck brace or have psychiatric expenses, I had no money damages. What Kevin and Martha did was disgusting, but if a person wrote the "N" word on the office wall of an African-American the victim would have to prove damages in order win anything. Being an asshole was not actionable per se. Further, in California, since punitive damages were a factor of actual damages, they couldn't be awarded either.

When I told Stu that working for a small newspaper in Santa Maria vs. a big metro newspaper set my career back at least five years and that my job as vice-president at a larger newspaper paid double or triple the $75,000 I made in Santa Maria, Stu said that was speculative.

Invasion of privacy was another matter. That was a topic a jury could understand. And damages could be explosive. So, Stu wanted me to be happy. Damages are less if you're happy.

"Are you happy in your position there?"

"I like my boss. It's a good company."

"Are you happy in your position?"

"I'm doing fine."

"Are you happy, or pleased?" He was annoyed.

"I live there because I lost my job here. So I live in Santa Maria, not the most interesting town. I make do."

"Forgetting about the location...," he said.

"Forgetting how I got there," I interrupted.

"Let me get a question out. Are you happy in the job you have?" he asked, leaving out Santa Maria.

"Sure."

In the end we reviewed the company's employee manuals and training standards. I was asked to acknowledge seeing them and receiving training. Normally, it was helpful for a company to say that a bad person violated training standards, so he wanted it on the record that I received Human Resources training. The problem for Stu was that I was the only one who used the training. Kevin, Martha, Greg, the lady working late, and the lady with the desirous posterior, all contrary to training, never contacted Human Resources and never put anything in writing until I was gone. I, in contrast, had two problems in two years: I recounted the butt conversation in writing for my files and after losing my job, I wrote a letter asking the Vice President of Human Resources to investigate. Stu didn't get it and worked methodically through employment manuals he may have authored.

In eight hours the two-day deposition was over. Stu still didn't know what the defense should be. He had ideas, but none fit tight. He had to say, "You quit," since the investigation said nothing more. The problem: I had a modest sum in my checking account, no other job, and I was getting my foster care license the next day. It didn't compute. He wanted to say I was a bad person, but three promotions and no negative letters in my file while I worked there gutted that option. He dabbled with Kevin being supportive of my adoption classes, like he was trying to help me, but cutting half of the responsibilities of a parent-to-be to "help" them was simple discrimination.

Stu's best bet was that I did not suffer damages. It had promise, but it was risky because it's hard to predict what a jury might award for invasion of privacy. Plus, unbeknownst to Stu, or the company, I did not feel like I needed damages to win. I was happy removing Kevin from his job, inspiring the company to be family friendly, exposing Martha's hypocrisy, and causing the company damage in the form of giant legal fees and a diminished reputation.

The deposition ended. My brain was tired. Stu said he was glad to be going because his family was waiting down the road. Mine waited down the state. Mark and I took the elevator and talked on the sidewalk.

"How did it go?" I asked.

"You did fine. Better than fine. They would be fools to not settle."

"They may be fools; don't be surprised. You're right that most companies would try to protect their reputation but with these guys, I'm not sure what's left to protect."

I went to my hotel and slept before sundown, drapes drawn. Stu must have agreed the day did not go well. The man who said it was outrageous that I would accuse Kevin of coming between a man and his family went home to his family with a plan: interfere with Santa Barbara County placing children in my home. There was no way, he'd say, that Kevin would ever do to you what I am about to do to you now.


A few months later, Keith, an attorney from Mark's office charged with developing the lawsuit war plan, called to tell me that Stu was trying to get my Santa Barbara County adoption records and the files for Javier, Adriana, and Craig. This was the nightmare I feared. From here, I imagined they'd try anything...private detectives, tapped phones, or worse. Did my instinct to fight put my children in danger?

"Call Santa Barbara County Social Services right now," he said. "Tell them you expect them to resist the subpoena on privacy grounds. Then, send them an e-mail to make it official."

"Tell Mark I want him to keep those people away from my kids."

"I'm filing a motion to quash the subpoena. I'm going to crush them."

I called Scott. "My lawyer says that the company I sued is trying to subpoena the adoption records here."

"There is no chance we'll comply. I can't believe they'd be that stupid. It's an invasion of the kids' privacy, for starters. We don't like lawyers bothering our kids. I'll know if a subpoena arrives. When it does, I'll let you know, and I'll let them know this is a confidential placement and that it's none of their business."

Do. Not. Mess. With. Scott.

Mark said he'd go to court to stop Stu. Mark was disgusted, professionally embarrassed, that they would stoop that low. Worse, if they got Shrek's Monterey Bay Aquarium fake ID they could get him thrown out of preschool and we couldn't use it to go out drinking.

Keith called with an update. "Those idiots served the wrong people!"

"How did they miss a county?"

"That's what I mean. I can't believe they get paid for this. They sent the subpoena to some guy in Santa Barbara, the city. I called the number. His answering machine sounds like he runs an adoption service from home. Mark will be in court tomorrow."

Keith called to tell me what happened. The judge was an African-American female. A woman represented The Firm. Stu couldn't make it.

"The judge granted the motion to quash almost immediately," Keith said. "Mark didn't even get a chance to say anything. When the attorney for the other side asked the judge if she was losing because they served the wrong people, the judge said, "I read the file. I saw what you did to this man the first time he tried to adopt. You won't be doing that again."

"Then," Keith continued, "their attorney asked if she could fix the subpoena, send it to the right people, and come back. The judge said, "Don't bother.""

That evening I sent an e-mail to Mark: "Thank you for keeping them away from my kids."

He replied, "You're welcome."

The Firm, allowed one objection to the judge assigned to the case, had her removed. After two settlement conferences and a deposition about the reader contest, the lawsuit was settled. With the money I took the children to Puerto Rico to meet my father's family. And I bought new tires.

In 2006 Kevin called my employer about newspaper software he was selling. He was transferred to my office phone. He launched into a sales pitch. His software cost thousands of dollars.

"How long have you been in the business?" he asked.

"About 20 years."

"Me, too. Maybe we know some people in common. Did you ever work in the Bay area?"

"I did. I worked at the Oakland Tribune. I worked for you."

"What's your name again?"

"David Marin."

Silence…

"A few months ago," I said, "we paid a computer science student $600 to write a program for us. It works fine. Thanks for calling."


I didn't know it when I sued, but with 70% of households having one or more working parents (up from 20% in 1960), a new legal cause of action called Family Responsibilities Discrimination (FRD) was taking form based on mistreating parents because of their parental responsibilities. According to a 2010 study done by Cynthia Thomas Calvert at the Center for WorkLifeLaw, FRD lawsuits have increased by 400% in the past decade, with 88% filed by women.

With more single parents, companies must recognize that employees need time to care for families (children, the sick, or elders) and that punishing them for that is actionable in court. Moreover, companies that recognize this and give people room to breathe will find a more productive workforce with less turnover.

For males, the change is sloth-like, slow motion if we're noticed at all. Even experts don't see through the stereotype, like one quoted in a 2010 Associated Press story about FDR lawsuits: "There's a clear penalty to motherhood and care giving in this country. Basically, we've said to women, if you can conduct yourself in the workplace as if you were a man, without any other responsibilities, being available day and night, then (and only then) will your pay and opportunities will be similar."

How about using the word 'parent' instead of 'women'? Men run to the store at lunchtime for a loaf of bread. Trust me; I did it Thursday. If we react to discrimination by removing age, gender, ethnicity, sexual orientation, or religion from the way we look at people we'll instead look at ourselves as what we are, humans, unique each one, judged, if at all, by character and deeds, not by shade, status, or past.

# 16. Visiting Santa Barbara?

I recommend the downtown four-star Andalucia Hotel unless you have four Mexican children with you. We arrived with Maribel. I sent the kids into the lobby while the valet and I unloaded the Land Rover. I watched the kids sit quietly and I watched a man in a suit turn his head like a tank turret, staring at each child, ready, aim, fire. He met me at the counter.

"Are you with them?"

"They're with me."

"Are you staying here?"

"We are."

"Our, um, rooms are very small. I can find another place for you to stay. You'll be more comfortable."

"We'll be fine. This is not the first time we've been in a hotel."

I asked the check-in woman if the roof-top pool was heated.

"You don't want to go the pool," he answered. "It's very small, and crowded."

I took the kids swimming. The rooftop pool was not small or crowded. It had four people in it, all little and brown, the youngest in a Spiderman swim outfit with red webbed fins. He was adorable.

The pool was, however, adjacent to the Andalucia's rooftop "perch," as they called it, now hosting a private party for Santa Barbara's finest. The Man in the Suit tried and failed to spare them the indignity of looking at what he saw.

I sat in a lounge chair reading the Wall Street Journal, watching Craig tease the delighted young women watching him "swim."

He arrived. Eight feet away. "Who's watching these kids?" he yelled.

"Excuse me. Over here. From downstairs."

He simmered.

"We need four extra towels, if you don't mind."

He called the people and had four towels sent to our room.

After we swam, brushed up and left our room to wander down State Street he was outside our door. He turned and walked away.[21] The next morning, as we left the room for breakfast, he was outside our door. He turned and walked away.

Bev didn't tell us in adoption training that we couldn't swim near the perch or that people would stare at us like we're a freak show or that some people never learned their manners. At a Thai restaurant a woman with her back to us turned, rested her chin on her forearm, and watched. The woman in the kitchen of a Utah restaurant who yelled, "Those aren't your kids!" could have learned her manners from the people at a Utah Burger King who stood polite in line, six deep, waiting to ask questions.

Bursting with curiosity, some people skipped me and went directly to the children. I hadn't talked to the kids about talking to strangers because I wasn't sure what to say. I didn't know what they knew and I didn't want to goof up what they learned in school. On a grocery store trip, I sent Adriana and Javier to sit on a bench 15 feet away while Craig and I waited to see how much I owed. A lady spoke to Adriana and Javier. I watched them squirm. After I paid, the lady told me she knew the kids' names, ages, adoption status, my name, where I worked, and that I was single.

"I told the kids I have a cat," she said.

"I see."

"Where do you go to church?"

"We don't."

"What do you do on Sunday mornings?"

"We go to the beach."

The latest is a waitress at a Mexican restaurant we used to frequent because you get an extra half pound of delicious carnitas if you buy a

21  I complained to corporate. They sold it. It's now Canary Hotel. Nice pillows.

pound first. She queried me about where the kids came from, then about me having a wife, or not. The last time, she came at us before we sat down.

"What are you going to do if the mother comes back?"

"She doesn't know where we are."

"What if she finds you? What if she finds you and says she wants the kids?"

"They're not available."

"What if she wants them?"

"We'll have a pound of carnitas."


Part of the joy of adopting chocolate children is that with every step you take, you help the world get closer to the place where how people look doesn't matter. It's the content of their character, like Martin Luther King said. But after being harassed by the California Highway Patrol, fending off a social worker wondering why I would take "these kids," asked by a fancy hotel to go elsewhere, and listening to a cook in a Utah restaurant yell, "Those aren't your kids!" I wondered where society was headed.

Retired NBA basketball player Magic Johnson once suggested the NBA Most Valuable Player award be split into three halves so I'll try that. I'm half Republican because private industry is more efficient than bureaucrats; I'm half Democrat because the field is not level; and I'm half independent because I don't trust Republicans or Democrats to handle power responsibly. That's my politics.

I had tears in my eyes when Barack Obama won Pennsylvania and then the Presidency of the United States and I looked at my children and I thought this is us, this the only place on the planet where this can happen and that was great for a few weeks until Newt Gingrich, political operative Karl Rove, and media hosts Glen Beck and Rush Limbaugh slithered forth, conservative family values advocates with eight divorces and eleven marriages between them—not to each other—although you have to admit there'd be poetry in there somewhere.

Unable to advance their interests at the presidential ballot box and legitimately concerned about the direction of a nation in the worst recession in 75 years, conservatives directed vitriol not towards society's most powerful and getting richer[22], but at the weakest, the tired and poor.

Eager to disgorge illegal school children and return to constitutional values they defy constitutional authority—the United States Supreme Court—which ordered the education of illegal immigrant children. And they ignore bigger education challenges, such as those in California, where money is scarce because the public worker pension debt is ten times higher than what the state spends on K-12 education.[23]

Wanting to unclog hospital emergency rooms they oppose mandated health insurance that would...unclog emergency rooms.

If the anti-immigration crowd prevails, our nation will become a culturally stunted, shrink-wrapped vanilla hive with a perpetual sub-class of uneducated drones. Our children are watching and learning that the United States, taken and built by immigrants whose work, cunning, and merit ruled the day, is now retooling based on who was here first, ignoring Indians and Mexicans or, to summarize, white people. If the police stop me for rolling through an Arizona stop sign do I have to show them my children's papers? What if my children were white?

Growing up without a father, I searched for ideals. I was chastened to learn that the Constitution excluded women, Martin Luther King had flaws, George Washington owned slaves, and the heroes of the American revolution killed Indians. A boyhood hero, Kansas City Royals baseball player Amos Otis, smooth as silk in centerfield, admitted to using a corked

---

22  From 1976 to 2007, while the average hourly wage decreased 7%, the earnings of the top 1% of society grew from 8.9% of the nations' total income to 23.5%. New York Times, October 2010.

23  Governor Arnold Schwarzenegger. Los Angeles Times. August 10, 2010.

bat his entire career. All human; all flawed; such is life. I found only one ideal, carved in bronze at the base of the Statue of Liberty: "Give me your tired, your poor; Your huddled masses yearning to breathe free; The wretched refuse of your teeming shore. Send these, the homeless, tempest tost to me, I lift my lamp beside the golden door." The woman who wrote that, and the 151 foot tall copper clad woman welcoming strangers to an American harbor, were emblematic of the difference between reality and hope. It was love's pure light. It's why any child in an emergency room is treated or any child left at the school gate is educated. It is the difference between what is and what could be.

It says tempest-tossed because when Emma Lazarus wrote that the world was covered in storms, political and otherwise. The planet had issues with ethnicity, the wretched refuse, homeless and wandering. That's why it says that. The invitation was extended anyway. The Liberty plaque didn't say tempest-tossed to me if your paperwork is in order and you know what the Pilgrims had for dessert. That's the language of little people, bumbling bureaucrats, government loving process servers: the opposite of what the Republican Party used to be.

That's the shame of it all, the party of small, stay-out-of-my-yard government is at the gate in Arizona or Texas, looking under women's skirts for swollen belly buttons because if there's one thing we hate, it's mothers looking for a better future for their children.[24]

Airport screeners could also check for a bulging female tummy, or

---

24 Another thing we appear to hate is young people educating themselves or defending our country. In 2010, after passage by the United States House of Representatives, the United States Senate defeated the DREAM Act, first proposed in 2001 by Republican Senator Orrin Hatch. The DREAM Act created a 10-year long path to citizenship for the non-citizen children of illegal immigrants if the children complete at least two years of college or join the armed services. Hatch, and Arizona Senator John McCain, a prior supporter of the DREAM Act, voted No in 2010, ignoring Secretary of Defense Robert Gates' support of the Act as a way to "maintain and shape" the armed services.

better, require or perform pregnancy tests for all non-citizen females entering the United States.

In 2010 a commotion arose from a Pew report revealing that 350,000 (8%) of 4.3 million U.S. births in 2009 were to illegal immigrants. So what? They're not spayed and neutered. 340,000 is a tad more than one tenth of one percent of the U.S. population, 0.1%, a tenth of a penny on the dollar, like a 200 pound man going on a diet to shed 3.2 ounces.

And 'anchor babies', such an endearing depiction of human beings born to non-citizen mothers, cannot petition to bring family to America until they're 21 years old. In my experience about half would prefer their parents stay as come, if you know what I mean.

Armed at rallies like an old west carnival act, the anti-illegals crowd touts their second amendment right to bear arms. But the second amendment isn't in the Bill of Rights because the founders feared tool-less hand farmers from Mexico, it's there because it feared people like the political far right in 2010, unable to achieve objectives through elections, frustrated standing in line at the emergency room, trampling on others— the poor, the homeless, the least hopeful—pick on someone your own size—oops, sorry!—while imploring the government they despise to please help them achieve their objectives or they'll start shooting. The second amendment wasn't written to protect them, it was written to protect the rest of us from people like them.

And yet, the anti-immigration crowd may prevail. That's why I can't wait for the right-to-life religious right to become engaged in the debate.

The world is full of nations with street children picking through garbage searching for coins, brains stultified by the chemical stench. Ours isn't one of them, yet. Our common integrity, uniting liberals and conservatives, is to treat people with respect, be they poor or brown, from here or not. If children are drowning and a woman takes off her shoes to slip into the river we don't stop her and ask if she is a Republican or a

Sign at bus station. Rome, Georgia. Esther Bubley, photographer. 1943.

Democrat. We don't ask her where her parents were born. We jump in the river with her. We hold hands on the bank. We bring blankets. We help each other. We hold a flame when we want one more song. This is us.

Freckled with red hair, I'm the son of a blonde Missouri mother and a Puerto Rican father. In my youth, I was ashamed to tell people I was Puerto Rican because of Puerto Rican jokes. As a boy I saw no successful, nationally recognized Puerto Ricans outside of Chong and Cheech, with whom I shared a last name. A therapist would say adopting Hispanic children was my way of saying sorry, it's okay to be who you are.

But be careful. Last year, accused at school of being a Mexican, ten-year-old Adriana said, "I'm not Mexican, I was born in Santa Barbara." And eight-year-old Craig was told by children that he couldn't be on a recess soccer team, that he couldn't play because he was Mexican. And now the constitutional values people want to defy the, um, constitution, and strip citizenship from the children of illegal aliens like, for example, mine.

Strip their citizenship and we'll have second class citizens and with their children, third-class, the back of the bus. We've been there before.

Who will track these perpetual runner ups? Two million of the 11.9 million illegals in the country now overstayed their visas. We have no idea where they are. We'll need another bureaucracy to hunt people. When they're captured, we can keep track by marking them in an obvious place and we can call them "colored people." Can colored people run for school board or attorney general, win scholarships, or keep their place in line at the emergency room ahead of a full citizen, or buy land if a full citizen is bidding?

The colored children earned their citizenship the exact same way 95% of U.S. citizens earned ours, they were born here.[25] There is no

---

25  The other 5% are foreign-born naturalized citizens.

constitutional difference between them and us.

If, for example, as in Arizona, laws are made by legislators inspired by donations from private prison companies seeking new revenue, we can cage the kids at the Phoenix Zoo, former grounds of one of Arizona's three World War II POW and Japanese internment camps.[26] We have the infrastructure.

We can feed them pellets and a chicken on holidays. At night, they can howl at the moon. What do we care?

In 2010, a coalition of major corporations, including Boeing, Disney and NewsCorp, owner of Fox News, called for a pragmatic approach, reminding people of the American dream. Disney CEO Robert Iger: "It's our great strength as a nation, and it's also critical for continued economic growth. To remain competitive in the 21st century, we need effective immigration reform that invites people to contribute to our shared success by building their own American dream." Immigrants start businesses at twice the rate of native-born Americans and apply for patents 30% more often.[27]

Pragmatists favor sensible reform, a border more secure than not, a path to citizenship, and a work program for adults, including fieldworkers a few years older than thirteen. If they are invited to work with a specific employer (make them do the paperwork), there's no need to hike through the desert. What the business coalition sees is that for a society, an economy, to grow, it needs new consumers, new professors, new artists and new ideas. The world is tempest tossed, that's why people try to escape it. It's been that way for ten thousand years. That's why my family came here. Yours, too, unless you're the last of the Mohicans.

26  In 1988, former President Ronald Reagan signed the Civil Liberties Act, paying reparations and apologizing to American citizens of Japanese ancestry for interning 110,000 of them, citing "race prejudice, [war] hysteria, and a failure of political leadership." He was also the last president to grant amnesty to millions of illegal immigrants.
27  Kauffman, Index of Entrepreneurial Activity, 1996-2008.

# 17. Pulverized Bullion

After arm wrestling the law firm and with Santa Maria's summer winds blowing patio umbrellas through town, I took the colored people north on Highway 1 to see elephant seals and the Monterey Peninsula, the only perfect place in the world, and my home from 1985 to 1999. I wanted to practice being out there with the kids and try to do it better. Plus, the holidays neared and instead of turning off my lights on Halloween or having a bread bowl of clam chowder by myself at the Monterey wharf on Christmas day, I had holiday things to learn lest my children think they were adocted by a moron.

Anticipating car sickness, The Advisory Board recommended a drowsy pill for kids so I bought a package in San Luis Obispo at the last gas station before Highway 1. I'd always trusted gas stations for quality pharmaceuticals and that day was no different. I broke a pill into three pieces.

On the beach south of Hearst Castle we stood quietly in the area marked "Colored People" and watched elephant seals in the sand below the hard, rising dune. The males averaged 16 feet and 6,000 pounds, like two Volkswagens Bugs bumper-to-bumper. Males guarding harems chased other males away. The chase, however, at 6,000 pounds, or three Clydesdales, was brief as they moaned, groaned and lumbered for 20 feet, rested, and then chased again and rested. Fifty feet took five slow-motion minutes.

Highway 1 to Monterey was an asphalt roller coaster plunging to the sea and then rising high enough to see blue whales in January or ships leaving white foam prop ribbons 25 miles away. We drove on the right, in the lane for Colored People. The children awoke near Big Sur and The River Inn. We walked in the river and found the benches in the river we wanted. The water was so clear it was like seeing stones and fish in slanted air. There were fish and there were children. The children smiled.

We had lunch on the patio, next to a couple with a boy about nine years old. The couple knew exactly what they were doing. I felt bad I didn't know as much. My mother told me that a child with two parents gets 100% of each, or 200%, while she, raising five kids by herself, gave only 20% to each. Me with three was 33; it rhymed and that was nice and more than I got. After the family finished lunch, the dad told the boy to clean up and when the dad turned away the boy put his fingers in dad's glass of water and when the dad turned to see the boy he was incredulous. For five minutes he queried the boy, "Why," and his mother, "Did you see that?" Neither the boy nor the mom wanted to discuss it, making dad more upset. I felt better because my kids did not have their fingers in my water even though the percentage they got was much lower than the boy's.

We stayed in a Carmel lodge with a pool. The kids had water wings, and we swam in it. The next day we went to the aquarium Members Entrance where I told the people we were members but didn't have our membership cards because of the mail, and they let us in anyway. The kids loved the circling sardines. They put their hands in the water, rubbing the backs of the manta rays in the shallow sand bottom pool. We went to the playroom and made shark hats and wore them.

In the evening we visited the marina and walked the docks among sailboats and fishing boats. The sounds of seagulls, water lapping, halyard clinking against masts and voices from the hold made my heart beat quicker. Why that happened to a kid who grew up in Missouri I've never known why, but I always said that when I die[28] I'll do that in Monterey, where the fog horn blasts at 2 a.m. and you can hear seals bark all the

28  Spread my ashes where the Carmel River meets the Pacific, listen to Van Morrison sing Shenandoah and know, my three angels, that no man was ever filled with the joy you brought me.

way to El Dorado street. When I lived there I bought a sailboat across the bay in Moss Landing, a decomposing fishing village with more boats abandoned on land than resting in water. The boat I bought was the first sailboat I was ever on and I bought it that day.

At the wharf we saw the man with the monkey who'd been there for 20 years. If you wanted to take a picture with the monkey that cost extra, and when you took the money from your pocket the monkey took the money not the man.

Home and refreshed, I prepared for the holidays. I had to make sure we were happy, like Stu the lawyer wanted, and that I followed parenting protocol, from carving pumpkins to making gravy. Halloween was first, meaning it was time to grab a six-pack and a bat and drive around town bashing mailboxes. No wait, that was my childhood.

At Kmart, I purchased a Professional Pumpkin Carving Kit for $6. I didn't want an amateur kit; I wanted the best. Directions to patterns on a password protected web site were hidden under the scoop because the company did not want people stealing their patterns and who could blame them? It was not easy making pumpkin patterns and you didn't want people stealing your intellectual property when you could make $6 off them. I went online, entered my secret password (*****) and tried to print a pattern but my computer crashed. After printing one pattern, my printer ran out of ink.

For $33, we got pumpkins from a field off Highway 101. I'd never bought pumpkins before so I didn't know if that was a lot. I bought $6 worth of corn with rust husks and put them on the kitchen table in case anyone came by to see if I was doing a good job. At Circuit City I bought ink for $65. I'd spent $110 to carve three pumpkins and that seemed like a lot. My PC crashed four times so I drew a bat, an arched backed cat, and a witch using one inch tall Examples of the Patterns they teased me with on the package. I cut the top off the first pumpkin and made the hole bigger to put the candle in there but oops, the lid was too small and Stu was right, I did need a support structure. I was glad Carmen was there to help us.

We were better off in the hands of professionals, so for our next holiday trick we took Maribel to see Cinderella at the Santa Barbara Ballet. It was an overcast day. When we arrived at McDonald's the children were asleep in the car. Maribel was there with Miguel, his wife, and a baby nephew. Miguel slipped a $20 into her pocket, like always. Bless her heart; Maribel brought the photo she'd promised. She was in it, along with big sister Emine and my three children. The photo was about two years old. Craig was a baby. All five children wore fear on their faces like the faces of the damned Michelangelo painted on the ceiling of the Sistine Chapel. I made a copy because it was all they'd have.

When I asked Maribel if she'd called Emine lately, she said no. "I can't afford a phone card."

On the way to the ballet, I stopped at a gas station and bought her a card. A few minutes later, Maribel said, "I spoke with Emine yesterday. She lives in Reno."

"Did she ever receive the photos and letters we sent?"

"I don't know."

We arrived at the Lobero Theatre early to eat lunch before the ballet. The theatre, California's oldest still operating, was built in 1873. It was one of Santa Barbara's unique treasures and thank God for that. Compared to Santa Maria, Santa Barbara was like Paris. We walked to State Street and began our hand-holding march looking for a child friendly place to eat. I saw a sign for the Paseo Restaurant. We went through a maze of offices, stairs, plants, windows and vines, and found the door. There were no other adults with kids. As we followed the hostess through the garden and past a waterfall, all under the open roof, people stared like there'd been a breakout at the fieldworker's camp. Birds flew to trees. Adriana, my Cinderella, wore a pink princess dress and a diamond and red tiara.

It was brunch only day with a long table with silver platters filled with chicken, fish, enchiladas, eggs, bacon, and potatoes. I helped Shrek fix his plate of French toast, bacon, and a strawberry and showed him back to his seat. The other kids loaded up and we sat and ate in peace. Maribel accidentally called Adriana "Brianna."

Javier marveled at the dessert table with cookies, marshmallows, fruits, carrot cake, cheesecake, chocolate mousse, chocolate cake, and little muffin pastries with frosting and decorations on top. For some reason, the cornucopia and the colors and the sky and the music reminded him of the days when he rubbed food on his lips, he said, to lick when he was hungry. "I did that too," Maribel said.

"You showed me how," Javier said.

"When I went to foster by myself," she said, "because it took a few weeks for my dad to get me, the foster home was dirty. They always ate fast food. There was a dead dog on the floor."

As she ate her chicken and fish she said, "I'm going to be a vegetarian when I grow up. I like animals."

The ballet was a delight, but I forgot to tell the kids no one would speak.

"When will they talk?" Adriana whispered.

Shrek sat next to me, but the seat folded him so his shoes were next to his ears and it was hard for him to see so he sat on my lap, next to Adriana. At intermission we bought water and brownies and sat on the green grass fresh from the rain. After the ballet we went to the beach. The kids ran barefoot in the sand, waved sticks in the air, and chased seagulls that didn't care.

Thanksgiving was the perfect holiday to showcase homemaking skills or, in my case, not. At Safeway, I plucked a big frozen turkey from the tub and put it in the cart. At home, the label puzzled me. Not only had I failed to grab a turkey, but the label didn't even confirm that it was a bird. It was a capon. Seven pounds, $23. I didn't know it, but they put other things in the turkey case besides turkeys and that wasn't right. I had no idea what a capon was or how to cook it or cut it. I worried that in Santa Maria a capon might not be a bird at all, but a large rodent, like an armadillo. It had an armadillo build, round and humped in the middle, like a frozen football. I was upset, wondering what I was doing trying to run a household when I couldn't even buy a god-damned turkey.

I sat down with Brittany and discovered that my capon was a bird after all, and a juicy bird at that. I learned in a capon chat room that people who raise capons were very excited about them. I learned, for example, that "Cooking capons takes the same attention and care as growing them!" These were things I needed to know!

To execute the excitement, however, I needed gourmet-type skills and an oven bag. I had neither. I had a stove and a long, low gray pan. After plotting my approach with the Advisory Board, I gave up. Like a friendless drifter, I was last in line registering for the prepared turkey meal offered at Safeway for $39.99. Prepping a baking sheet for buttermilk biscuits, I accidentally sprayed PAM into my root beer, dulling the taste. The Thanksgiving meal itself was fine, except for the burning. I hadn't noticed a hole in the oven re-heat bag included in the package. Moreover, I served four plates with enough food to feed eight people, yet I sat with three kids with stomachs smaller than my fist. Worse, I learned the children had never heard of mashed potatoes or gravy. They were Mexican. They didn't even have turkeys there for all I knew. What did they care about Thanksgiving anyway? Plus, they were already full from the banana-chocolate milkshakes and the shrimp cocktail appetizer. I could have peeled three slices of turkey out of the sliced variety-meats pack in the fridge, fried that and saved two birds, two hours, and $63. I am selling a capon cheap, by the way, which is why I'm writing this book.

I had a Plan B for fun. We'd go to Guadalupe Beach in our coats and on the west side of the dunes we'd hunt for sand crabs in the white foam of receding waves. We'd watched fieldworkers who lived in the dunes capture crabs for eating, storing them in the folded up bottoms of their wet, sandy shirts, and we wanted to try it.

After feeding we loaded up, buckled down, and got on Main Street, heading west through Santa Maria on a road trip to Guadalupe. A billboard in a neighborhood populated with Mexican field workers invited them to snow ski in the Sierras. We passed through fields with the green velvet November leaves of strawberry plants poking through plastic covered mounded rows. The mounds made the strawberries knee high. This thoughtful accommodation meant that pickers didn't have to pick near their ankles and delayed the ache from the stoop. The space in between the rows was just wide enough for little field worker feet.

At the streetlight in Guadalupe I saw railroad barriers coming down and lights flashing, so we waited for the train. But there was no train; the mechanism was broken. I backed up, drove on the opposite side of the road and passed around the barrier, causing waiting people to honk, upset I'd broken the rules. I looked back in my rearview mirror and saw the barriers go up and then quickly down again, trapping the honkers. The road to the dunes cut through more fields. Five foot wide irrigation ditches lined both sides of the road. The western hills were bright green and glossed by fog like white icing. The fog rose to mist and then to clouds, blocking the sun. A house on the right near the river had checkered latticework across the windows and a dirty white tractor.

We passed through acres of woods. I warned the kids to look out for bears, raccoons, and hawks. Javier watched with binoculars, but didn't spot anything. Soon the paved road turned to sand as dune blow covered the road, making it impassable but for bulldozers pushing the sand to the side. Fresh grains stole my friction, causing the tires to spin. We crested the hill at a clearing that overlooked the winding river meeting the sea near cattle grazing in the open field. The grass was green from the rains, and the dunes were gold and soft, like pulverized bullion. The river spilled into the sea, but the sea was more powerful, pushing back at high tide, making the river turn back into itself, forming another, which didn't bother the cattle one bit, except for the crossing.

At the beach we parked among the battered cars of fieldworkers looking for Thanksgiving dinner in the surf. The sky was gray. Wind blew the clouds and I saw a warm opening coming. The kids took off their shoes in the car and walked on the asphalt softly until they reached the sand. A man and his friend walked by with a dog. An old Mexican couple sat in their jalopy, watching us pass, not hiding their stares. The kids ran towards the high, cold, pounding surf. They knew not to go near the water because of the rip current and because of the drowning. Javier found four sand crabs; Adriana three.

I found a twelve-foot-high hill of sand made by the bulldozer and we ran over to play, jump, and slide. It was cold; we wouldn't be there long. Javier spotted a seagull resting in the sand and with a run down the hill chased it until the gray-and-white bird was airborne, flying to the sunny opening in the clouds. At the car I brushed the sand and the cold off the kids' feet with a towel, wiping sparkled grains from brown little toes. We returned over the dunes past the cattle and the river overlapping. It was a good Thanksgiving after all. Their bellies were full and they had sand in their hair.

Soon it was time for our first Christmas tree! This was the excitement I'd been waiting for. We wore our coats and drove to Nipomo, a little town north of Santa Maria. I'd buy a tree using the coupon I had, but the coupon was no good the lady said, pointing to Weekdays 9:00-5:00. We got a handsaw off the rack, picked a row of trees, and walked in. The trees were tall, full and green and we found one and we cut on it. We got our tree, dragged it to the end of the row and waited there for the men on the tractor to take us and our tree to the shack. After we paid, good men wrapped our tree in plastic and put it in the trunk. At Walmart we got decorations like tinsel, the vacuum destroyer. We bought lights and the kids picked ornaments. At home we decorated the tree. We ran out of decorations about two-thirds of the way down, but it was our tree so who cared?

The kids had never seen snow except in the Rudolph the Red Nose Reindeer movie and that was fake. Using directions Brittany gave me, we drove to Mount Abel off Highway 166. We had new warm gloves and hats and I dressed the kids in layers and had extra clothes for the wet and cold. I brought bottles of water and Fig Newtons, enough to survive three days if we plunged over a cliff without witnesses. The day felt strange. It was 68 degrees.

Around a bend and under a bridge I got 100 yards notice that the exit for Mount Abel was near. We turned east, but still hadn't found snow. We entered Los Padres National Forest. Soon I saw a sign that said "Chains Required." Later, another read "Icy Roads 26 Miles." My car thermometer still read 68 degrees. We drove through an empty mesa and glided up a hill brown from exposure to the sun with no trees for shade. When I turned back I saw a giant valley covered with snow-white fog and I told the kids, "That's snow!"

Looking ahead two hills, I saw white between the trees. The temperature plummeted to 61 degrees. I had to hurry or the snow would melt before we arrived. Hawks circled at our level because we were high. We drove until we saw snow near us. It was dirty from the mud splash of the tires. We drove higher and found snow six inches deep and then a foot and then we saw an area where people like us stopped to play and we did that until we were asked to leave because we were trespassing. We drove further and found a spot to build a snowman and we were happy and we threw snowballs and walked the woods looking for bears.

The kids were wet so Mr. Prepared stripped them to their underwear in the trunk and re-dressed them in warm clothes, brought special. Down we went over the snow fog fields, through the hills, back into warm weather under gliding hawks. In New Cayuma, I made a u-turn and pulled into a perfect spot in front of a restaurant. There were four Harleys ahead of us and two behind. I saw a large, bearded Harley man squint through the window and rise. I got out of the car and opened the door behind me and took out my little girl. I circled around and took out my little boy and then I helped my smaller boy and we held hands on the sidewalk. The guy watching followed me and Craig into the restroom. Watching three-year-old Craig reach for a brown paper towel, he tore one off and said, "Here you go, little fella." We sat at the table next to him and ordered cheeseburgers and milkshakes.

## 18. Beads of Mercury

After severing the rights of the parents it was time to formalize the adoption. I was so tired of dealing with Social Services I worried it wouldn't feel like anything more than a legal maneuver a long time coming, more relief than joy. I called Scott to inquire about the next steps and tell him about our road trips.

"You're not allowed to take the children out of the county without permission. Next time, send me an e-mail before, or after."

"Okay."

"Have you heard from Melinda?"

"No. Why?"

"Well, she failed to notify one of the parents about the severance hearing. If we don't fix it, you may have to start over."

"How come I'm finding out from you? Why didn't she tell me?"

"She told me she thought you were too busy. I'm going to get involved. We'll file a motion in Superior Court, a higher court than Juvenile Court, and ask the judge to sever the rights of the man Melinda missed. We'll ask the judge to do that while preserving the original decision."

I bypassed Melinda and called the department director, Nancy Geffen. She agreed to help. A manager below Nancy called me. I was grateful for the quick action and happy to hear her voice. I'd met her very early in the adoption process.

"Why did you call my boss?"

"Well, um, Melinda missed notifying someone of the severance hearing again, and I want things done correctly. Did you know about that?"

"What's the big hurry?"

Let's review… One of the biggest law firms in the nation was coming at me. I had a Social Services person, or persons to be named later, opposed to me adopting. The mother was coming back soon, or not. I wanted to write a will to provide for the children, but if I did that before they were adopted where would the money go? The company I worked for, Pulitzer Newspapers, was sold that very month and executives often went out with the tide. Conservatives were rewriting adoption rules and who knew where that would go? I had three children I wanted to call my own forever, a doctor's office pretending they were dealing with the old regime, and a son with last name of a famous drug dealer taped to his desk. I knew every day that things could go wrong and I wondered how bad the political right wing could make it. Would they try, for example, to deny citizenship to fieldworker children born in the United States? Why, yes, they would try and those were the reasons I was in a hurry.[29]

"I want the legalities to be over so the kids and I can get on with our lives."

"The delays are irrelevant. You already have the kids."

"Do you think it's important that the legal steps are properly taken?"

"Maybe no one will appeal the decision."

"But they can't appeal a decision they don't know about. Has the error wrecked the original decision?"

"I don't know."

"How do I find out?"

"I'm not sure. We're overworked here and understaffed."

They were understaffed because if two or more stood adjacent they merged like beads of mercury. They were understaffed because many became one.

"Alameda County, where I came from, had 5,000 kids, you have 150."

29   Bills introduced in the United States Congress in 2005 and 2007 would deny citizenship to children born in America to parents who are not citizens. A bill introduced by Senator David Vitter (R-La.) would prohibit the U.S. Census from counting undocumented immigrants. In 2010, "moderate" South Carolina Senator Lindsey Graham spoke of mothers "dropping babies" for citizenship.

"They have a bigger staff than we do."

"So what's the next step?"

"We'll send the severance hearing paperwork to Sacramento. They need to approve it. That could take months."

"The paperwork was flawed. You failed to notify someone. Why would you send flawed paperwork to Sacramento?"

"I don't think anyone will notice the error. You'll just have to put up with it. You'll be lucky if anything happens this year."

It was no mystery why California had 98,000 children stuck in foster care. There were not 98,003 because I was stubborn. The process was slow from the start. Investigating people before issuing a foster care license so children could be placed in a home took six to nine months. Police behind a car vet it in thirty seconds. Presidential cabinet appointees are vetted in six weeks. From start to finish, the classes, applications, fingerprinting, report writing, notification to possible parents, court hearings and all the rest took about 100 hours, spread over years. It was a deeply flawed process that hurt kids who wandered from home to home, ate bread dipped in milk like cats, worried about lost siblings, hauled possessions around in trash bags and wore ten cent shirts.

The national tragedy, exposed in the 2002 National Survey of Family Growth, found that with 129,000 children available to adopt, there were 600,000 women desiring to adopt, nearly five mothers per child. In a Washington Post op-ed, Listening to Parents founder Jeff Katz did the Alice in Wonderland math. 351,600 women were open to adopting a child between six and 12 years old while 46,136 were available. 521,400 women said they would adopt black children, 12.5 mothers for each of the 41,591 black children available. And 185,400 said they would adopt children older than 13, six mothers per child with 30,654 available. Yet the explosive demand resulted in only 8,000 children being adopted by parents like me, without a previous relationship with the child. Jeff Katz, in a separate study, found that for every 1,000 people contacting Social Services about adopting, only 36 did so.

My first phone call to Social Services, easily the most important call I'd ever made, done after contemplating a family, bunk beds, and holding hands, ended after a bureaucrat, indifferent to my excitement, told me incorrectly that living in a one bedroom condo disqualified me from taking the training classes. I needed a bigger place, obviously, before children were placed with me, but not, I learned later, before I even attended orientation.

Mr. Katz dug deeper and found that many of the 964 people who called but didn't adopt were stifled by bureaucrats, explaining that people in San Jose, California—welcomed to a happy orientation meeting— were 12 times more likely to adopt than people in Miami. After having to provide personal and financial information to a bead of mercury on the phone, the Miami curious were lined up at the first introductory meeting and fingerprinted, like a mass arrest. The fingerprinting can be done later or, like it was with me, three times.

A few days later Melinda called and confessed.

"I'm going to tell the judge I couldn't find a person who could be the father of Javier."

I called Nancy Geffen, the Director.

"You missed notifying someone."

"I'll need to check and see what happened. They may have made a mistake."

"Who are they?"

"Social Services."

"Isn't that your department?"

"Yes. I'm not handling the case. We've had budget cuts."

"I'd like you to assign Scott to my case. He's the only one who gets things done."

No response.

"What I'm trying to do is make sure the process goes as required by law. I don't want people in a van in my yard in a year's time taking my kids away. Do you understand that?"

No answer.

"How will I know it's fixed?"

"I'll check it out and call you." I didn't expect to hear from her and I didn't.

"I have a question for you. Do you think I should hire a lawyer to make sure your staff is doing their jobs correctly?"

"You wouldn't be the first."

"By the way. My kids are not comfortable with your people visiting our home. The last one tried to buy my daughter's furniture. Half the time no one comes after telling us they're coming. I have to de-program my kids each time there's a visit. They have not had good experiences with your people."

"If the kids are not comfortable around strangers you should send them to counseling."

She was so matter of fact it struck me that she was right. Maybe I should have sent the children to counseling. I planned on it. When I got them I asked Scott to recommend a therapist. He said don't bother, if they're happy leave them alone. His advice surprised me, so I asked Bev, my training social worker, and I asked our pediatrician. Both agreed with Scott. Leave them alone. They're children. They'll adjust. But here was the division director of Social Services, maybe she knew something extra. I assumed she was a health-care professional, but wait. Weren't kids supposed to be suspicious of strangers? Wasn't that the rule? Worse, my children knew these people. They weren't strangers, they were robbers.

At 7:30 p.m. on a Thursday evening, I heard the front gate squeak. It was Melinda, an hour late. She was such a nice young lady I couldn't get mad at her. She greeted the children. They were happy to see her. Even they knew that if she meant harm, she couldn't do it.

"We're going to try and get the home visits cancelled."

"What about the could have been dad missed for the severance hearing?"

"I have good news."

She must have found the donor. What a relief.

"The judge didn't notice I missed someone and approved it anyway. We're going to go ahead and send everything to Sacramento. They probably won't notice, either."

Should I call the judge? Was that allowed? Should I wait and see what happened? I wouldn't risk my family's future on a bureaucrat feeling lucky. Maybe I'd call the county lawyers who appeared in court on behalf of Social Services. Did they know they'd misinformed a judge? I began to see social workers as one mercurial blob. I didn't want to do that and occasionally a dose of kindness pulled me back. On Craig's birthday, I picked him up from preschool to take him out for lunch and cherry pie. Social Services offices were on the floor above his school. Outside the building we met two polite and happy women who said to Craig, "We know you."

And to me: "We were in court for the severance hearing. We work for Social Services."

They were two of the smiling women on the wall.

"We're thrilled at what happened," they said. "We knew the family for many years."

"Thank you. We're having lots of fun." Maybe they could help me. "Do you know the kids' older sisters?" I asked.

"Yes."

"I spoke with Emine and we sent pictures, but now the phone is disconnected. We've seen Maribel a few times. She's great. If you ever hear of the older two girls in trouble, not of their own making, find me, I'll take them."

"We will."

Soon, Scott called to tell me he was assigned to my case. "I have good news. Sacramento approved the adoption."

They did it. The end was near. Until Social Services got it together, I was not 100 percent sure I'd get to keep my children. Now I was a Life-long Dad with whom you can talk about Important Things. I finally felt safe talking to the kids about how they came to be with me. I knew from conversations with Melinda that she and Social Services took this part seriously. They were open and honest, Melinda told me, about what happened to the kids and told them during Family Practice why they were no longer with their mother. I didn't have to go there, but to be sure, I double-checked at dinner.

"Do you remember talking to Melinda about why you are with me and where your mom is?"

"No," Javier said.

"We never talked to her about that," Adriana said.

*Oh, Melinda.*

I told them what Melinda told me she told them. "A few months ago, in the spring after you came to live with me, Social Services told your mom that you are with me."

"What did she say?" Adriana asked.

"She said that's good. Not all parents can take care of their kids. Sometimes they don't have a place to live or enough to eat."

"If she doesn't have any food," Javier said, "maybe we can go to a restaurant and buy some and take it to her."

"I don't think she lives here anymore," I said.

"Did she go to Mexico?" Adriana asked.

"I think that's where she is."

They were relieved. They didn't ask to see her or talk to her. They never have.

"Who will take care of us if you can't?" Adriana asked.

"I'll take care of you, but if something happens to me, Aunt Diana volunteered to take you to live with her in Colorado."

"Colorado? Yippee!" Adriana said.

"I don't want to go back to foster," Javier said.

"That will never happen."

"When I was in bad foster," he said, "they made me sit in the crib on the floor if I got in trouble. There were spiders and rats down there. Bad foster never cleaned."

"You're safe here."

I felt good addressing a difficult topic. I was inclined to keep difficulties quiet—I didn't speak to my mother or siblings about my father's death for nearly 20 years—but knowing Sacramento approved the paperwork boosted my confidence. I did it the right way and my children knew Daddy would talk about anything and they learned that sometimes even the robbers did something good, like Robin Hood.

Two days later, at a lunch meeting with Scott, he told me that Sacramento discovered that Melinda missed notifying someone. "The severance was flawed. We need to go back to court and then send the whole thing back to Sacramento again for approval. It will be another six months, maybe a year. Your foster care license has expired. You need to be fingerprinted again."

"This will be the third time I've been fingerprinted in two years. What do you do with the fingerprints?"

"I don't know where they go. But we'll keep this set forever. We'll always have this set."

I worried that Social Services would hover forever.

"Even after I've adopted the kids?"

"No. When it's over, it's over. I also need to update your income. You need to get a physical again, too. So do the kids."

"They had a physical a few months ago."

"I know, but we have to update it for the final paperwork."

"But with the flawed hearing we can't use this final paperwork until next year."

"That's true."

The meeting that began with the end in sight ended at the beginning. I called Nancy, the Director, the woman who told me to send my kids to therapy.

"Have you been following my case?"

"Not really."

"Your staff botched the severance hearing. After two tries and postponements, you failed to notify one of the candidates."

Nada.

"I have two questions for you: 1) Who is in charge of the legal issues in my case; and 2) What is the timeline for you folks to finish your work?"

"I'll get back to you."

The next day she called and left a voicemail telling me Scott was in charge of my case. I knew that. She didn't answer question #1, or question #2. I called her back.

"I have a few thoughts. One, I knew Scott was on the case. Scott is on the case because Scott is the only person in your division who does anything. He's on the case because I asked for him to be on the case after watching your people botch the case ever since we met over a year ago.

"Second, I called you to find out which lawyer is handling this case because I'd like to talk to the lawyer. One of us should, to find out whether the severance was botched, or not. I can't tell from here. One person says, 'botched', the other says, 'no one will notice'.

"I am not trying to get away with something, hoping a judge

or Sacramento doesn't notice. I want the legalities clean. In a perfect world"—I assumed she was still listening—"Social Services would either pick up the phone and call the County Counsel's office, or for all I know, walk across the hall to the County Counsel's office, but no. Here, I, who have no god-damned idea who is in the County Counsel's office, will call the office for you and ask them my question, for you.

"Third, I called to see what the timeline is for your people to finish your work. We've known each other for over a year. In that year your staff needed to do two things: 1) get into court and take care of the withdrawal of services hearing and 2) complete the severance stage without a miscue. It took you months to do the first. Here we are, in October, four months after the severance hearing took place, six months after it should have taken place. That's half a year and no one knows where we stand. I've been patient. If I worked like you my boss would have fired me twice. You have no idea what's happening.

"I'm tired of babysitting your department. I'm tired of listening to the pathetic stories of people in similar situations. We rely on you to do your jobs in a timely manner. Last week, after a year being an advocate for adopting kids, I had lunch with a local lawyer who used to work with you. I told her adopting kids is awesome, for sure, but I also found myself telling her about the dark side: you have to work with Social Services and it's a nasty, drawn out brawl. Worse, half the time Social Services doesn't even know they're in the fight. I need you to finish your business. I need you to finish your business and I want you to tell me the name of the lawyer handling my case."

"I'm not sure I have the name."

"I can go higher than you. You don't run the county, do you?"

"The lawyer is Carol Haines."

"And her number?"

She gave me the number.

"And my second question…?"

"When will we finish?"

"Right."

"Probably next year."

"It's October. When next year?"

"It'll probably take another year."

The attorney I had lunch with told me that the long sordid history my kids' mother had with Social Services was bad, but not the worst. The record, she said, was a family reported to Social Services nearly 100 times. She said Social Services and the County Counsel's office had an adversarial relationship and that Social Services workers had standing orders to never contact the County Counsel's office unless there was 100% certainty that the County Counsel's office would prevail in court.

That evening, I called the adopting mother of Jeremiah and Flora, Mimosa's other foster children.

"It's a nightmare," she said. "I'm waiting to complain because I don't want them to ruin our holidays. Now I'm going to move forward. I'm going to tell them we're tired of waiting. I have no idea when it will end. It's taken so long our license has expired. They told me we have to get fingerprinted again."

"Me, too."

"And I have to take the kids for check-ups again. We're doing that. And we have to take classes again. You'll have to go to the classes, too. Come to the ones we go to. They're at a church. The classes are only an hour long, but you get two hours credit."

Nice return, two for one, but how sad to make people go through that again because Social Services was slow. No one told me about more classes, anyway. If they did, I'd tell them I won't go. Maybe a Highway Patrol-Vuarnet showdown would get their attention.

"There was a young lady at the last class," she continued. "She was eager to learn from those of us with kids about when she could actually adopt a little girl recently placed with her. None of us had the heart to tell her the truth."

Scott soon sent an e-mail telling me I had to take eight hours of classes since my foster care license was expired. I didn't sign up. Instead, I called Carol Haines, the county attorney, and left her a voicemail saying that one person (the division director) had told me the severance miscue would be dealt with next year and another (Scott) had said it was done last month. I asked her to clarify.

I got fingerprinted again to prove I hadn't robbed a bank since the last time. I filled out the old forms again for Scott, writing "See Home Study" on most. I could have written "See Last Time," "See First Time," or "Enough Already," but "See Home Study" seemed more professional. The only difference between this time and last time was $280,000 in new life insurance.

Relief arrived—a competent lawyer.

"David, this is Carol Haines, I'm a county attorney. I apologize for not calling earlier. I've been out of town. I am very familiar with your case and I want to tell you everyone here is thrilled that you've taken these kids in. It's an inspiration to all of us."

"It's my pleasure."

"How are the children?"

"They're fine, thank you. Yesterday Craig said he doesn't like hard-boiled eggs because of the cheese inside. Javier won Student of the Month."

She laughed. "That's great. Congratulations."

"Thank you."

"A person, a possible father, who should have been notified of the severance hearing, was not notified. I've known this all along. I re-filed papers just for him months ago. I don't know why no one knows what's happening. I am going to go to court myself and look in the file. I'll go to court on Friday with a copy of the document in hand. If the court has no record, I'll re-file. I'll call Friday afternoon to let you know what happened."

Carol called on Friday.

"The special order was never signed by the judge because someone forgot to take it out of a folder and give it to her. I took it out of the folder and left it for the judge. When I get a signed copy, I'll send it to Scott."

Smart. Friendly. Helpful.

A few weeks later, eight months after the kids entered my home, I found three, three-ring-binders on the ground near the front door, each colorfully emblazoned with a child's name. A bright blue sticker on the front of each read BINDER TRAVELS WITH CHILD TO EACH PLACEMENT. The folders, called a Health and Education Passport, were a snapshot of their little lives. This was it! This was what I'd been waiting for! I'd learn about my children. Most adoptive parents got these binders before they met children so they'd have some idea what they were dealing with, but not in Santa Barbara County, no sir, not in one of the wealthiest communities in the world. Here, they were understaffed, so you got the binders long after you got the children.

I placed the binders in my bedroom without opening them. I didn't want to spoil the excitement. I'd see why the kids were taken from their mother. I'd see the impressions the other three, or however many, foster families had of my children and I'd see Javier's kindergarten report card. I'd learn what they did for fun when they were little and learn about their health issues, habits and more. What if there were photographs! I'll grab a root beer, sit in my wing chair, and read one at a time. I'll savor each word. What a weird way to learn about your children…I'd take the best pieces and make scrapbooks. I'd build them a bridge, like the one I dreamt about my father building when I was seven.

I put the children to bed. Each binder contained sections: Placement Info, Health and Dental, Develop/Social, and Educational Information. Develop/Social looked to be the most fun and the best place for photos. The Introduction listed two of the main reasons for the existence of the binders: 1) Provide school officials with vital information and, 2) A folder for medical records. A historical medical record also "prevents the unnecessary and cruel repetition of vaccinations."

It was like a sailing logbook, with forms foster parents filled out to chronicle the kids' lives. It was a terrific idea. But as I turned the pages of the first binder and then the second binder and then the last binder I found nothing but blank forms. There was no mention of my children except for their names on the cover and on papers I already had that someone crammed into the sleeve in the back. I had three blank binders I should have had a year earlier. Melinda must be back in town. I wondered if I should fill out the forms, but how stupid was that? I was the person the binders would help. I was the end; the last man.

A cynic would say "Wake up, David, someone is playing you. What surprises you more, things going right or things going wrong? Be honest. And, delays are not the worst thing. You get information about the children only after knocking on their door with a sledgehammer."

Soon Willie was in the kitchen to renew my license. It was the same house, nothing had changed except I had more towels and toys and next to Shrek's dining room chair there was a new vacuum cleaner with the hose permanently poised like a cobra in strike position. I liked Willie. He was the only Social Services employee I met in two years who made a point of meeting the children he dealt with. He sat down and asked me for the children's binders. I brought him three.

"Here you go. I got them last week."

"You got what last week?"

"The binders. Someone left them on the ground outside the front door."

"You're kidding me, right?"

"No."

"Who left them?"

"I have no idea."

"Did anyone call to tell you they'd leave these on the ground?"

"No."

"You were supposed to get these in February. Oh, well. At least the information helps you understand the kids better. And what they went through. Your kids went through a lot."

"The binders are blank."

"What do you mean?"

"There's nothing in them. Other than the sticker on the front, there's nothing about the kids."

He was surprised and embarrassed. Something went wrong.

"Well. It's a well-intentioned process."

"I suppose."

"If people would fill out these forms, it's a well-intentioned process."

"I agree."

"You should start filling them out."

"I thought of that. But I already know the kids; they're mine. Why would I fill out forms on my own kids?"

"Yeah. You're right. What difference does it make now?"

He went through the paperwork.

"Have you been attending classes?"

"No. Scott told me last week I could put off going to classes until as late as possible. I assume he's trying to finalize things."

"I don't know about that. I'll have to issue you a temporary license, with "B" level deficiencies. It expires in 45 days. You need eight hours of training. If you want to go this Saturday, there's a class in Solvang [a town

30 miles south]. You can get the eight hours done in one day."

"Do they have child care?"

"No. The next day-long class is in January. We do have Friday evening classes. They're held at a church. If you don't go to the all day class, you'll need to attend four of the night classes. Your first aid certifications are expired. You'll need to attend a two-day training course again."

I had no intention of taking any classes or spending two days breathing into the rubber mouth of a blown up doll. I wondered if Willie could tell I was not going to go.

"I'm surprised you have to be fingerprinted again," he said.

"It will be third time in 18 months."

"That's not right."

"I tell people I've been fingerprinted more than anyone they know who is not in jail."

We walked around the house he licensed before. He asked me if I had guns or a swimming pool. He asked to see where I kept drugs (all for the children) and we checked the smoke detectors, fire extinguisher, and first aid kit. He issued a temporary license with Level B deficiencies.

"I'll say one thing. Whenever I ask you about your children you get a huge smile on your face."

"I'm lucky; they're great kids."

"We almost never see kids go to a good home."

After Willie left I called Scott.

"Willie was at the house and issued me a temporary license because I haven't taken the classes. Do I have to go?"

"No. I'm going to take an important legal step soon. It will change your status to adoptive placement, meaning no more classes and no more home visits. We may be through in January."

A few days later Scott sent an e-mail telling me that on December 6, one day short of a year since I met the kids in Mimosa's foster home, he'd place the children in adoptive placement status. I would not have to attend classes. He asked to visit as required for his report. We still didn't have an adoption date, but it was closer. The Minutemen were running out of time. I was going to beat them.

Scott arrived at 6:30 p.m. I talked to the kids about shaking hands and we practiced making people feel welcome in our home. Scott got the full tour of the house, race car bed, Adriana's room, and the garage. He was professional and polite, he didn't try to buy our things, and the kids were happy to see him, especially after I reminded them that Scott helped me adopt them.

"I'll call you in about two weeks. We'll need to meet so you can sign paperwork, lots of it."

After his tour, we stood out front.

"Seeing the kids so happy makes me think about adopting some myself," he said. He already had two children who filled him with pride and he'd organized his life around them, like I was trying to do with mine. Once again, and for the last time, he said, "You need to tell me if anything goes wrong."

A few days later, Scott called to ask me the new legal names of the children.

"You can change their first names if you want."

"Why would I do that?"

"It'll make it harder for their family to find you."

I did not want the trauma of new first names. However, I didn't mind entertaining them with new middle names. I called my mother for recommendations. Her name was Diana, my sister, too, so I named Adriana, Adriana Diana Marin. I wanted to honor my father so I added Juan to Javier. He'd be Javier Juan Marin. And I wanted to honor my uncle, a surgeon. He had died recently and had a son, also a surgeon, of the same name, Pedro, so Craig Pedro Marin it was. With three names I honored five people. That night, I wrote the kids' new names on pieces of paper and taped them to their bedroom doors so they'd know who they were when they went to bed.

New names were a mile marker, a time to ponder our progress as a family. It felt great. I was now less worried about people interfering, trying to wreck us. I reflected on my battles with Social Services. Was I too combative, like the old days, paranoid, or overprotective? I needed to decompress and stop making every encounter with Social Services a movie scene.

A few days later a lady called.

"I'm with Social Services. Is this David Marin?"

"Yes."

"I work in the licensing division. I'm looking over some files and I just noticed that your foster care license has expired. Do you know your license is expired?'"

"I do."

It was Sandy, the social worker with the walnut fetish, calling from her second-floor office above Craig and Adriana's preschool. She pretended she didn't know me.

"You can't have kids without a license."

*Ouch.*

"Are you going to stop being a foster parent?"

"I'm adopting three children."

"But, according to the file, you were supposed to take classes and renew your first-aid training."

"I skipped that part."

"That's not allowed."

"I'm working with Scott, he knows everything. He's doing the paperwork now."

"So you're going to let your license lapse?"

"That's right. Talk to Scott if you have a problem."

"Well, I haven't read the whole file. I have no idea what's going on."

"You can talk to Scott if you have any questions."

"Are you saying that you won't be taking any more kids in to your house?"

"I'm adopting three kids; that's enough for now."

"I came to your house."

"I remember."

"I watch you and your kids out the window every day."

"That's nice."

"Scott's a great social worker," she said. She either had all she needed to cause the trouble she wanted, or she was giving up.

"I'm glad to be working with Scott."

"The kids look bigger now from when I first watched them."

"It's funny what happens when they get a plate of food each."

I never heard from her again.


A helpful accounting of my relationship with Social Services requires me to address what I could have done better. I could have attended the picnics so my children were more comfortable around them and they were more comfortable around me. Or hired an attorney and not wasted energy figuring out legalities. I might have joined an adoption support group or attended the license re-training sessions with the thoughtful woman who adopted the two other children from Mimosa's foster home. I don't remember her name. The fake name I gave her in this book could be her real name and I wouldn't know, and that's not good.

Instead, after learning what my children went through and watching them trying to escape memories, I thought of nothing more than leaving town. Sandy was right for the wrong reason.

Had I been more engaged, I'd realize that the challenges I had were not the worst case. I didn't travel to Russia and give $15,000 to a block-jawed scammer, and I didn't experience a backfired open adoption like a friend and his wife, forced to give their baby back after he spent months in their home.

I dealt with nine social workers and an attorney over my three year journey—half were good. Having spent many years in business, I knew a 50/50 split wasn't unusual. The dedicated half wanted to help people. I gained a lasting respect for them. They practiced in a noble profession.

The other half, at ground zero of domestic abuse, homelessness, hunger and murder,[30] could not give what was required. Time again I heard complaints about social workers being understaffed, but I've never seen an organization assert it was overstaffed. People work hard and that's the way it is. No one carried Scott's coat. Bev worked without complaint.

Adopting children is the thrill of a lifetime. The karma lasts longer. In addition to the emotions a parent feels being loved and trusted, the joy giving hope to children hiding in cabinets or eating pet food is better than a thousand Christmas mornings. Removing fear from children's lives, filling their bellies, holding their little hands, or watching them disappear inside a kindergarten door is pure joy.

Relying on social workers, like relying on doctors or accountants, is terrific if you have good ones. If not, it's important for adopters to know that they are free to request different social workers, or they can adopt from a different county, or state. All are possible. My adoption, predicted by Social Services management to take another year, or more, was completed in several months after Scott took over at my request. The struggles were frustrating, but the sweet smell of a two year old's hair and the gap-toothed smile of a little girl holding her first frog made it better.

30  From 2007 to 2009, the Los Angeles Times reports 68 deaths of children from families reported to Social Services before they died.

## 19. She Will Break Our Mouth

On February 23, days away from the one-year anniversary of my children moving into our home, I met Scott at the café next to preschool on the ground floor of the Social Services building. I looked for Sandy in the window.

The end was near for me and Scott. I wanted to finish and get out of Santa Maria. He'd purchased income property back home in Tennessee and wanted to move his family there. He stayed for now because his children liked their school, and he needed to care for his sick father.

He had more files. "It's all I have."

I took the one on top. With a glance I noticed that Adriana, who was four when we met, had been in four foster homes, not two like they told me. I saw the mother's name again.

"What are the rules about future contact between the kids and their mother?" I asked.

"Everything goes through us."

"How?"

"In order for there to be contact, both sides need to send us a letter requesting contact."

"Will you tell the kids if she has contacted you?"

"No."

"Vice versa?"

"No."

"So the time between one side contacting Social Services and the other side contacting Social Services can be twenty or thirty years."

"Right. If the mom writes the kids a letter, I'll leave instructions in your file to send the letter to you. You decide what to do with it."

My heart sank thinking he'd be gone.

"Have you heard anything from her?"

"Nothing."

I looked for the file chronicling the kids' final days with their mother. I wanted to know. My children will want to know.

"We are going to issue new birth certificates. We do this for this kind of adoption."

"How many kinds of adoptions are there?"

"Some adoptions are open, where the new parents know the old parents and the kids see the old parents sometimes, or a family member. This is the other kind. We're going to change the children's past so no one can find you."

"Like a witness protection program?"

"Something like that."

He had his reasons.

"How do you issue a new birth certificate? They have old facts."

"We change the facts. The parents' names will be erased. Your name will appear like you were there for the birth. We'll get their school records, medical records, everything we can find. It will be like they never existed as their old selves."

I wondered about Shrek's aquarium ID card.

Scott showed me the three official Adoption Orders the judge and I would sign on adoction day. There were papers that changed peoples' lives, like diplomas, deeds, or peace prizes, but each was a reward for a job well done. Mine were a gift for a job to do and I did it with joy, because whatever I gave them they returned three times.

Each Order said the age of the child was three. "Oh," Scott said. "I'll have to fix that."

I signed a few documents. Scott gave me the rest of the files. Adriana's was three inches thick, crammed with medical records about her two-week stay in the hospital after she was born. Javier and Craig had next to nothing in theirs.

"There isn't much here."

"Most of the family files are property of the District Attorney. They're criminal files. You'll never get access to those."

I didn't complain. I wasn't adopting the parents. All I needed to know about them I figured out at the severance hearing they skipped. Finally, a year and a half after first asking, Scott gave me two Special Reports written by Social Services covering the days when my children's mother lost them for good. They were too long to read with Scott sitting there.

"It's possible their mother was a prostitute, for a while. Or, not."

"That might have mattered before I met the kids. It doesn't matter now."

"You need to pay $60 for a court filing fee, $20 per kid."

I pulled $60 from my pocket.

"I can't take cash. We prefer a check."

That night I sent the check in a card thanking Scott for his hard work—a modest gesture. Scott did his job. I had a license; the children needed a home; he did the math. But his effort was bigger than that. What did he endure that led him to warn me repeatedly that he was under pressure, threatened almost, saying 'people think I'm crazy'? He fought resistance; trapped in the bureaucracy I railed against—the overworked and understaffed.

A Siberian tiger that appeared from nowhere left 500 lb. footprints in the hills southeast of Santa Barbara. The children were intrigued, so I gave them updates. There was no point telling them I had signed adoption papers: they thought I'd already adocted them. The tiger was more compelling. I had a stupid notion that people would leave the tiger alone. Send a female tiger in after him and reimburse farmers $900, 30 times a year, for lost cattle if the farmer provided documentation, like a ransom note. It didn't occur to me that I might have to explain an alternative.

"The tiger," I said.

"What happened?" Adriana asked. "Did they catch it?"

"He's dead. He was shot by rangers."

"Why did they kill it?" Adriana was sad.

"He was near a school."

"Was he killed near Taylor?" That was her school.

"No, sweetie, it was killed down past Santa Barbara."

"They shouldn't kill it. It's one of God's animals."

"How do you know it's dead?" Javier asked.

"I read the news."

"Who tells the news?" he asked.

"People go to where things happen and they write about it in the newspaper, like where I work."

"Newspapers are smart," Adriana said.

"I'm smart," Craig added.

After the kids went to bed, I reviewed the files. In August 2003, two months before Scott called me about five children, Social Services finally put it together, writing a comprehensive report about the family and their troubles. It began with a list of the children's names and ages: 1, 4, 6, 9 and 10. It stated the reason for the August hearing: On July 22, 2003, the police found the mother drunk at home. The kids were gone. The report writer said the mother had not attempted to find them, didn't know where they were, and that the mother's continued substance abuse negatively affected her ability to take care of the kids. The report briefly recapped the ten year history of the family's contacts with Social Services and noted that the criminal records of the alleged fathers were "unavailable at this time." Like Scott said.

An adult witness in the July 22 report, a relative, told police the mother was a good person and that to cope with the loneliness of not living in Santa Barbara, 70 miles south of Santa Maria, she drove to Paso Robles, 60 miles north of Santa Maria, and got drunk. The mother called the relative when the police were at the mother's house and asked her to come from Santa Barbara to watch the children while she dealt with the officers.

The social workers interviewed the kids. Javier was first, taken from his school classroom. He said his mother was drunk on July 22, the day police arrived, because she almost fell down in the kitchen. He said he felt sad when she was drunk and that he and his siblings prayed for their mother to stop drinking. The older sisters were interviewed at home. They said their mother was drunk on beer and brandy and that they called a friend to come over and help them because they were scared. Adriana and Craig were not interviewed because they were too young.

The social worker interviewed their mother in the home and wrote that "the mother immediately explained to the social worker that she was remorseful and felt bad that she had drank again." The mother told the social worker she had three beers. She said she called the police because an adult the kids called "a church friend" came to her home and told her she was taking the kids. The mom said she had not been drunk in months and that she was willing to cooperate with services offered to her and that she did not want to lose her kids. In the summary recommendation, the social worker said it was clear the children have been, and were now at risk.

The door was closing.

It was clear, the worker wrote, that the mother loved her children, but her continued substance abuse put her children at risk of physical or emotional harm. The mother was told in March 2003 that the children could be removed from her if she continued to abuse alcohol. The report said the mother had complied with previous services offered to her, including counseling, parenting classes, and drug and alcohol treatment. The worker wrote that the mother was cooperative and agreed to comply with any new services offered so that she could have the children remain in her home.

The door was opening.

This report, the final chapter, I presumed, in the family's long saga, instead ended with this: "The Child Welfare Service Worker recommends that the children remain in the home while the mother participates in outpatient substance abuse treatment."

It was a colossal failure; a private-sector career ender; a Santa Barbara tsunami. Six weeks later, according to the next report, the mother was arrested for beating our children. A small note in the second report asked the court to please dismiss the first report. It wasn't easy being in Social Services where they were understaffed.

Written by three social workers not associated with the first report, the second report chronicled the last days in chilling detail. This one would hurt me. I recalled interrupting an armed robbery at a pharmacy years earlier and feeling the warm steel circle of a handgun pressed to my temple. Worried the robber might shoot me if he thought I could identify him, I repeatedly told myself, "This is real, don't look at him; this is real, don't look at him." I went into emotional hibernation. This would be a good time for that.

The police were called to the home the day before the report was written. "On October 2, 2003, the child, Emine, stated to the Child Welfare Worker that her mother hit her twice across her back with a belt, slammed her face against a metal bed frame, and pulled out her hair."

Murray, the day I took my children from Mimosa's foster home: "This is such a disappointment."

Emine said her mother was drunk and hit her for calling her father and telling him that her mother had been drinking. "The undersigned observed that the child had two sets of linear bruises two inches apart and six inches long which resembled belt marks, bruising around her right eye, and a bump on the back of her head. The mother was arrested and charged with inflicting corporal injury to a child and failure of county probation for willful cruelty to a child. The mother's anger problems and substance abuse have resulted in the abuse and neglect of the children." The report didn't say who called the police. Was it Emine?

"On October 2, 2003 the child, Emine, stated to the undersigned worker that her mother had hit Adriana with a belt."

Just like the pharmacy. A warm steel circle. Social Services on the trigger....

"The undersigned observed that Adriana had two linear bruises two inches apart and six inches long, which resembled a belt mark on her right thigh. When the undersigned asked Adriana about the bruises she stated that her mother hits her when she soils her pants."

The two older kids were quoted:

Nine-year-old Emine: "Mom always tells us that if we tell someone the truth she will break our mouth."

Seven-year-old Maribel: "If we said anything to anyone she would hit us very bad and she didn't care if she went to jail."

Emine: "She pulled my hair so hard I saw a lot of hair in her hand when she let go."

Six-year-old Javier was interviewed, too. He neither saw nor heard a thing. When asked where he was when the police were at his house the night before he said he didn't know or that maybe he was sleeping. Ricochet. He said his mom did not threaten him or tell him what to tell Social Services. Maribel, on the other hand, said their mother was drunk and hit Emine twice with a belt. She said her mother kept beer in her bedroom and had been drinking for three days. The writer of the first

217

report said the mother consumed three beers.

Emine provided greater detail. She said mom drank all the time and that she, Emine, took her siblings into her bedroom and, "they sleep so mom won't hit them."

Baby Craig…sealed in his chamber, coated in anechoic tiles.

Emine said her mother hit Maribel the most but that Maribel hid the bruises because she loved her mom, "and she thinks that she deserved to get hit." Emine said their mother took them to stores and told them to steal things.

Then the mother was interviewed. She said she called Social Services on September 29 to tell them she would miss a substance abuse class because her car broke down in Santa Barbara. The social worker noted that throughout the day of October 1—the day the mother was beating the children—the mother called the social worker and said everything was fine and that they, "did not need anything."

The mother said problems began when ten-year-old Emine tried to hit her and that she did hit Emine with a belt, but could not recall hitting "the eye or pulling her hair." The mother said that she saw the belt marks on Adriana's leg, but explained that the other kids must have seen her hit Emine and "were copying her in play." The mother denied drinking and said this was the first time she'd ever hit her kids.

Social Services interviewed Angela, the long-lost aunt Scott told me wanted to take the kids. She said the police were in the home on September 27 because the mother was being beaten by Craig's father. The mother called Angela and asked for help, so Angela drove from Santa Barbara and found the children hiding and the mother in the shower. Angela searched the house and found a 24 pack of Bud Light in a diaper bag in the mother's bedroom closet. She left the house, Angela said, to go to school and when she returned the mother was drunk and there was a burning pot of chicken in the kitchen. The mother said she didn't remember cooking a chicken and blamed Emine. Angela asked her about drug abuse, drug testing, and classes, and said the mother was often drunk when she took drug tests and that if she tested positive, counselors would "cover for her" and tell Social Services she tested negative.

Murray: "We really tried to work with the mother."

The mother said she disguised her breath with gum or by wearing perfume.

The next day Angela called the social worker and said the mother had been drinking the night before and that she did hit Emine with a belt. She said Emine's father in Santa Barbara called the police after Emine called him to tell him her mother was beating her. Emine also called Angela. She arrived from Santa Barbara, 70 miles away, at the same time the police arrived from seven blocks away. Angela said she asked the police to check Emine's back where her mother hit her with a belt, but that the officer declined because he was not called out "for that reason."

Adriana: Look, it's the police. It's okay...we can get away.

The next day, Angela called Social Services and said she'd like the children to live with her and that she'd be willing to move to a larger apartment. But, the report stated, the children have not been placed with her "due to Angela having a criminal history including inflicting injury upon a child seven months earlier." The report said that Angela was now applying for "an evaluation of criminal exemption."

We'd meet soon.

Somewhere in there my file landed on Scott's desk. He called me at work and said he had five kids that needed a place to live. I regret saying, "No."

A week after the report, Scott called Maribel's dad in Santa Barbara. He agreed to take her. After her arrest and the children were gone, the mother called a social worker and admitted drinking a beer. She said she was enrolling in an Alcoholics Anonymous group and an Anger Management class in jail. But it was too late. Two weeks later, Scott sent Emine to her father in Nevada. The report ended with a brief note that the adoptions worker, Scott, "has identified a prospective adoptive placement for Adriana (Brianna), Javier, and Craig (Chris) and was arranging a meeting between the children and the prospective adoptive family."

I was that family.

## 20. Smoke Under the Door

In February we returned to the Milpas Street McDonald's in Santa Barbara so Maribel could join us on Javier's birthday. Meeting at the same spot made me nervous. I usually stopped at the nearby gas station after the drive from Santa Maria to focus and review fight or flight options. I wondered if the mother was nearby, hanging out with the addicts and alcoholics. I could stand next to her and not know it. If the old regime wanted my children they were unlikely to offer me a glass of Chablis first, so I exercised caution. I never woke the children until we were safe, and I prepared to speed away if something didn't seem right. When I entered the McDonald's parking lot, I scanned for strangers with a bottle or a gun. I looked for a slight tug on a sleeve, heads turning our way, or cars parked, like mine would be soon, with the front pointed towards the exit.

After we got Maribel, and her family said goodbye, several children needed to go potty. Inside, a lady with a little boy recognized Adriana.

"Wow!" she said, and then, "Javier!" and "Craig!"

The kids didn't recognize her. They hadn't recognized their sister either.

"We're part of the family," she said. "I heard about you. My son used to play with Craig."

"Do you remember me?" she asked Adriana.

"No."

"We're here to see Maribel," I said.

"What's your name?"

"David."

"It's great to see the kids. They look so healthy."

"Thank you." My radar detector told me it was time to go.

"Look," she said. "I want to give you a phone number. It's the kids' grandmother. Her name is Lagrima."

Then she whispered, "Thank you. Thank you for taking the kids. We couldn't do it."

None of the people who knew them could take even one.

Outside, I asked Javier if he knew the lady.

"No."

I wondered if she was the aunt with the child abuse conviction who wanted the children.

"Do you know her, Maribel?" I asked.

"I've never seen her before."

"Do you know the grandma?" I asked. Grandmas were good, but was she the mother of the mom, or one of the fathers?

"I don't know her," Maribel said.

As we passed an outdoor garbage bin I wadded up the paper with the phone number. There was a breeze so I tossed it high and right and made the shot. I felt bad afterwards, but either the kids didn't know the lady, or worse, they knew her but wanted me to think otherwise. I was unsure why they would mislead me, but it gave me no reason to call and get together.

The next day, I took the children to Mimosa's to play with her girls so I could golf. After I picked them up and paid her, Mimosa walked to my car door and gestured for me to roll down my window. With Javier translating, she told me that while I was gone a Spanish speaking woman called and asked Mimosa if "David Marin" was there.

"Ask her what she said," I told Javier.

"She says she said you weren't here."

I looked in my rearview mirror.

"Ask her what the lady wanted."

"She asked Mimosa to call you and tell you to bring us here."

The caller didn't know the kids were already there. I looked up the street and down.

"Ask Mimosa what she told the lady."

"She says she said no, she wouldn't call you."

"Then what happened?"

"The lady wanted your phone number."

I started the engine.

"Did Mimosa give it to her?"

"She says no."

Santa Maria was shrinking. I called Scott.

"A woman called Mimosa's and asked her to tell me to bring the kids over."

"That's not good."

"The kids were there. I was playing golf."

"Maybe if it's the mother you can meet her."

"What?"

"And tell her about the kids. Show her pictures. Hey, you never know."

What the hell? He told me not to contact the old regime until their rights were severed and to use his address so they couldn't find me and he asked me if I wanted to change my children's first names to go deeper undercover. Now he imagined their mother and I might enjoy connecting and seeing a movie?

"Maybe if it's the mother she's here in violation of a court order and should be arrested, right?"

"Well, she would be arrested if she did anything to get arrested."

"But doesn't the fact that she is here make her subject to arrest? The order says go away and don't come back. Why wouldn't she be arrested?"

"I suppose she would, if someone told the police."

"Why wouldn't you tell the police?"

"Well, I guess I would."

"Well, if her intention is to visit and get pictures, that's one thing, although I am reluctant to discuss even that. What if she wants to hide the kids in the trunk and drive them over the border?"

"She may just want to see the kids."

"The last time she saw the kids she slammed Emine's face against a bedpost. I think the next best step is to see if it was her. Could you ask Willie or Melinda to call Mimosa and see what happened? Someone who speaks Spanish needs to call."

"We can do that. Do you know of anyone else who may have called Mimosa?"

"No."

"I'll check it out," he said. "I'll let you know."

"Thanks. I'll be curious. Are we all set for the adoption?"

"We are, but the date was postponed. It's March 7th."

"I haven't figured out what to tell the kids. They thought they were adopted a year ago."

"Just tell them this is the final step."

"The truth, you mean?"

"Right. You know, the older two kids are old enough that the judge may ask them if they want to be adopted. Wouldn't it be funny if one of the kids said they didn't want to be adopted? There would be some embarrassed adults there."

"We'll be fine."

"I'll have someone call Mimosa and I'll call you."

At home that night I read an e-mail from Scott. A Spanish speaking lady from Social Services called Mimosa. Mimosa told her the caller asked for Davey Marin. The caller wanted to know if I was there or ever lived there. Scott said Mimosa said nothing.

My showing the children that their sister didn't disappear after the robbers took her brought us too close to the old regime. McDonald's was unnerving. Now their mother wafted in like smoke under the door. They could change my children's identities, rub their fingerprints off with 320 grit sand paper and give me a new name—it wouldn't change this: Santa Maria had one white guy with three brown ducklings in tow. Adoption day would be a singular and momentous event. It would also be the first day we could legally leave town. Prior to the stranger calling Mimosa, she used to call us once a month to say hello. After the stranger those calls stopped. We never saw her again. Maybe Mimosa stopped calling so she could tell the truth if she was harassed: "I don't know where they are and I have not talked to them." She was a sweet old lady doing her best with no income I could see outside of payments for several foster children; an insufficient sum.[31]

If their mother was sober and thoughtful and she wanted the kids healthy and happy, perhaps we could meet and she could see them – from 25 yards away. On the other hand, if she was like most addicts and stood holding a sign on the corner, or worse, on our porch, I would not allow it. How would my children cope? I took them away from that. If I needed three tanks of gas to get away and a new job in a new town where people didn't call when I was playing golf then that's what I'd do.

I'm sorry when any mother loses her children, but I had no feelings towards their mother. I didn't wonder what she thought. I wasn't curious if she taught Javier to play marbles before, or after, she made him beg and steal. I thought about the 50% of foster children of mothers with a criminal record having their own record before they were 18 years old.[32] I thought about her tip-toeing past Adriana in the maternity ward, telling the nurse she'd be right back; or Craig in his chamber; or Javier hiding

31  In 2010, the 9th Circuit U.S. Court of Appeals ruled that California Department of Social Services payments to foster care parents at just 80% of the cost to raise foster children violated the Child Welfare Act. The court ordered the state to reimburse foster homes for the true cost. No worries. At the time of the ruling, California was planning on changing the payments, from 80% to 70%.

32  Crowe. 1974. 50% is ten times higher than average.

in cabinets, clutching Kitty, clenching his teeth to make it all go away. And I thought about Maribel not recognizing her siblings, and Emine, the battered fifth grader I never met, ignored by Social Services when she asked for help, teaching the children to pray while pretending to sleep.

In the long run I don't wish the mother harm; I wish her well. My children wish her well. That's four people wishing, and that's enough. As of this writing, none of the children have heard from her in seven years. She may be in jail. She may dead. She may be around.

If you know, keep it to yourself.

## 21. Color in Their Lives

After a postponement Scott blamed on the length of singer Michael Jackson's Santa Maria trial, adoption day was slated for March 31st, three years after I first called Alameda County Social Services. The end was near. I wouldn't have to worry anymore about The Firm, Melinda, Murray, Nancy, Sandy, their mother, the Minutemen, or Florida's Governor Jeb Bush. Mr. Bush was in court defending[33] his state's 1977 law prohibiting gays from adopting because Florida wanted a mother and a father. But what about singles wanting to adopt? And what did Mr. Bush think about single women having biological children on their own?

I invited Carmen to join us for breakfast and court. We'd reconnected after breaking up so she could spend more time with her teenage daughter and we often met at home on the sly for "lunch." We were growing closer again now. She spent the night. I put her name on the emergency notification card at preschool. Before bedtime, she sang Spanish songs to the children and at the bowling alley, when I entered Daddy and Mommy on the video display, she squirmed in delight even more than the kids. She was a wonderful and beautiful companion, full of love for life. Plus, we had the same brand of vacuum cleaner and that meant something, she said. At Morro Bay, after Craig got his head stuck in between wrought iron rails above a 500 pound sea lion circling below, Carmen pulled him out and held him when he cried. She was too good to be true, but she was. She had the kids for overnights and she taught me how to cook better and she said, "I love you" often and I said it back. I called her during the day and asked her what she was wearing, and when

33  In 2010, Florida became the last state to allow gays to adopt when it declined to appeal a ruling by the 3rd District Court of Appeal that found the Florida ban an unconstitutional violation of the equal protection rights of the children and potential parents.

she told me I said, "I mean underneath that."

I knew Scott was leaving Santa Maria. Carmen talked about moving back to New Orleans because life was better there for her daughter, and her ex could help. Carmen and Scott did not know each other. I was the only one who knew all three of us might be gone by August. The support structure Bev told me to build was about to collapse.

The afternoon before the adoption, I picked up Javier and Adriana at the YMCA, but I didn't say anything because I knew court would frighten them. Nearing the final turn to Craig's preschool I rationalized being a coward as waiting so Craig could hear me explain what was going to happen, like a three-year-old would appreciate the legalities. At preschool, Adriana and Javier asked to go inside to visit. Adriana, the graduate, rushed inside. On the sidewalk outside a lady passed me and Javier.

"How are the kids?" she said, smiling.

"Good."

"Is everything going okay?"

"We're fine, thank you." I presumed she was a social worker. "The final adoption is tomorrow."

"Oh my gosh, that's great. How long has it been?"

"About a year and a half."

"Oh. Well, congratulations," she said, shaking my hand. She spotted Javier, who turned back to watch us. "Congratulations," she yelled. Oops. Javier wrinkled his nose, wondering.

"He doesn't know," I told her, soft enough so Javier couldn't hear me. "I told the kids when they came into my house over a year ago that I was adopting them then."

"Oh."

"It's okay. I'll tell them later. Thanks for your kind words."

In the car I told the children. "We're going to court tomorrow so the adoption can be finalized. We're going to talk to a judge."

"I don't want to go to court," Adriana said.

"Scott will be there. And Carmen. I'm not going to work. When we're done we'll go to Morro Bay and feed the seals that bark for fish. Then we'll ride in a real submarine." A clever diversion.

"What's going to happen?" Adriana asked.

"Well, a judge will be there. He may ask you if you want to be adopted."

The car burst with silence. A Wizard of Oz twister picked us up, spun us around, and set us down in the place where children realize their father tricked them. We'd lived together for over a year with them knowing they'd been adopted. Now they wondered. But the alternative, when Adriana asked me in Toys R Us if I was going to adoct them, was to answer maybe, or someday. Then I could have updated them about missed hearings, botched court dates, and Sandy watching us from the window. I could have offered Adriana 30 percent of the bedroom furniture money, or 50 percent. I could have told the truth.

"What will you say, Javier, when the judge asks you if you want to be adopted?"

"Yes."

"How about 'yes, your honor?'" I suggested.

"Yes. Your honor." He was scared. His voice trembled like he spoke underwater.

"How about you, princess, can you say it?"

"Yes," she said, in whisper. "Yes, your manners."

"Yes, your honor, you mean."

"Yes, your honor."

"What about me?" Craig asked.

"Oh, I'm sorry. What do you say Craig?"

"Yes."

"Yes, your honor," I said.

"Yes."

"Yes, your honor."

"Yes."

After baths, while the boys were allegedly using Q-tips, Adriana climbed onto my lap as I watched the TV news.

"And Daddy?"

"Yes, love."

"Tomorrow, are they going to take you from us?"

"No, sweetie. That will never happen."

"What if the man, the man who helped us…"

"Scott."

"What if Scott tries to take us away and put us in another foster?"

"That's not going to happen."

"What if they try to take you?"

"They can't take me, princess, I'm too big. We're a family now. I'm going to take you to first grade and second grade and third grade and fourth grade and fifth grade and sixth grade and seventh grade and eighth grade and high school."

She nestled in tight. El amor.

"Then I'll take you to college and then you'll find a boyfriend and get married and have a baby and we'll live next to each other."

"Can I marry you?" She wore a little Made in China ring she called our wedding ring.

"No, princess, you're too little. If you're scared tomorrow just hold my hand, everything will be okay."

It rained in the morning. Still in her pajamas, Adriana asked me again if they'd take me away. I told her not to worry and that I'd be next to her holding her hand. We met Carmen for breakfast. I was nervous, but there was nothing left to do.

It was still raining when we arrived at the courtroom. I had one umbrella for five people. Carmen held Craig. I held the umbrella over their heads as we walked to the wrong building. The correct building was half a block away. Back in the car, we started over. This time we knew we were in the right place because people overflowed the small lobby. We sat in three seats. Scott was not there. I wondered if I'd made a mistake. A lady I did not know welcomed us.

"Scott will be here shortly," she said.

Scott arrived wearing a suit. His long hair was long gone.

"I forgot your files. But it's okay. If the judge doesn't give you the adoption papers today, call me in a week because it should be mailed by then."

The children were frightened. They didn't speak. They didn't play or ask for a snack. Javier looked at the floor. Adriana stared at the door like she was waiting for someone she knew. A group of ten people, including two babies, went in first. There was an adoption in there because Scott went in with them. After twenty minutes they came out in tears, happy tears. I wondered if I'd cry. Then it was our turn. We entered the same small judge's chambers Carmen and I attended when the children's parents lost their rights, but this time there were no women along the wall. There was a judge, a young handsome Hispanic; a court reporter; the judge's assistant; and a bailiff in case we tried to steal their articles. Scott told me to sit at a large table 15 feet in front of the judge. There was a microphone chin high. Carmen sat directly behind me with Craig on her lap. Adriana was on her right and Javier next to Adriana, by the door, his specialty. I turned to the children and made faces to ease their fear. Adriana smiled. We'd be okay.

"Are you ready?" the judge asked me.

"I am."

"Who do we have here?"

"Well, this is Javier. In the middle is Adriana and this is Craig and this is Carmen."

"How do you do?" the judge asked.

"Good," Javier responded.

Carmen smiled and nodded.

"Let's get started," the judge said to Scott. Scott rose. He made an opening statement telling the court reporter and the judge why we were there.

"I'd like to ask you some questions," the judge said to me. "Would you mind if I have you sworn in?"

"Not at all." I stood and raised my right hand.

Like the judge in the severance hearing this one saw good. He spoke about responsibility and life-long commitment.

"Are you ready to finalize the adoption?"

"I am."

"No regrets?"

"None. We're ready. We've been a family since the kids came into my house and we're a family now."

"That's good. For the record, we are here to finalize the adoption petition for Javier Fuentes, Adriana Fuentes, and Craig Rullan. I'd like to ask the kids some questions. I need them to be sworn in."

I turned and told the children to stand. The assistant asked the kids to raise their right hands. Javier and Adriana got it. Craig stood and watched. The assistant read the same swear-in statement she read to me. The kids said, "Okay," and sat down, Craig back on Carmen's lap.

"Hi," the judge said to the kids.

I turned around. Javier and Adriana were afraid. I made more faces.

"Can you tell me your names?" he asked.

"Javier Marin."

"Adriana Marin."

"Craig Marin."

They hit a triple. I'd never been so proud and grateful in my life.

"Do you know why you're here?"

They mumbled.

"We're here for the adoption," the judge said.

"Who is that man sitting there?" he asked, pointing to me.

"He's our dad," said Adriana. My eyes moistened.

"Do you want to be adopted, Javier?"

"Yes."

"Do you want to be adopted, Adriana?"

"Yes."

"Do you want to be adopted, Craig?"

"Yes."

"All of this is fun," he said, "but there is a bad side to adoption."

I turned to the children.

"The bad side is that when Daddy gets old, you have to take care of him. An adoption lasts forever. When your Daddy gets old, instead of him taking care of you, you have to take care of him. Javier, will you take care of your dad when he gets old?"

"Yes."

"Adriana, will you take care of your dad when he gets old?" Adriana sat high and proud, set to answer when the bailiff said, "I bet she takes care of him now." Everyone laughed.

"Adriana. Will you take care of your dad?"

"Yeth," she said. It was an ideal retirement plan. Three people, under oath, with witnesses.

"Mr. Marin, I am going to ask you to sign the adoption petition in front of me. Or, three adoption petitions in this case." He handed them to the bailiff; she passed them to me, along with a pen. I signed each one.

"Let the record show that Mr. Marin signed the adoption petitions in front of me. I am reading the petitions and his signature. Now, and this is the exciting part, I am going to sign the adoption petitions."

"Thank you," I said.

"This is a great thing you are doing," he said. "You should write an article for Readers Digest. There are people out there who would try to save their sperm or hire a surrogate mother, but you didn't do that. You could have incubated a woman."

I hadn't thought of sitting on a woman until she hatched.

"But you went out and found kids who needed a home, and I am impressed with that."

"Thank you. My kids have added depth and meaning to my life."

My walk through the desert was over.

"There is a stigma attached to adoption," he said. "This court date, for example, is confidential and secret and it shouldn't be. To protect the kids, sure, but adoptions like this should be open and celebrated."

"When I told people at work I was adopting children, a few people told me, all quietly and in confidence, that they were adopted or had adopted their kids. It's something people try to hide."

"It shouldn't be that way, it's a good thing."

"I've become an advocate of adoption. I haven't met anyone who, upon hearing that I've adopted three kids says, 'Hey! I want to try that!' but I have helped a few people get started."

"That's good. Well, we're finished here."

"I'd like to do something before we go," I said.

"Okay," he allowed.

"I don't know how I could have pulled this off," I said, as I removed an engraved black marble column from a box, "without Scott's help. So I have something for him and I'd like to read it for the court."

"Be my guest."

Scott Reeves
The World's Greatest Social Worker
Thanks for Everything
David Marin
Javier Marin
Adriana Marin
Craig Marin
April 2005
Santa Maria, California

I turned to a stunned Scott, gave it to him and shook his hand.

"That deserves a hug," the assistant said. I gave Scott a hug and said thank you.

The kids were up and leaving when the bailiff pulled out a basket of candy. They asked me if they could have some.

"Two each," I said. "You can put it in your pockets."

I leaned down to the kids and told them to tell the judge, "Thank you, your honor." Like a chorus of cicadas, all three said "Thank you, your honor."

I turned to him and said, "Thank you, sir" and left. It was over. The rain stopped. Outside, a group of people I didn't know congratulated us. We got in the car and took Carmen to hers. She had a doctor's appointment. I thanked her for coming. Our experience was better because she was there.

The kids and I drove north on Highway 101 to Morro Bay to visit the aquarium and feed sardine fragments to seals in foster care. You couldn't buy the fragments from the clerk standing in front of you next to the fragments. You had to walk past her, through a door, and turn around and stand at the window behind her. Doing it this way they avoided people buying sardine fragments for personal use.

Four adopted seals lived in three tanks separated by chain link fencing. If the seals wanted to change tanks, they jumped through basketball size holes above the waterline. All it took was a push of their tails, or rear parts. A seal jumped and splashed us. After the feeding and barking we looked at the science room. We saw a red octopus longer than Adriana, a horseshoe crab and three moray eels. We walked past a display case with a small, stuffed, great white shark and two stuffed little brown sea otters.

"Are they alive?" Adriana asked.

"They were. People keep them here so we can learn about them."

"Why are their eyes open?" she asked.

"That's how they lived."

We held hands on the empty street. I was comfortably numb. No one rushed up and said, "Your wife must be really, really dark." Social workers weren't spying on us or trying to buy our things. Not a single Highway Patrol officer lied to us and we weren't selling Chiclets. We were different from other families, but not by much and not for long. Single parent households—I'm not an advocate—have increased from 10% in 1965 (primarily due to divorce) to 27% today.[34] Depending on immigration levels (legal and illegal) the percentage of Hispanics (and Asians) is expected to double as the U.S. population zooms from 310 million in 2010 to nearly 439 million by 2050.

The only group in danger of shrinking—not as a percentage, that's happening now—but in total, are non-Hispanic whites, like in Russia.

The percentage of mixed race/ethnic marriages (like my mother and father) has increased from 0.4% in 1960 (against the law in 41 states and the Census counted Hispanics as white) to 6.8% in 1980 (counting

---

34  Custodial Mothers and Fathers and Their Child Support: 2007. U.S. Census Bureau, 2009. I'd love to be married and believe researchers like McLanahan and Sandefur (1994) who found that children with two parents did better in school, went to college more often, and earned more as adults. Those findings could be tied to household income rather that marital status, but the result is the same.

Hispanics) to 14.6% in 2008, one in seven. The Supreme Court gave a boost in 1967, forbidding the illegality of mixed marriages in Virginia and the 15 other states where it was still outlawed.

The doubling of mixed marriages from 1980 to 2008 will double the number of mixed children. That's a lot of Colored People.

We were the new All-American family—multi-ethnic parent(s) raising multi-ethnic children—all natural born. Like all minorities, however, we prefer not to be judged by looks or pedigree like entries in the Westminster Dog Show. The 2010 census form was a comedy of racial/ethnic/part racial/part Tongan questions. I wanted to note that two-year-old Craig looked like an Eskimo but there was no place for that. Who cares and what's a Tongan[35] and what does that have to do with contributing something to society, doing more good than harm?

So, two recommendations: First, eliminate ethnicity questions from the census and our lives and if you're interested in improving the economic conditions of fellow citizens focus on… economic conditions. Second, when people ask where you were born, say "Savannah, Georgia." It works for me.

The new All-American families are the best hope for melding segments of society cracked by fear, making whole something broken. It's a decades old wave spreading from home to neighborhood to state and country, like a sonic boom. Me and my three are for that.

After lunch we found the yellow submarine and put on life jackets. The children's had a half moon shaped handle on top for yanking. We rode to an area the captain called the "secret spot," and we went down the steps below the waterline to look through acrylic walls. We saw a school of fish. Suddenly, we heard the captain yell "Octopus!" and there it

---

35  They come from a chain of Pacific Islands and have the highest obesity rate in the world.

was, among the fish. It went up and down and up and down. I wondered why the octopus moved like that instead of pushing itself forward like the octopi on National Geographic channel and then I wondered how a captain could see an octopus underwater and I looked up the hatch to see him holding a string that went into the water. His arm moved up and down. It wasn't easy being a captain, especially if you were understaffed.

On the way home we stopped at Mervyns and bought 14 pairs of little pants without anyone's help. When I first got the children, I recruited a young cashier to help Adriana while I shopped for the boys. We drove to Target and I bought them their fifth pair of shoes in 13 months. At Marie Callender's we got four pieces of pie and four glasses of milk for $28, including the tip.

"You could have bought an entire pie cheaper than that," my sister Joy told me over the phone that night.

At home the kids tried on their new clothes and we had dinner. We were tired. I asked them to tell me their favorite part of the day.

"I liked it when the seal jumped in the water and splashed us," Javier said.

"What about you, Craig?"

"I liked it when the seal jumped in the water and splashed us, and when the lady gave us candy."

"What about you, Adriana?"

She paused and smiled. "I liked it all. It was a good day."

That night, I went to sleep thinking I could do anything in the world. My children had color in their lives and music and poetry and they went outside when they wanted and they had a chance, more than before.

## 22. Where We Were

Scott sent me to the Social Security office to change the children's names on their cards. The man looked at Javier and Adriana's last name, Fuentes, and said a lot of "them" were changing their names.

"Them? What does that mean? Do you mean because of Fuentes, the cocaine dealer?" Mexican Amado Fuentes was renowned for transporting drugs in his 27 private 727 airliners. I'd read about him years earlier when he died during plastic surgery to alter his face.

"Didn't Social Services say anything?"

"No."

"Oh, well. It's probably nothing…"

I didn't have a formal list of reasons to leave Santa Maria, but if I did, a Fuentes assassin slitting my throat would be in the top five. Maybe Scott was right about giving the children new first names.

The children's annual medical checkups were scheduled in early May. I took Craig first, cheerfully toting the Utah papers to show the receptionist that the children I'd been hauling around for more than a year were mine. I gave her the papers. She placed them on the counter, handed me a form, and asked me to verify the information from the old regime.

Not to be outdone, two months after adoption day, I saw Melinda outside Craig's preschool.

"Hi," she said. "Do you have a date yet for the final adoption?"

That week the newspaper invited readers to submit a short essay about why they loved Santa Maria. One person responded.

In mid-May I visited Fischer's Fine Jewelry to buy an engagement ring. I had no idea what to choose: white gold, platinum, or regular gold and solitaire, wedge, oval, princess or a heart so I asked the lady what to do. She said buy a fake diamond ring and bring Carmen in to choose what she wants after you propose.

"How many men do that?"

"More than you think."

"How many come back?"

"Less than you think."

Santa Maria had no special places to propose. We'd have to leave town. My fantasy was to put the ring in a treasure chest and bury it mostly and when we walked in the sand she'd see a key and then Wow!, a treasure chest! She'd open it and we'd live happily ever after in the jungle.

I took a week off work to celebrate the adoption. I volunteered to chaperone Adriana and her class on a field trip to California State University, in San Luis Obispo, because they had a farm with animals on it. We met in the morning. There were 50 children from two kindergarten classes and about 10 parents. I was one of them now.

Adriana's teacher gave me a scrap of paper with the names of the kids I was responsible for written on it. The first was a whirling dervish of a girl. The second was a little boy with a baseball cap. The third, Lorna, was an adorable little girl, tiny and sweet. She wore the clothes of the poor and liked to hold my hand. The fourth was Adriana, excited that her daddy was coming along, showing her friends.

The bus was long and yellow and the driver had her rules: 1) be quiet, and 2) sit still. We drove up the coast past the cliffs with coots circling near Shell Beach and we went around a bend with fields of yellow mustard. We drove past the Avila Valley Barn where we had taken Carmen to feed goats and buy fresh pie and past San Luis Obispo proper because the university was on the north side below the hill. In the parking lot we lined up for a head count to make sure no one fell out of the bus.

The farm was a dairy farm where students learned Dairy Science. They didn't call it farming anymore, they called it Dairy Science. I took two little hands in mine and we walked through the parking lot. We smelled cows and we saw the buildings where we'd go. We walked past a sixteen stall Herringbone milking parlor. That's what they called it and they were in college. Each stall had a digital machine with four rubber tubes to attach for the milking. When the machine sensed no more milk it disengaged. There was a one story tall, 10-foot radius tank with water in it to wash everything afterwards to comply with the licensing.

Fifty feet down a dirt embankment pocked with chipmunk holes and studded by clumps of withered weeds, we saw two rows of 20 little calf houses. The children ran to see the calves. The plastic houses were off-white and four feet tall, three feet wide and six feet long. In front of each house was a little fence, same size. Baby bottles were stuck in a sloping tin slot on the front of the fence. Each house had hay and a calf. Half the calves were deer-colored Jerseys and the other half black and white Holsteins—a design shamelessly pilfered from Gateway Computer packaging. Each calf got to lie in the hay or stand in the hay. The teacher invited the children to stick a finger through the fence and feel what it was like for a calf to suck on it.

Each house had a card with the calf number, the dam number and the sire name. Only the sire got a name; the mom and the calf only got a number. One sire was named Monty. Another calf had a sire named "Bull?" Bull must have been messing around because if they knew it was Bull for sure they wouldn't put "Bull?" on the card. This was the kind of thing that pissed off Dairy Scientists.

We, er, the children played with the calves and then we walked north 50 feet to stand next to three larger sheds, each twice as big as the smaller sheds. After weaning at two months, calves were moved to the larger sheds as roommates to be socialized. If they skipped this part they wouldn't have to worry about problems caused by bulls like Bull?.

My cell phone vibrated in my pocket.

241

Each shed had four older calves in it. Here, they could mix the Jerseys
and the Holsteins because the animals were immature, or else you'd have
a coupling between a deer calf and a Gateway calf, called a Macintosh.
The only way to prevent this was not to mix males and females. I couldn't
tell which was which by looking and I didn't ask because of the privacy.

It was Carmen, crying.

West of the little sheds, down the hill from the calf sheds, the
socializing sheds, and the steel hay barn were two, massive, tin-roofed
barns where the calves became heifers and bulls. Each was 100 yards
long and two stories high although most of the space was open air for
the ventilation. Each heifer and bull wore an ear tag and they were much
larger. Some heifers had the result of socializing inside them.

"I have cancer," she said.

A loudspeaker attached to a beam mounted computer hung from the
roof of the big open barn. Every minute the loudspeaker screeched like
a red-tailed hawk to keep the birds away so they wouldn't steal the oats.
The loudspeaker was the boss of them. A thousand birds waited outside
the barn for the red-tailed hawk to go away but it never did and the birds
waited their whole lives for something they never got.

One bird flew away. It went to get what it wanted.

Back on the bus we listened to the rules and rode to a park to eat
lunch. All of the other adults brought lunch with them. I ate a kid lunch
out of a brown paper bag. Under the trees I saw a group of eight new
mothers with babies in strollers and blankets. It was a peer group. I
wondered if they'd let me join.

After lunch we boarded the bus. Lorna fell asleep on one shoulder
and Adriana the other. I stared out the window like Mimosa. Our time
in Santa Maria was over. I carried Carmen's ring around in the Land
Rover bought special, but I couldn't make myself give it to her because
she was busy making plans to go back home because that's what you do

with cancer. We talked and made plans not to give up and then we met at the International House of Pancakes and gave up and she left. I cried in the car driving away.

Scott's father died and he went back home. Carmen went home and we needed to go, too, but there was no back home for us. Then I realized back home was where we were. It was the four of us and we were happy and lucky.

# Epilogue

We left Santa Maria. In 2006, I became the vice-president of a California media company.

Since meeting Maribel at McDonald's, we've returned to Santa Barbara every year to celebrate a birthday, sail, or ride horses in the hills.

In 2008, five years and a month after the robbers separated Javier, Adriana, Craig, and Maribel from their oldest sister, Emine, she made her way from Mexico to Santa Barbara and called crying on the phone, wondering how her brothers and sisters were doing. As I suspected, her father had been jailed. Not wanting to risk another five years passing, I told 15-year-old Emine that I'd read the files. She cried softly.

"I read about you. I read about you helping your brothers and sisters. I read about you getting in trouble for that and I read about the things you went through. I want to thank you for what you did."

She continued crying.

When the kids were with their mother and she was gone in the morning, Emine walked Adriana and Craig to a friend's house to be safe and she walked Javier and Maribel to school. Emine was nine years old. She's 18 now and gets up at 5:30 a.m. to walk 45 minutes alone to high school.

"I want you to know that you're a hero to me," I said.

Within weeks, I took all five children to Disneyland to ride down magic mountains. They stared at each other and through the years at siblings they used to know and wondered in silence about what life might have been. But that was then.

At dinner, Emine surprised me with three photo albums she made of my children's early days. She did what Social Services couldn't do and she did it well. The photos included one of Adriana in a bassinet on the

244

couch of the foster home she entered after her birth. Another showed the children's mother sitting on a couch. Emine said no one had heard from her in years.

Since coming into my home and filling it with April light, the children have been healthy, happy and good. Guided by Janet the nanny, all three have been on the honor roll for years. They've become good little soccer players and learned to swim and ride horses. At a local shelter, we adopted Jack, an abandoned three-year-old Pointer dog, a walking rib cage, a 48-pound stripe. We play fetch at the park every day. If it's raining we wear hats. If it's dark we're alone under the light.

Javier, a less shy and more confident big brother, was ranked number one in his class of 205 sixth graders. At fourteen years of age, he aced the college placement test and rides his bike to a college-level math course. A child of illegal immigrants, he won a local essay sponsored by the Veterans of Foreign Wars. The gentlemen at the hall didn't ask us for our papers or spy on us with Minutemen night vision goggles. In fact, they seemed to not care at all about leprosy or car pool lanes.

The essay topic was "Heroes." Javier wrote about me and Emine.

Adriana still skips through the hallways, singing her happy songs and wiggling her lucky toes. She's the proud mother of Emmett, a dwarf rabbit she walks in a stroller around the neighborhood. Adriana is a Justin Bieber fan and dreams of her first iPod. She is a thoughtful, sweet person, and makes friends easily. She wants to become a veterinarian when she grows up and adopt three kids, ages two, four and six; two boys and a girl, she says.

Craig has a zest for life and endless curiosity.

"Daddy, how does electricity work?"

"Time for bed!"

He still hides a flashlight under his blanket, not to spot the robbers, but to read the books he's grown to love. He hopes to attend Stanford

University and become a prospector. At nine years old, he is three years older than Javier was when I met the children. He's still my baby, but bigger.

In December 2008, I found Carmen on Facebook. We rushed to see her, living a quiet life on the coast. She read the manuscript and she was happy.

In March 2011, Emine was admitted to a California State university. She'll be the first in her family, but not the last, to go to college.

I, finally a father, sought unconditional love and found it. I will not be alone on a Carmel Valley porch.

# Famous Adopted People, or Whatever

Adriana Marin, veterinarian
Alexander the Great, politician
Alonzo Mourning, NBA player
Aristotle, philosopher
Art Linkletter, comedian
Babe Ruth, baseball player
Bill Clinton, U.S. President
Charles Dickens, writer
Cher, entertainer
Craig Marin, prospector
Crazy Horse, Lakota war chief
Dave Thomas, founder of Wendy's
Duante Culpepper, NFL quarterback
Eddie Murphy, actor
Edgar Allen Poe, poet, writer
Eleanor Roosevelt, First Lady
Gary Coleman, actor
Gerald Ford, U.S. President
Ice-T, actor
Ingrid Bergman, actress
Jack the Pointer
James Dean, actor
Javier Marin, firefighter
Jesse Jackson, minister
John Lennon, musician
Leo Tolstoy, writer
Louisa May Alcott, writer

Malcolm X, civil rights leader
Marilyn Monroe, actress
Mark Twain, writer
Maya Angelou, writer
Nancy Reagan, First Lady
Nat King Cole, singer
Nelson Mandela, Nobel Peace Prize winner
Priscilla Presley, actress
Ray Liotta, actor
Richard Burton, actor
Steve Jobs, King of Apple computer
Superman, reporter
Spiderman, perpetual student
Tarzan, King of the apes

*The Story Continues . . .*

# A Conversation With David Marin

*Q: You've characterized your book as being about "a man without a meaningful past who adopts three children without a meaningful future." That's catchy, but really . . . what made you decide to tell your story?*

A: My children had a tough early life, eating pet food, hiding in cabinets, sent around the neighborhood begging for quarters, attacked by the adults who should have cared for them. As foster care children, statistics said one would graduate from high school, another would work in the fields at age thirteen, and the last would go to prison. Even though I was a single male with zero parenting experience, I couldn't let that happen.

My children now fulfill my life every day, in small ways. And with someone to fill their bellies, keep the nightlights on, and provide the unconditional love they deserve, they are full of joy. Their spirit, their zest for life, and their willingness to "adopt" me as their daddy, is a source of great pride and astonishment for me and, I think, will be a source of inspiration for all who read our story.

Yet the future is not clear. Instead of our society being colorblind, where you're from and what you look like matters now more than ever. When I began the book and researched discrimination and anti-immigrant fervor, I dismissed mentioning a crackpot who called for stripping the citizenship of fieldworker children born in the United States, like mine. Now, it's a to-do item in both chambers of the United States Congress.

We are at a crossroads. We need to decide if we are going to close ranks and close our hearts. Or, not. The next few years will set our course for a generation. I'd like *This Is US* to be a compelling argument for us to go the way we came: a melting pot of people, ideas, songs, literature, and histories.

*Q: You're half Puerto Rican, but redheaded and to all appearances, completely Caucasian. How are you able to help your Hispanic children cope with racism?*

A: A pale male, I've never experienced racism. And I assume people are not racist, so I'm always off-guard. Just last week, a person I introduced to my children asked me if they spoke English. Yeah, they do. I tell my children that there are people who decide how they feel about others based on how they look. I ask them if they do that. No. And I asked them if their favorite teacher would be better, or worse, if she were taller or shorter. No. Or darker, or thinner. No. We talk about being nice to people and we talk about judging people by how they treat others, not by how they look. And we've had a rule for years: whenever there's a new kid in school, the Marin kids make friends with him or her first, so they have one friend until they have many. We try to do good in the space we're in. If a lot of people try that, we win.

*Q: You were born in Georgia, grew up Wisconsin and Missouri, went to prep schools in Maine and Virginia, college in Denver, law school in California, and have traveled extensively. Your children have been in California their whole lives and you've lived there for many years, but it is also one of the epicenters of the national immigration debate and you're very open about the prejudice your family experienced in Santa Maria. Now that you're in the San Jose/Santa Clara County area, do you think you've found a more tolerant environment?*

A: I'm not sure if Santa Maria is less tolerant or the first place I began to pay attention since I had three Hispanic children under wing. But you're right, 36% of the population of Santa Clara County are immigrants—the highest percentage in the state—and people are more tolerant. Most want to be and the rest have to be.

Tolerance is born from confidence; intolerance from uncertainty. As people become more comfortable around people who are different, I trust that things will improve. It's difficult, though, in this environment with weak politicians playing to boisterous crowds, turning immigration reform into a blunt instrument. The last president to grant amnesty to millions of illegal immigrants wasn't Lyndon Johnson, or Jimmy Carter, or Bill Clinton. It was Ronald Reagan—he thought people who were here and working and honest deserved a better future. America has, instead, turned on the weakest and most vulnerable, the opposite of what we were and can be.

*Q: Despite the fact that your children's early years were filled with abuse and neglect, they don't seem to have experienced too many behavioral problems. Did you take any special steps to help them settle in as well as they have?*

A: In the book, I talk about how I planned to put all four us in therapy as soon as I got them and how surprised I was when the social worker assigned to me, the social worker who taught my foster care license classes, and the kids' pediatrician all advised against that, telling me to just leave them alone and let them grow up. It was clever advice. I did immediately surround my children with responsible adults, first in their pre-school program and then by hiring a nanny I employed for five years. She, and her husband and neighbors, as well as my sisters and friends, have all been healthy role models for the kids. More role models have entered into their lives over the years including teachers, coaches, and new neighbors.

Most importantly, I helped them gain confidence, in little ways, like sending my five year old to get extra napkins at a restaurant counter or being silent when a waiter asked me what they wanted to eat so they could order their own food. When they nervously questioned whether we could do one thing or another, I said, "We can do whatever we want. No one tells the Marin kids what to do." I became one of them, trying to see the world through their eyes.

Being loved is a boost. When they were younger, we used to play a game where we'd try to convince each other who loved each other the most. I'd tell Javier, for example, that I loved him more than spaghetti and ice cream. He'd tell me that he loved me more than dogs and books. I told Adrianna I loved her more than the moon and the sky. She told me she loved me more than cats and worms.

*Q: You've also made a very real effort to keep your children connected to their two older sisters. Why did you think this was important for them?*

A: I thought it was important to them because my two sisters are important to me. And the kids spoke of their missing sisters with such heartache—like they were ghosts or gone—because they had been split from their siblings, and each other, numerous times, when they were just one, or three, or five years old. Imagine watching a sibling being taken by a stranger in the night. You can't call, you can't text, you can't even spell your name.

I was in a big hurry to reunite them and I knew I had to do something as soon as I was allowed, but I had to wait until the legalities were clear.

*Q: Sandra Bullock, Meg Ryan, and Angelina Jolie are just a few of the celebrities who adopted children as single parents, and overall, single parent adoptions are on the rise. Still, single men are stigmatized when it comes to adoption. Why do you think that is?*

A: I think men are more ignorant than stigmatized, simply unaware that they can adopt on their own. I was ignorant, asked advice, didn't believe it, and called Social Services to see if it was true—yes, single men can adopt.

To stigmatize is to condemn. Single male adoptions are so rare, only 2% of the total, that there aren't enough of us to condemn. Moreover, people are stigmatized if they care what other people think of them. If you're going to do what I do, you need to be in a different place. I didn't care what negative people thought about me adopting. I didn't need their permission and didn't seek their approval. For more sensitive men adopting children, I encourage them to focus on the kids—don't look up—they'll keep you busy.

*Q: You endured years of red tape before the adoption became official. Based on some of the statistics you cite, the system is obviously broken, in need of more staffing, more funding, and it would seem, in dire need of employees who actually have the best interests of the children they represent in mind. What can be done to fix this?*

A: The story does touch on my journey through the maze of Social Services, the inspiration I found in social workers who care about what they're doing, and the frustrations I felt parrying with indifferent bureaucrats. It is vital that flaws in the system are addressed because there are hundreds of thousands of children in foster care. A 2005 study found that 240,000 people a year contact Social Services about adopting children (but only three percent do so) and over 10 million families (one in ten) have considered adoption. Regardless, adoptions from foster care have more than doubled since 1990. To encourage this trend, the system itself shouldn't be discouraging.

My hope is that through stories like mine, social workers will see the difference between good work and bad, and feel the impact their decisions have on children in the system.

While there are staffing and resource issues, I'm talking about changes at the micro level. For example, social workers should spend time understanding what children go through and modifying their actions accordingly. In their defense, though, it would be easier for them to make the hard decisions about removing children from a home if they knew there were loving homes kids could go to. In that vein, we can help social workers and foster children by adopting more of them. Or, all of them. There are around 100,000 available for adoption today. With 120 million households in the United States, if 1 in 1,200 adopted a child, foster homes would be empty.

*Q: Many people would consider rescuing three children to be a heroic act, but you ran into very real resistance from your employer. Do you think that adoptive parents experience more discrimination in the workplace?*

A: No, I don't. I faced workplace challenges because I was (going to become) a single parent, not an adoptive parent. My boss was concerned about my ability to do my job and be a dad. He guessed wrong and got sued and his job ended two weeks later. I've been a business executive for more than 20 years. The personal lives of my employees are none of my business. However, I do acknowledge that if they have a healthy, pleasant life, they're more fun to be around. So whatever takes them there, being a parent, or not, or whatever, is a good thing.

*Q: You also make it pretty clear throughout the book that you're not necessarily the "hero" of this story and it's your children who deserve that honor. Can you tell me a little about the ways in which they've changed your life for the better?*

A: I appreciate the hero sentiment. But, in my view the book has seven heroes: my three children; their older sisters who at eight and ten years old protected them, fed them and hid them; my mother who raised five children by herself when her husband died young; and my social worker who plowed ahead and supported me against resistance and opposition among his own co-workers.

As for my life being better, it goes far beyond that. It's a dramatic and powerful change, more than I imagined, and I feel it every day, going on eight years later. My experiences are deeper, my emotions more developed, and my sense of joy, of pride, at watching my children grow and learn and become good people isn't just better, it's a revolution, a personal paradigm shift. I'm in a whole different world now. For my birthday this year, I got two cans of Vienna Sausage and a flyswatter.

*Q: You freely—and colorfully—admit that, "there are small mammals who knew more about parenting than I did." What are the most important lessons you've learned?*

A: I knew at the outset I'd make mistakes and really, I couldn't have made any more than I did, but I convinced myself that it was okay because if at the end of the day the children were safe, fed, and sleeping soundly, I was doing okay. I guess I had very low standards, but it was the best I could do to survive at the outset, with so many things happening. I'm not complaining, it was amazing, but a blur for years.

The most important lessons are patience (I still work on that), being open-minded to their feelings and desires—especially as they grow older and can voice them—and to not give up if you want something badly enough. I made up my mind when I met them that we would be a family. Now, when I look back, I can't believe I did it, and I'm not sure I could do it again. I was on a once-in-a-lifetime mission and I made it home.

*Q: You tell an amusing story about your first Thanksgiving with the chil-
dren—mistakenly buying a capon instead of a turkey. Now that you have a
few holidays behind you, what traditions have emerged?*

A: We still go to the beach every Thanksgiving, now in Monterey, or we
walk the coastline in Pacific Grove, looking for crabs and sea stars or
driftwood to make a raft we tie with wet kelp. We visit their sisters before
Christmas and we open a gift on Christmas Eve, just like I dreamed we'd
do.

And on the 4th of July, I take the children to the Pajaro Valley, where
we walk the fields, picking strawberries. There's some poetry in there
somewhere.

*Q: What's next for the Marin family? Will it be getting bigger anytime
soon?*

A: Next year, I'll have one child in elementary school, one in junior high,
and one in high school. Unbelievable. I'm prepared though, having endured a Little League season with three children on three different teams
playing at three different parks at the same time. We have no master plan,
other than to live and grow and do well in school and be good people.

My biggest regret, which I think about too often, is that I said no
when I was asked to take all five children, my three and their two older
sisters. They went to live with their fathers, which was okay back then,
but it's problematic now. I often think of getting all five together just
so they all can be in one family, in one house, at peace, even for a little
while, a summer or a year, or celebrate holidays in a place all five can call
home.

*Start Your Own Conversation . . .*

# Reader's Guide

1. What do you think of when you hear the phrase "All-American family"? How do you define "family"? How does David Marin define it? Do you think the definition of family has changed over time, and do you think it will continue to change?

2. How does this book compare to others you've read about families? How is this story different? How is it universal? What role can one family play in the structure of society?

3. Do you particularly identify with anyone in the Marin family's story? With Javier, Adriana, or Craig? With David? Or with someone outside of the family?

4. Holidays and "traditional" family activities play a big role in the Marin family's life. David especially feels creating traditions are vital to the growth of a family. Do you agree? What traditions do you try to observe, or change, within your own family?

5. David is honest about being completely unprepared for parenthood. Do you think his efforts to develop a support system made up for his early lack of knowledge and experience? How did he grow as a parent after taking the children into his home? Do you think he did a good job of helping the children understand and reconcile themselves to their troubled past?

6. Why do you think David felt it was important to tell the story of how he came to adopt Javier, Adriana, and Craig? Do you think his experiences would be a helpful road map for couples or individuals considering adoption?

7. David relates a great deal of his story through dialogue, much of which comes from conversations he recorded at the time. Do you think this was an effective way to narrate the story? Do you feel it's important to be 100% accurate when it comes to remembered conversations?

8. What did you know about the issues surrounding adoption prior to reading this book? How has this book changed or enhanced your view of the subject? Does reading *This Is US* affect how likely you would be to look into adoption?

9. Do you think Social Services helps or hinders adoption in the United States? Have you had an experience where one dedicated person in an otherwise bogged down bureaucracy made the difference? How do you think the system could be improved?

10. Did reading *This Is US* change your perspective on immigration issues in the United States and if so, how?

11. If you found yourself at the restaurant David describes at the beginning of the book, seeing his family without any context, how do you think you would have reacted? If it were your family, would your response have been the same as David's? Do you believe that as multicultural families become more common in America, that families like David's will face the same kind of scrutiny?

12. Do you feel this story would have had more or less impact if it included photographs or were presented as a documentary film instead of a book? With omnipresent media influences around us all day—cable television, talk radio and blogs, as well as traditional media outlets like newspapers and network television—what do books offer that other media cannot?

13. Meg Meeker says David's story "opens our eyes to the profound significance men make in the lives of children." Is this a common view of the family or do mothers still get the most credit? Is there still a stigma attached to being a single parent? Do you feel that traditional parental roles are changing?

14. What did you learn from this book that you would pass on to a new parent, adoptive or otherwise?

## Acknowledgments

The calm courage of two California social workers enabled my journey to parenthood: Bev, my Alameda County training social worker, and Scott, assigned to me and my children in Santa Barbara County. My Parental Advisory Board—the ladies in Accounting at the *Santa Maria Times* newspaper—and other *Times* colleagues were incredibly helpful during my transition; as was Curtis, the smiling director of the YMCA; the physicians who cared for my children; Willie, the Santa Barbara County Social Worker who spent the most time in our home; and the social workers and county attorneys who helped me over the hurdle of their colleagues. I am grateful to all.

Brittany, you were incredible.

My sisters and mother, stronger than me, provided continual support and good cheer. Carmen was a loving friend. Tod Davies (she's a she), the energetic, freethinking publisher of Exterminating Angel Press, took *This Is US* from a BB to a bazooka. Your aim is true.

DAVID MARIN (pronounced "marine") is half Puerto Rican, half Irish, and all American. Raised in the Midwest, he went to prep school on the East Coast, college in Colorado, and law school in California, where he has spent the past twenty years. A media company executive by profession and an adventurer by nature, he has traveled to eleven countries and visited thirty-six of our fifty states. He has skydived in Arizona, water skied on the Caribbean, and rescued olive ridley sea turtles in Costa Rica.

By far the greatest adventure of David's life is fatherhood.

Spend Quality Time With The Marin Family
Photo gallery, adoption resources, and much more:
*http://www.thisisus–davidmarin.com/*